# BIG MEDIA, BIG MONEY

# BIG MEDIA, BIG MONEY

## Cultural Texts and Political Economics

RONALD V. BETTIG and JEANNE LYNN HALL

ROWMAN & LITTLEFIELD PUBLISHERS, INC.
*Lanham • Boulder • New York • Oxford*

ROWMAN & LITTLEFIELD PUBLISHERS, INC.

Published in the United States of America
by Rowman & Littlefield Publishers, Inc.
A Member of the Rowman & Littlefield Publishing Group
4720 Boston Way, Lanham, Maryland 20706
www.rowmanlittlefield.com

PO Box 317
Oxford
OX2 9RU, UK

British Library Cataloging in Publication Information Available

**Library of Congress Cataloging-in-Publication Data**

Bettig, Ronald V.
  Big media, big money : cultural texts and political economics / Ronald
V. Bettig and Jeanne Lynn Hall.
     p.  cm.
Includes bibliographical references and index.
  ISBN 0-7425-1129-4 (cloth : alk. paper) — ISBN 0-7425-1130-8 (pbk. :
alk. paper)
  1.  Mass media—Economic aspects.  2.  Mass media and culture.  I.  Hall,
Jeanne Lynn, 1958–  II.  Title.
  P96.E25  B48  2002
  338.4'730223—dc21

2002008623

Printed in the United States of America

In memory of Herbert I. Schiller

# CONTENTS

# ACKNOWLEDGMENTS

We owe debts of gratitude to many people, far more than we can name here. Nonetheless, we'd like to single out a few for special mention in the form of a loose narrative about how *Big Media, Big Money* came to be written. It began when John Dickison invited us to coauthor a column of media criticism for our local alternative newspaper, *Voices of Central Pennsylvania*. We began writing a monthly column, which we called "Beat the Press," in the fall of 1998. A number of our students, colleagues, local shopkeepers, taxi drivers, and friends read it regularly, prompting many lively conversations over the next two years. These columns provided the seeds for a number of the chapters that follow.

Brenda Hadenfeldt, acquisitions editor at Rowman & Littlefield, recognized the significance of our work and encouraged us to write the book. She was the perfect editor: patient when we wanted her to be and impatient when we needed her to be. Her critical acumen, editorial expertise, and excitement about the project helped us every step along the way. Siho Nam took on the daunting task of cataloging hundreds of newspaper clippings and helping us formulate our rants against Big Media into coherent chapters. Sojourner Ruth Marable spent hours in the library and online to help us nail just the right quotes. Cheryl Adam polished the text with precision and tolerance for the occasional vagaries of our prose. Jason Proetorius orchestrated production with what we assume was only apparent ease. Chris Jordan, Darryl Davies, Ann Zirkle, Tobin Bettivia, Rhiannon Bettivia, Fred Bettig, Lydia Von Imm, and Skip and Joyce Hall were supportive of the project throughout. We love them all.

Finally, we want to give special thanks to Jennifer Proffitt, our graduate student, research assistant, and friend. Jennifer embraced the project as

ix

her own in both word and spirit. She sifted through piles of articles, conducted countless online searches, and read each chapter as the book took shape. Her extraordinary research skills were matched only by her boundless energy and enthusiasm. We couldn't have done it without her.

# 1

# INTRODUCTION: BEAT THE PRESS

This book began as a series of essays on media criticism entitled *Beat the Press*. We'd like to begin with an explanation of that title: what it means to us to beat the press in terms of theory, method, and practice. By "press," we mean more than just journalism. We use the term to include our entire mediated environment: movies, broadcast and cable television, music, books, the Internet, advertising, fashion, education, and the many other means we use to communicate. We use "beat" as a *sensitizing concept,* a qualitative research strategy suggested by Cliff Christians and James Carey, to "capture meaning at different levels and label them accordingly."[1] They liken this strategy to peeling "the onion of reality down to different layers."[2] Over the course of the twentieth century, this "reality" became increasingly defined by the mass media, which have in many ways usurped the traditional role of family, friends, and religion in shaping how we make sense of the events and experiences of our daily lives, so much so that we risk thinking of our mediated existence—and the particular form it has taken under global capitalism—as somehow natural or inevitable.

In the first section of this chapter, we use a number of different meanings of the word "beat" to examine the emergence and development of the mass media, from the invention of the printing press to the weaving of the World Wide Web. We explore the growing influence of the mass media on our shared perceptions of reality and investigate some deeply held beliefs about the free press in the United States. In the second section, we briefly outline the tradition of mass communications theory and research. This is important because communications scholars have sought to study the role of media in society in a number of different ways and toward a variety of different ends. Our work is no exception. We conclude with a description of our approach and a survey of the wide range of local and global media texts we will examine as we attempt to "peel away the layers" in the chapters that follow.

1

## MEET THE PRESS

Under capitalism, the media are structured so that their primary goal is profit. This means beating the competition, whether at the newsstand, box office, or *New York Times* bestseller list. For the news media, beating the competition involves a long history of getting the scoop, as in "You saw it here first." The news business first emerged in the Italian city-states of the late fifteenth century with the rise of capitalism and the development of the modern printing press. Early printers found that there was a tidy profit to be made in providing merchant capitalists with news about markets and political conditions. The industrialization of the news business in the nineteenth century resulted in the transformation of news into a mass-produced commodity. With this development, the range and scope of news content expanded to cover a wider range of human events and social behaviors. Competition at the newsstand resulted in increased sensationalism and even fabrication of news. The motivation to get the scoop remains a dominant influence in the news business today, as evidenced by the premature projection of the results of the 2000 U.S. presidential election by television news networks. Although it is difficult to prove whether such broadcasts sway voter behavior, the election was nonetheless followed by congressional hearings at which network news directors promised yet again to regulate their election coverage more rigorously.

The rise of the book publishing industry is also tied to the invention of the modern printing press and the rise of capitalism. As with the news business, book printing and publishing flourished in the capitalist city-states of late-fifteenth-century Italy, then spread throughout Europe. The earliest book publishers built their businesses with the publication of religious works, classic Greek and Roman texts, government documents, and educational materials. As Elizabeth Eisenstein discovered, however, printers soon found that there was a lucrative market for "scandal sheets, 'lewd Ballads,' 'merry bookes of Italie,' and other 'corrupted tales in Inke and Paper.'"[3]

The book publishing industry became increasingly industrialized in the nineteenth century during what is known as the "great age of the European novel." As in the newspaper industry, mass-produced novels took a new look at everyday human existence within the evolving social context of urbanization and industrialization. In the 1920s and 1930s the book industry turned to the mass production of books based on formulas such as the western, detective story, science fiction, and romance. The modern publishing industry took shape in the 1960s as large industrial conglomerates began buying up publishing houses and putting them on strict profit plans. This meant reducing risks by developing and promoting a stable of star authors—the Stephen Kings, Danielle Steels, and Michael Crichtons of the business. Prolific and predictable, such stars guarantee bestsellers on a regular basis.

Celebrity authors are not the only ones who command million-dollar advances from publishers. Public figures who write or ghostwrite manuscripts do so as well. For example, Simon & Schuster agreed to pay $8 million for Hillary Rodham Clinton's autobiography, and Knopf Books (a division of Bertelsman) promised Bill Clinton more than $10 million for his memoirs. The former president's advance was the largest ever for a nonfiction book. The effects of the star system in publishing are highly significant. Paying a small number of authors large sums of cash makes the industry more concentrated, and the prospects for lesser-known authors much smaller. There is simply less money allocated to the development and promotion of their works.

Five global media corporations dominated the book publishing industry at the turn of the twenty-first century: AOL Time Warner, Bertelsman, Viacom, Pearson, and News Corporation. Concentration at the retail level exacerbates the situation, as chain bookstores and superstores routinely drive out independent bookshops. Readers have fewer choices since large retailers, like publishers, concentrate on bestsellers. Any additional titles they offer are usually determined by buyers at corporate headquarters, rather than chosen by store employees or customers. The serendipitous discovery of a little-known gem on the shelves of a book superstore is rare.

According to Eisenstein, the printed book helped produce a revolutionary transformation in early modern Europe. The sheer abundance of texts proliferated new ways of thinking, leading Western civilization out of what was known as the Dark Ages. We may have an abundance of books today, but it takes work to find many that challenge existing ways of thinking or advance new ones. The book industry's reliance on a handful of genres and a stable of stars leads to the regular publication of all-too-familiar works. The same goes for movies and recorded music.

Both the movie and recorded music industries owe their origins to industrial capitalists of the late nineteenth century seeking to exploit new markets. They discovered the economic logic of capturing dramatic and musical performances on film or disc. The bulk of the costs of production went to staging and capturing the original performance; the costs of copying a movie or recording were miniscule by comparison. Film projection and recorded music quickly evolved from novelties found in arcades, nickelodeons, and vaudeville houses to become major entertainment industries in the mid-1920s. Motion picture palaces such as New York's Roxy Theater had more than 6,000 seats. Like book publishing, movies and music came to depend on the star system, the blockbuster, familiar genres, and outright imitations. Both industries also grew to rely on large production budgets and expensive promotion and marketing campaigns, though these costs are rarely associated with quality. Like the book publishing industry, movies and music have grown increasingly concentrated at the retail level, with the rise of theater and record store chains. Finally, all three industries are now adapting themselves to the Internet, which large media corporations first saw as a threat but soon began to view as an opportunity.

Radio broadcasting comes next in the history of the mass media. Wireless telephony evolved as an alternative to the telephone around the turn of the twentieth century. Until the early 1920s, radio was primarily a hobby of amateurs based on the simple pleasures and practical uses of point-to-point communication, much as the Internet was originally used mainly for e-mail. The new technology put dollar signs in the eyes of industrial capitalists, who wrenched radio from the amateurs and transformed it into a source of profit. At first, radio broadcasters provided programming for free to promote sales of receiver sets. Soon, however, most U.S. households owned radio sets. The market for receivers was saturated, and revenues from the purchase of replacement sets were insufficient to cover the increasing costs of radio program production.

Looking to the newspaper industry as a business model, radio broadcasters turned to advertisers to support program production and distribution. They also copied the network model, enabling broadcasters to share programs and therefore program costs. By the early 1930s, radio broadcasting had evolved into a commercially supported and networked industry controlled by only two firms, the National Broadcasting Company (NBC) and the Columbia Broadcasting Company (CBS). Beating the competition grew to mean having the highest ratings, or the largest audiences to sell to advertisers.

Television broadcasters copied the radio broadcasting model wholesale, building a privately owned and operated, commercially supported, and tightly networked industry. They even borrowed or pilfered the same radio shows along with radio stars. At first the film industry saw television as a threat and responded with big-budget widescreen spectacles, Technicolor, and 3-D. Soon, however, Hollywood capitalists saw profitmaking opportunities in the new medium. Today, the handful of major companies that produce movies and television shows are one and the same—Disney, Fox, Warner Brothers, Universal, and Paramount. Since the rise of television, the content of filmed entertainment has not changed all that much, just the means of delivery from cable and satellite television to videocassettes, DVDs, and the Internet. Meanwhile, the trend toward media concentration has accelerated, meaning more channels but not necessarily a wider range of voices.

The history of the mass media is intimately bound up with the history of advertising. While the book, movie, and music industries have traditionally relied more on direct consumer sales, the newspaper, magazine, and broadcast industries derive significant revenues from advertisers (around 50–60 percent for magazines, up to 80 percent for newspapers, and 100 percent for radio and television broadcasters). Advertisers exert two main influences over the programming they sponsor. First, advertisers determine the structure of media industries simply by choosing where to spend their money. They support media outlets that reach the right demographic groups—audiences that consume the most. Media producers seeking to serve "undesirable" audiences cannot count on advertising revenues to finance their operations and therefore remain marginalized. For example, advertisers have shunned urban radio stations with largely African-American and Latino audiences, a practice known as "nonurban dictates." When advertisers do patronize such stations, they pay less for ads than they do for stations with predominantly white audiences. In this way, advertisers contribute to the suppression of media diversity.

Second, advertisers exert direct influence over media content. There are many documented cases, and surely many more undocumented ones, of advertisers actually pulling or threatening to cancel their accounts because of critical reporting. This should not be surprising because advertisers have a vested interest in keeping consumers uninformed or misinformed. They prefer for us to make decisions based on emotional bonds with their products. If the primary goal of advertising is to maintain brand loyalty and keep competitors out of the market, then the giant media companies are their own best advertisers. They launch extravagant promotional campaigns in print and television media promoting the latest blockbuster books, records, and movies, turning them into "must-see" events. Again, advertising helps support an oligopolistic media structure by deluging audiences with information about a handful of media products and keeping them largely uninformed about alternatives.

Advertising is not only an economic institution operating for the benefit of a few major corporations and their owners; it is also an ideological institution that supports and negates certain ways of thinking. For example, advertisers had no interest in the vibrant working-class press of the nineteenth century, not only because working-class audiences had little to spend on manufactured goods, but also because the anticapitalist sentiments these newspapers expressed were obviously contradictory to their goals. Advertisers therefore shunned publications that challenged consumerism as a lifestyle, especially as it became more essential to sustaining the capitalist industrial system. First, people had to be convinced that there were an infinite number of unmet needs that consumption could surely satisfy. Advertisers began suggesting that social and personal relations could be improved by using new products such as deodorants and mouthwashes. Moreover, not just *any* brand of health or beauty aid would do; consumers also had to be persuaded that products manufactured by large, national companies with famous brands were superior to those made at home or in town.

In the first few decades of the twentieth century, big brand advertisers began to use national magazines to spread the virtues of consumption, not only through the ads themselves but also through editorial content. Since then, advertiser-supported media have been expected to promote consumerist lifestyles, largely based on credit, to enrich the capitalist class so that its members can enjoy consumption at the level of luxury. Such are the rewards of ownership and control of the few hundred multinational corporations that account for most of the world's advertising expenditures.

The advertising industry has proven itself voracious in its search for new venues and attractive demographics. Advertisers have even taken their anthem of consumption into the once-sacred realm of public education, where they have found a most lucrative captive audience. In the United States, elementary and secondary education belongs to the public sector. It is seen as both a guaranteed right for all citizens and the responsibility of a democratic society to provide. Increasingly, however, public schools strapped for cash are turning to the private sphere for sponsorship of academic and athletic programs and for donations of educational materials.

Education funding shortages have long been a problem in the United States due to the unequal distribution of tax money and the contradictory way the public thinks about taxes. The largest portion of public school revenues is generated from local property and income taxes, creating large gaps between rich and poor school districts. Although everyone wants their children to have a good education, those living in poor neighborhoods cannot afford it and those living in richer neighborhoods do not want to pay for it. Taxes reduce personal income and so are seen as an invasion of the right to consume. State and federal education funds have not been sufficient to close the gap, and advertisers have been all too willing to step in. Today's students are subjected to ads on school buses, in hallways and cafeterias, and in educational materials such as textbooks and news programs. The parameters of science projects are subject to the dictates of corporate sponsors. Market researchers have even bought class time to conduct taste tests and surveys, all to establish lifelong brand loyalties in children while they are still young.

While education in the United States is primarily a public institution, journalism has evolved as a private institution working under a general mandate to serve the public. Journalists are expected to "beat the bushes" (to return to our sensitizing concept) but more routinely they are relegated to "work the beat." The difference here is crucial. Beating the bushes, or searching out stories that aren't advertised or announced, requires time and effort. This raises the costs of news production. Working the beat usually entails covering the courthouse, police station, city hall, the White House, Wall Street, and so on. This ensures stories on a predictable timetable and at low costs. The result is that news and public affairs are defined by authority figures such as politicians, corporate spokespersons, and readily available experts from think tanks and research institutes. Such officials are prone to beating *around* the bushes—withholding information, spreading half-truths, or just plain lying. It was not the press corps working the White House beat that broke the Watergate story; they were being misled by President Richard Nixon's press agents. It took investigative reporting from outside to get the real scoop.

This leads to the most obvious referent in the title of our newspaper column and this chapter of our book, the NBC Sunday morning news show called *Meet the Press*. Along with other Sunday news shows—CBS's *Face the Nation*, ABC's *This Week with Sam Donaldson and Cokie Roberts*, CNN's *Late Edition with Wolf Blitzer*, and the Fox network's *Fox News Sunday*—*Meet the Press* serves as a site where Washington's elite meet to set government and media agendas for the week. The topics discussed on these Sunday shows invariably become the subjects of newspaper reports and analyses on Monday. Far from challenging authority figures, journalists have come to rely on them. The media thereby become the means by which officials define public issues and set the parameters of policy debates. Those in power also use the media to determine what *isn't* news and therefore what *won't* be debated. Important arguments are often left unspoken; significant news is unreported, buried, or banished to the last paragraph of a column or the final minutes of a broadcast. An analysis of the guest lists and topics of four Sunday morning news talk shows concluded decisively that issues of corporate power are not on the agenda.[4]

Finally, we use "beat" as a sensitizing concept to invoke reflection upon the long history of violence against journalists and other media workers. In *Violence against the Press*, John Nerone documents the history of violent censorship and suppression of journalists seeking to expand the public sphere from the Revolutionary War to the late twentieth century.[5] Both Nerone and Jon Bekken cite violence as a routine means of suppressing the working-class press.[6] Around the world, journalists continue to sacrifice their lives for the expression of ideas and the dissemination of information that threaten the status quo. In the 1940s and 1950s, Hollywood studio owners caved in to national anticommunist hysteria, blacklisting writers, directors, and actors deemed "Un-American" by virtue of their involvement in radical or even liberal political organizations. Authors have endured book burnings, book bannings, and even death threats. The suppression of nonmainstream music also has a long history. Conservative groups and government officials have consistently attacked alternative music genres, from early rock 'n' roll to heavy metal and rap.

Why the violent response to the press? Most of the time the marketplace filters out threatening ideas and information, but there *are* leaks in the system and the media *can* play a role in effecting social change. The muckrakers of the early twentieth century exposed corrupt and dangerous corporate practices. Their efforts contributed to laws and regulations governing corporate behavior, ranging from product safety standards to the oversight of mergers and acquisitions. Investigative journalism continues to have an effect, but there is not enough of it, and its findings are seldom put into broader social, political, and economic contexts. In the spring of 2001, for example, Knight Ridder Newspapers published a series of investigative reports on the use of child slave labor in the cultivation of cocoa beans, the essential ingredient in chocolate. The reports prompted responses from both the chocolate industry and the federal government.[7] After first denying that child slaves were cultivating cocoa beans, the Chocolate Manufacturers Association agreed to finance a study of such business practices. Hershey Food Corp., the largest chocolate manufacturer in the United States, pledged financial support for the study. The Labor Department began an investigation into the government's cocoa purchasing practices. The House of Representatives voted to direct the Food and Drug Administration to develop disclaimers guaranteeing that chocolate products sold in the United States did not come from child slave labor.

The publication of the two-month Knight Ridder investigation is in itself exceptional, and the political action it prompted even more so. The reports stop short, however, of any kind of critique of the larger global economic context that forces many more millions into slavery and billions to work at poverty or below-poverty levels of income. The idea of boycotting the purchase of chocolate products was dismissed by the series reporters, who echoed the industry line that a boycott could harm slaves.[8] In doing so, the reporters ignored the long history of successful boycotts in the struggle for human rights. These include the bus boycott by African Americans in Montgomery, Alabama, in 1955; the international economic, political, and cultural boycott of South Africa under apartheid; and the global boycott of Nestlé that forced the company to revise its marketing practices for infant formula to mothers in the Third World.

Instead of a boycott, the reporters recommended that readers express their concerns to the chocolate companies, U.S. Congress, and president. Meanwhile, the chocolate industry moved to quell any further action by Congress with lobbying efforts led by former Senate majority leaders Bob Dole, a Republican, and George Mitchell, a Democrat. The industry also enlisted major food manufacturers such as Kraft and General Mills to lobby lawmakers with operations in their home districts to help thwart the "slave free" label movement.[9] Ultimately, bad publicity forced chocolate manufacturers to create an action plan that sought to halt the practice.[10]

Although this example hints at the potential power of the press in effecting social change, it also reveals the limitations imposed by political and economic forces. Throughout human history, the control of knowledge and culture has been inextricably bound up with the control of wealth and political power. Therefore, in order to understand the communications system at any point in history, we must place it in its political-economic context. Not doing so can lead to misleading arguments, such as the one often made about freedom of expression within the U.S. media system.

It is commonly held that since the government does not directly control the media in the United States, and in fact is prohibited from doing so by the First Amendment, freedom of expression prevails. This ignores the role government officials play in setting media agendas, as well as more direct forms of intervention from laws and regulations regarding libel and obscenity to the allocation of radio and satellite frequencies. More importantly, it ignores what Edward Herman calls "market system constraints on freedom of expression,"[11] or the ways in which profit-making goals result in the suppression of diversity. If indeed the marketplace of ideas is prone to failure, then the assumption that "truth" will prevail becomes problematic. This raises the larger normative question guiding our analysis: Can a system in which culture and information are treated as commodities fully meet the needs of a self-governing, democratic polity?


## MEDIA TEXTS IN CONTEXT


Our criticism of the media is rooted in the tradition of mass communications theory and research. From this tradition, we draw upon the political economy approach to examine the production and dissemination of information and culture. This approach provides the context that informs our interpretations of media content. In this section, we briefly review the mass communications research tradition and explain what we mean by political economy and interpretive textual analysis.

The dramatic expansion of the mass media in the 1920s and 1930s led to questions about their effects on society. Government, business, religious, and parent organizations began funding research on media effects in hopes of using the media to better promote their interests and causes. Government officials were most interested in mass mobilization of the public during wartime. The U.S. military used media research to improve motivation of troops. Politicians sought polling data and studies of voter behavior in hopes of influencing election outcomes. Business was most interested in understanding consumer behavior to create more effective marketing and advertising campaigns. Religious groups and parent associations prompted research on the potential threat of the media to traditional morals and values. These efforts were often barely disguised attacks on minority or working-class media. In sum, the entire foundation of mass communications research was oriented toward better control and manipulation of audiences. This administrative research orientation dominated the field of mass communications studies well into the 1960s.

The rise of a critical challenge to administrative research paralleled the larger challenges posed by the civil rights, feminist, environmental, and anti-imperialist movements in the 1960s. Critical communications research dramatically reversed the focus, studying the ways in which the media perpetuated institutional racism, sexism, imperialism, and other forms of oppression. This required an inquiry into the relationship between the media and economic and political systems, prompting the development of a political economy approach to the study of communications. Concurrently, critical media researchers sought to expand the range of methods for the study of media content.

Traditional content analysis relied on quantitative methodology, basically counting obvious things such as the number of articles or column inches the press devoted to each candidate in an election and deciding whether the coverage was more or less favorable. Content analysts worked on a basic assumption that press coverage ultimately affected voter behavior, although research did not always prove that this was the case. Effects researchers found that, more often, the media reinforce preexisting dispositions, attitudes, and opinions. They therefore concluded that the effects of the media were limited. Critical communications researchers challenged this idea, arguing that the capacity of the media to reinforce existing beliefs is a powerful effect to the extent that it mitigates social change.

Critical communications research on audiences shifted the focus of administrative research from the study of how media texts affect behavior to the study of how audiences make meaning of media texts. Using qualitative methods such as focus groups and ethnography, critical audience researchers found that responses to media texts varied according to audience demographics including class, race, and gender. They found that audiences generally respond to media texts as producers intend them to, but may also miss the point if it is not clear. Some audiences understand the producer's intent, but resist it and replace it with an opposing meaning.

Most students of mass communications are familiar with the traditional model of sender, message, and receiver. Although not entirely breaking from this model, interpretive theories break the communications process down into phases of making meaning. They begin by analyzing the context within which the sender operates, how meaning is shaped at the point of production. Interpretive textual analysis examines how various levels of meaning are expressed—intentional meanings, but, more importantly, the hidden and often unintended meanings found in media content. Interpretive studies of audiences focus on how meaning is produced by receivers. By treating the making of meaning in phases, we are able to concentrate on both the context of production and the messages we find in the texts. That is, we can examine how media ownership, media control, and the profit-making motive affect what we read, hear, and see.

## THINKING LOCALLY AND GLOBALLY

We draw on a wide range of media to inform our analysis of the press. Our daily newspaper, the *State College (Pa.) Centre Daily Times,* serves as the source of our initial inquiry into many of the local, national, and global issues and events we use to examine how media structures and practices affect content. The newspaper serves the community of State College, Pennsylvania, site of the main campus of the Pennsylvania State University and the surrounding townships and boroughs. It is part of the second-largest newspaper chain in the United States, Knight Ridder, whose flagships include the *Philadelphia Inquirer* and the *Miami Herald.* Because it is a chain newspaper and serves a diverse university and local population, the *Centre Daily Times* provides a good sample of local, national, and international news for textual analysis. When we use the term "sample," we mean representative rather than random, as traditional content analysis requires. National and international news in the *Centre Daily Times* comes from wire services, primarily the Associated Press and Knight Ridder. The local press helps inform our study of the larger structure of media and educational institutions.

As the issues and events we study become more national and international in scope, we expand the range of our sample to include more national media, including the major broadcast and cable television news networks; upper-tier newspapers such as the *New York Times, Washington Post,* and *Wall Street Journal;* and the primary wire services and syndicates. Our analysis of media merger mania, for example, takes the merger of America Online (AOL) and Time Warner as an opportunity to examine how the national news media reported facts and opinions about the event. From mergers and acquisitions to going-out-of-business sales, we find that immediate economic ramifications, rather than long-term political or cultural implications, tend to be prioritized in the news. Side stories on big mergers focus on the personalities of chief executive officers and the effects on stock market prices. This is to be expected of the business press, but we should expect news media to be more vigilant in their coverage of concentrations of power—including within their own industry—as part of their normative mission of serving the public. Since this is not the case, we are often left with a handful of alternative media sources to put current events into perspective.

By alternative media, we mean the nonprofit, largely ad-free newsletters, magazines, and periodicals operating on the margins of the media marketplace. Because they are primarily reader-supported publications, they have greater freedom to provide a wider range of views, but because they are not a part of the mainstream distribution system, they are nearly impossible to find at the local newsstand. In terms of methodology, our use of the alternative press provides a comparative dimension that is also a key qualitative research strategy. We compare, for example, mainstream coverage of protests against the World Trade Organization (WTO) and the International Monetary Fund (IMF), written by reporters sent to the scene, to accounts in alternative media, written by activists actually involved in the scene. The differences are striking and the reasons for this will become more apparent in the following chapters.

Chapter 2 examines the process of media merger mania, as well as the logic behind it and news coverage of it, using two millennial megamergers, Viacom with CBS and AOL with Time Warner, as case studies. Chapter 3 looks at the effects of media concentration on culture, focusing on the structure and content of the movie and music industries. Chapter 4 examines advertising and journalism as ideological and economic institutions, exploring the effects of the symbiotic relationship between them on the structure and content of the news. Chapter 5 extends this analysis with an examination of the commercialization and privatization of public education as advertisers invade the classroom. Finally, in chapter 6, we turn to media coverage of those struggling to expand news agendas or to challenge the parameters of public debate. Specifically, we examine a surge of protest against global capitalism at the turn of the twenty-first century and media attempts to symbolically contain it. We argue that alternative voices will be more important than ever in the struggles to come.

## NOTES

1. Clifford G. Christians and James W. Carey, "The Logic and Aims of Qualitative Research," in *Research Methods in Mass Communication,* ed. Guido H. Stempel and Bruce H. Westley (Englewood Cliffs, N.J.: Prentice-Hall, 1981), 342–62.

2. Christians and Carey, "The Logic and Aims of Qualitative Research," 353.

3. Elizabeth L. Eisenstein, *The Printing Revolution in Early Modern Europe* (Cambridge: Cambridge University Press, 1983), 93.

4. George Farah and Justin Elga, "What's *Not* Talked About on Sunday Morning?" *Extra!,* October 2001, 14–17.

5. John Nerone, *Violence against the Press: Policing the Public Sphere in U.S. History* (New York: Oxford University Press, 1994).

6. Jon Bekken, "The Working Class Press at the Turn of the Century" in *Ruthless Criticism: New Perspectives in U.S. Communication History,* ed. Bob McChesney and Bill Solomon (Minneapolis: University of Minnesota Press, 1993), 151–75; and Nerone, *Violence,* 265–95.

7. Sudarsan Raghavan and Sumana Chatterjee, "Child Slavery Persists on African Cocoa Farms" (Knight Ridder Newspapers), *State College (Pa.) Centre Daily Times,* 25–26 June 2001; Sudarsan Raghavan, "The Slavery Trap" (Knight Ridder Newspapers), *State College (Pa.) Centre Daily Times,* 25–26 June 2001; and Sumana Chatterjee, "Chocolate Companies React to Slavery Revelations," *State College (Pa.) Centre Daily Times* (Knight Ridder Newspapers), 25–26 June 2001.

8. Sumana Chatterjee, "Consumers: Why Not Boycott Chocolate?" (Knight Ridder Newspapers), *State College (Pa.) Centre Daily Times,* 26 June 2001, sec. A7.

9. Sumana Chatterjee, "Chocolate Companies Fight 'Slave Free' Labels," *State College (Pa.) Centre Daily Times* (Knight Ridder Newspapers), 1 August 2001, sec. A4.

10. Sumana Chatterjee, "Chocolate Makers to Accept Responsibility for Cocoa Farm Practices" (Knight Ridder Newspapers), *State College (Pa.) Centre Daily Times,* 1 October 2001, sec. A3.

11. Edward Herman, "Market Constraints on Freedom of Expression," *Journal of Communication Inquiry* 15 (1991): 45–53.

# 2

# MEDIA MERGER MANIA: CONCENTRATION IN THE MEDIA INDUSTRY

One reason we write this book is to call attention to the biases, distortions, and gaps in mainstream media coverage of contemporary issues and events. In this chapter we focus on the way in which the media "cover" themselves. There are, of course, occasional acts of self-flagellation and *mea culpas* when news operations are caught fabricating stories or distorting facts and images to support a particular take on a news report. One need only recall the outcry surrounding flights of fancy in a Pulitzer Prize–winning "news" story or the infamous *Time* magazine cover "photo illustration" of O. J. Simpson with darkened skintone.[1] Critics within the media constantly condemn their colleagues' speculative and sensationalistic coverage of scandals and tragedies involving politicians and celebrities. But this kind of internal "flak," to use Edward Herman and Noam Chomsky's term,[2] only serves to reinforce the public's belief that the media are vigilantly policing themselves, and that the media marketplace is free and competitive enough to ensure that the "truth" generally prevails.

Unfortunately, such self-criticism leaves serious gaps in mainstream coverage of media issues. Most notable, perhaps, is the lack of any systematic analysis of the processes and effects of media concentration. Media mergers have implications that resonate beyond Wall Street, but these are seldom explored when they are announced. Such is the case of news coverage of Viacom's announcement in September 1999 of its intent to acquire the CBS Corporation for $37.3 billion, creating the second largest transnational media conglomerate in the world. America Online's (AOL) announcement in January 2000 of its intent to acquire Time Warner for $165 billion was characterized by a similar lack of analysis. The ways in which these mergers *were* covered warrant closer examination. In this chapter, we take a look at each.

## THE VIACOM-CBS MERGER

The transaction continued a trend that began in the mid-1990s when the Federal Communications Commission (FCC) repealed regulations that prohibited the major television networks—ABC, CBS, and NBC—from producing and syndicating their own prime-time programming. The FCC had imposed the Financial Interest and Syndication Rules (FISRs) on the networks in the 1970s when their viewing audience still attracted about 95 percent of U.S. households. At that time, the FCC found that the networks were forcing producers of prime-time television shows to give up portions of their revenues and their syndication rights to gain access to the airwaves. Also, prime-time schedules tended to favor the scheduling of shows in which the networks had a financial interest. By the mid-1990s, however, the FCC found that the decline in the share of network audiences to cable television, as well as the rise of a competing fourth network, Fox, made the FISRs unnecessary. The rules had also prevented the merger of major film studios with the networks when such vertical integration seemed necessary to improve the global competitiveness of U.S.-based media companies. Indeed, even before the rules were repealed, the Walt Disney Co. announced its intent to purchase ABC, confident of the federal government's approval. Disney's film and television studios planned to provide in-house programming for ABC's national broadcast network. Similarly, Viacom's takeover of CBS gave Paramount film and television studios direct access to the prime-time network audience, at both CBS and the United Paramount Network (UPN). The repeal of the rules essentially revived the practice of utilizing vertical integration to favor in-house programming on the prime-time broadcast schedules.[3]

### PROGRAMMING THE AUDIENCE FROM CRADLE TO GRAVE

Media concentration is an ongoing trend that follows the predominant tendency within capitalism toward centralization of economic power in the hands of oligopolies. The 1996 Telecommunications Act, which lifted a number of restrictions on media ownership and control, accelerated further concentration. CBS, for example, directly benefited from the removal of restrictions on the number of radio stations a single company could own. Until the mid-1980s, FCC rules permitted a single company to own seven AM and seven FM radio stations. In 1985, the FCC raised the limit to twelve AM and twelve FM stations. The 1996 act removed most restrictions on radio ownership and set off what Douglas Gomery called "the greatest merger wave in history."[4] The CBS-owned Infinity Broadcasting chain owned 160-plus radio stations when the Viacom takeover was announced. Many of these stations were concentrated in the same cities, giving Infinity up to 50 percent of the advertising revenues generated in these markets.[5]

The Viacom-CBS marriage included the consolidation of a number of media operations in addition to the CBS and UPN networks and Infinity Broadcasting. The deal involved cable programming (MTV, VH1, Nickelodeon, Comedy Central, ShowTime, and country music stations TNN and CMT); 17 owned-and-operated television stations; copyrights to the Paramount film and television libraries, and to more than 100,000 songs; Spelling Programming; Blockbuster Video; five amusement parks; billboard advertisers TDI Worldwide and Outdoor Systems Inc., with 210,000 billboards nationwide; and what was left of the Simon & Schuster publishing company. New media outlets included MTV Networks On Line and Marketwatch.com, CBS.com, and Country.com.[6] The estimated combined value of the advertising revenue generated by all Viacom-CBS outlets in 1999 was $11 billion,[7] far ahead of its nearest rival, Australia-based News Corp. At the time the deal was announced, the audience demographics of the merged Viacom-CBS ranged from cradle to grave, from *Rugrats* to *Touched by an Angel.*

JOINED AT THE HIP

So what about news coverage of this media megamerger? The *State College (Pa.) Centre Daily Times* signaled the significance of the merger with a front-page story from the Associated Press (AP).[8] The headline, "Giants of Media Join at the Hip," acknowledged the magnitude of the deal while playing on the dominant theme of the story—the merger of "hip properties like MTV and VH1" with the "old line network" known for *60 Minutes* and *Murder She Wrote.*[9] The report cited two sources. The first was Viacom Chairman Sumner Redstone, who ranked fourteenth on the *Forbes 400* 2001 list of the richest people in the United States, worth an estimated $10.1 billion.[10] Redstone declared that Viacom-CBS "will be the global leaders in every facet of the media and entertainment industry, financially strong from day one, with an enviable stable of global brands."[11] The second source, an analyst from PaineWebber, gave his approval: "It's a good deal for everybody. . . .You need to be big.You need to have a global presence." No sources questioning the political and cultural implications of the deal are cited. This is typical of the mainstream news media and reflects their reliance on a "Golden Rolodex" of sources for expert commentary.

Since the AP account of the merger was framed as a business story, it is not surprising that CEOs and Wall Street experts were the first consulted, but the *CDT*'s follow-up story—provided by Knight Ridder and buried in the back of the Sunday business pages—was just as disappointing.[12] Again, the commentary flows entirely from media analysts and executives, while the entire process of media concentration is treated as natural and inevitable—as "part of an evolutionary process leading to a day in the near future when four to six companies control most of what the world hears on radio, watches on television and sees on the big screen."[13] The report does not even begin to touch upon the significance of this reality. It was written by a reporter for the *Atlanta Journal-Constitution*, which published an extended version on the front page of its business section, but the additional text narrowly focused on the emergence of Melvin A. Karmazin, CBS's chief executive, as a "new media kingpin."[14] This is in keeping with the mainstream media's tendency to favor personality profiles of CEOs over substantive analyses of institutional structures.

Network news coverage of the Viacom-CBS deal followed the same formula. We focused our attention on *NBC Nightly News,* since the merger left NBC as the only network not owned by a major Hollywood studio. NBC news producers left it up to anchor Tom Brokaw to raise the question of the impact of media concentration on diversity, creativity, democracy, and freedom of expression. His expert witness, however, was yet another Wall Street analyst who quickly dodged the question and returned to the economic dimensions of the deal.[15] Foremost for Wall Street, of course, is how the integration of the two companies could potentially reduce costs by increasing "efficiency" and hence raise returns to company shareholders and lenders. As Herman argues, such mergers produce no real benefits to society, only to investors.[16]

The *New York Times* coverage of the Viacom-CBS merger also cast the story as a business matter. Almost all of the reporting on the merger was printed in the business pages. The front page of the "Business Day" section was dominated by two articles featuring the biographies of Redstone and Karmazin.[17] Still, a very careful reader might have caught a glimpse of the economic, political, and cultural implications of the deal. One article, for example, predicted another round of major cuts at the CBS news division and a further erosion of the line between news and entertainment. The conglomerate owners of the major news networks expect these divisions to be profit centers. In order to cut costs, they favor the cheaper news magazine genre over more costly foreign, investigative, and documentary news.[18] Another suggested that the deal would enhance the likelihood of privileged access for Paramount productions to CBS's prime-time schedule to the exclusion of more creative independent producers.[19]

A report on the impact of the deal on the music business hinted that the combination of MTV, VH1, TNN, and CMT with Infinity Broadcasting's 160-plus radio stations would give the company a dominating presence in the music industry, and that this domination would extend to the Internet, given the brand recognition that has made MTV's websites among the most popular.[20] Stuart Elliot, the *New York Times* advertising columnist, cited sources expressing concerns that Viacom's control over so many media outlets would drive up advertising rates as the company extracted a premium for access to its many audiences.[21] Finally, the day after the deal was announced, the *New York Times* ran an editorial written by an in-house "Editorial Observer," who concluded that the deal promised benefits for stockholders but merely "more of the same" for audiences.[22] The editors of the *Times* effectively dissociated the paper from this opinion by including the author's byline and placing the piece beneath the unsigned editorials, separated by a black border.

Despite the apparent concerns, a *New York Times* report on how federal regulators would respond to the deal found "a widespread consensus that at the end of the day Washington will bless the acquisition."[23] Immediately after announcing the deal, Redstone and CBS president Karmazin headed to Washington, D.C., to seek exemptions from the remains of the FCC regulations that the merger would violate, confident that these hurdles could be cleared. Karmazin declared that ownership limits on broadcasters were outdated and needed to be modified due to the proliferation of cable and satellite television and the Internet.[24] Viacom also challenged broadcast ownership limits on First Amendment grounds, arguing that they constituted an arbitrary regulation that violated the company's freedom of expression. When the FCC approved the deal in May 2000, the *New York Times* quoted an "ebullient Mr. Redstone" as saying, "This has really worked perfectly. We basically got everything we had wanted."[25]

Not quite. Existing FCC rules still required Viacom–CBS to sell off some of its television stations. The merged company would control more than 40 percent of the national television audience, exceeding the 35 percent limit. FCC rules also prohibited a single company from owning two national broadcast networks, in this case CBS and UPN. Viacom's challenge to the rule limiting its share of broadcast households to 35 percent gained momentum when News Corp. (controlled by Rupert Murdoch, number twenty-one on the 2001 *Forbes 400* at $7.5 billion) announced its acquisition of Chris-Craft's ten television stations from Herbert Siegel (211th on the *Forbes* list with $1.1 billion) for $3.5 billion.[26] The acquisition also put

News Corp.'s share of the U.S. broadcast audience over the limit and violated FCC cross-ownership rules prohibiting one company from owning television and newspaper outlets in the same media market.

Like the Viacom-CBS merger, the FCC approved News Corp.'s takeover of Chris-Craft under the condition that certain properties were sold or traded to reduce its broadcast reach to 35 percent of U.S. households. Meanwhile, Viacom and News Corp. took their case to the U.S. Court of Appeals for the District of Columbia. The court is responsible for ruling on the legality and constitutionality of FCC procedures and regulations. In April 2001, the D.C. court of appeals granted Viacom's request for a suspension of the date by which the company was to divest some of its television stations. The FCC had to defend the rules before the court in September 2001, but it was clear that under President Bush's newly appointed chair of the commission, Michael K. Powell, son of Secretary of State Gen. Colin L. Powell, they already were on their way out. Powell, called the "Great Deregulator" by the *Washington Post,* was criticizing the rules even as FCC attorneys were obligated to defend them.[27] The *New York Times* concluded that the sharp tone of the judges' commentary during oral arguments suggested that the FCC was going to lose this case.[28]

On February 19, 2002, the D.C. court of appeals handed what a front-page story in the *New York Times* called "a huge victory to the nation's largest television networks and cable operators."[29] The rule prohibiting a broadcast television network from reaching more than 35 percent of U.S. households was sent back to the FCC for reconsideration. The court struck down another rule preventing companies from owning a cable system and broadcast station in the same market. Given FCC Chairman Powell's open skepticism of the need for ownership restrictions, the *New York Times* predicted that the 35 percent rule was all but certain to be watered down or abandoned. The decision was a setback for smaller owners of broadcast stations and consumer groups advocating more diversity in media ownership. As the *New York Times* noted, it was likely to "open the door for a new wave of megamergers in the entertainment and media industries and a continued concentration of power among the biggest media companies."[30] Broadcast chain ownership rules date back to the 1930s, when NBC and CBS dominated radio airwaves. The court's action therefore called into question seventy years of government regulation of broadcast network concentration.

Although the question of Viacom's television station ownership remains unresolved at this writing, its challenge to the rule preventing ownership of two television networks was successful. In April 2001, the FCC voted 3–1 to repeal the 50-year-old rule preventing a single company from owning more than one national television broadcast network. The decision primarily hinged on Viacom's claim that the 200-affiliate UPN network would not survive if divested, and diversity would be lost since the network targeted African-American audiences and employed African-American talent. Following this logic, only the deep pockets of a major media conglomerate can enhance diversity. Robert L. Johnson (number 172 on the 2001 *Forbes 400,* at $1.3 billion)[31] argued the same when he sold his BET Holdings II Inc., which owned Black Entertainment Television (BET), to Viacom for $2.9 billion in 2001. Johnson received $1.3 billion in Viacom stock from the deal and a five-year contract to remain head of BET. At the time of the acquisition in January 2001, BET reached 70 million homes and had become a main medium for reaching black consumers. Over half of its programming schedule was made up of free programming—music videos supplied by record companies. Most of the remaining schedule was made up of reruns of black situation comedies and monologues by black stand-up comedians. Johnson expected to draw on Viacom's resources to enhance the quality of the programming and silence those who criticized the network for exploiting African-American audiences with cheap programming.[32] For Viacom, the takeover of BET gave the company a lock on music television from urban to country, with MTV, VH1, and its two country music networks, CMT and TNN.

A year after the announced Viacom-CBS merger, it was confirmed that the deal was about synergy and not diversity. The *New York Times,* reporting on the scene of the 2000 MTV video awards, noted that while a "rap artist hip-hopped around with the back of his pants worn at thigh level, revealing his gray undies in all their glory" on stage, Viacom executives up in the first mezzanine were sipping champagne and dining on lobster, "fully attired in business suits, pants belted at their waists," apparently enjoying the show.[33] Rather than a culture clash, the report found that the Viacom executives had much to celebrate as the first fruits of the deal began paying off. Thus far, CBS had run promotions for the MTV awards during its season finale of *Survivor,* Nickelodeon planned to provide children's programming for CBS's Saturday morning schedule, VH1 would rerun CBS concert specials, and Viacom programming was being regularly promoted on Infinity radio stations.

## THE AOL–TIME WARNER MERGER

While Viacom pursued government approval of its acquisition of CBS, in January 2000 America Online announced its intentions to acquire Time

Warner for an estimated $165 billion, at that time the largest merger in world history. As one industry analyst put it, only a merger of AT&T, Yahoo, and Disney would have been of equal significance.[34] This merger brought AOL's 20 million Internet subscribers together with Time Warner's 35 million HBO pay-cable subscribers, 13 million cable system subscribers, and 120 million magazine readers, including readers of *Time, People,* and *Sports Illustrated.* Time Warner's cable news network, CNN, reached a global audience of 1 billion at the time. Its Warner Brothers film and television division and Warner Music, with over forty labels, are global leaders in their respective industry sectors.

MERGING TO MAKE A BETTER WORLD

The significance of the AOL–Time Warner merger made front-page headlines. The *State College (Pa.) Centre Daily Times* reported that the merger between the world's largest Internet service provider and the world's largest media empire "means whenever you pick up a magazine, turn on the TV, flip to a cable channel, go to the movies or log on to the Internet, AOL Time Warner will probably be there with you."[35] The reporter might have been referring to AOL's penchant for monitoring the proclivities of its customers, but considering the total lack of any critical assessment of the deal, this is doubtful. Rather, the sole sources, AOL chairman and CEO Steve Case (number 211 on the 2001 *Forbes 400* list, worth $1.1 billion)[36] and two financial analysts, celebrated the merger as a historic transformation of the media and Internet landscape. A follow-up article from Knight Ridder further celebrated the deal as a boon to Silicon Valley.[37]

On the PBS *NewsHour with Jim Lehrer,* Case and Time Warner CEO Gerald M. Levin put a similar history-making spin on the merger.[38] The script, according to *New York Times* television critic Walter Goodman, cast the merger as an altruistic endeavor that had nothing to do with power and money. "This is not trying to have control for some self-serving reason," Case was quoted as saying. "In business, you can have a social commitment." Levin agreed: "This company is going to operate in the public interest." When Case announced his commitment to creating "the most respected company in the world," Levin did him one better: "We want to make a better world."[39] In their world, this meant integrating Time Warner brands with the marketing and delivery power of AOL. As Goodman concluded, nothing in the script suggested improving the quality and diversity of the merged company's output.

MERGING AS MATING

Despite the global implications of the merger for media and democracy, much of the *New York Times* reporting and commentary remained superficial. The dominant themes involved fashion, cuisine, and romance. For example, the day after the merger was announced, the front page of the paper included a large color photo of Case and Levin. In identifying the two CEOs, the photo caption accompanying the lead story described Case as "with tie" and Levin "without tie."[40] Another accompanying story, also on page one, explained how strange it was for Case to wear a suit and tie while announcing the takeover of Time Warner, since he was known "for clinging to his casual costume of denim shirts and khakis on even the most formal occasions."[41] A third front-page story noted that Case had once appeared in a Gap ad.[42] Levin, it was noted, removed his tie before the news conference, then welcomed the "suits from Virginia," home of AOL's headquarters. A next-day lead article in the *New York Times* business pages described an AOL senior executive as expressing relief that Time Warner had casual dress days five days a week.[43] The article is accompanied by a large color photo of AOL's president, Robert W. Pittman, without tie—an accessory that, the reporter notes, was required at *Times* editorial offices in New York until the beginning of the 1990s. A senior executive from the Time Inc. division predicted the merger would be smoother than the one with Warner back in 1989, since the AOL management was made up of "Dockers guys" rather than "Hollywood killer types."[44]

In addition to the fashion hook, *New York Times* reporters used a cuisine theme to interpret this merger of "old" and "new" media and to speculate upon the potential clash of corporate cultures. The AOL model is cast in the image of Case, who once worked for Pizza Hut,[45] was known to hold "regular beer parties" on Fridays at AOL headquarters,[46] and had a penchant for popping jellybeans during interviews.[47] Time Inc. once exuded an image of Ivy League gentility. In the 1950s and 1960s, the closing of an issue of the magazine was heralded by a waiter with "a cart of wine and hard liquor for a celebration."[48] The ascension of Levin to the top of Time Warner, however, is said to have "brought about a certain anodyne quality, almost a neutral environment," and there is reportedly no drinking at the "big, rather bland" Time Warner headquarters at Rockefeller Center in midtown Manhattan.[49]

The cuisine theme reemerged when AOL announced its profit forecasts. One article quoted "people who know both Time Warner and America Online," who predicted the first culture clash between the two companies would be in the advertising sales area. A former Time Inc. president stated that Time Warner had developed "an implied code of civility," while at AOL civility was frowned upon. She compared AOL's pursuit of advertisers to "the bar scene in *Star Wars*: everyone is a character, and a tough one."[50] The same Time Warner senior executive who commented on the pants worn at AOL did not foresee such a conflict, describing his future colleagues as "latte-drinking nice guys."[51]

The most prevalent metaphor for the merger in the *New York Times* was that of romance. Reporters typically described the deal in terms of courtship and marriage. The courtship process, we were told, included regular dinners between Levin and Pittman along with their spouses.[52] In an article headlined "The Online Generation Courts the Old Guard," Case is described as a "prickly suiter." He rebuffed overtures from AT&T but was still "on the prowl" for a "major-league partner" in media or telecommunications, though "unwilling to get together with just any admirer."[53] Case was attracted to Time Warner and reported to have had long phone conversations with Levin, "wooing him with his vision of the wired future."[54] Time Warner had its chance to merge with AOL when it made its promising debut in the mid-1980s. Now, with AOL's far greater stock value, it was Time Warner shareholders who, as the *New York Times* reported, "leapt in celebration, like some waif rescued by a wealthy benefactor."[55]

Not everyone approved of the marriage, however. One article cast investors as skeptical parents seeking to rent the couple asunder, believing each had greater value as single entities.[56] Within three days after the announcement, AOL investors signaled their disapproval by selling off their stock, dropping its value by one-fifth. This, in turn, reduced the value of the deal to Time Warner shareholders, who were to be paid off in AOL stock. Under the terms of the merger contract, however, Time Warner was altar-bound regardless of the price of AOL shares, locking the companies into going forward "for richer or for poorer."[57] Additionally, the marriage had the blessings of Janus Capital, an institutional investor that owned $12 billion worth of AOL and Time Warner stocks. Finally, a key partner in the marriage was Ted Turner (number 62 on the 2001 *Forbes 400* list at $6.2 billion), then the largest individual shareholder in Time Warner with 6.7 percent of the company's stock. Bringing together the themes of money and romance, Turner approved the deal, later declaring: "When I cast my vote for 100 million shares, I did it with as much excitement as I felt the first time I made love some 42 years ago."[58]

A closer analysis of the *New York Times* coverage of the merger does reveal some strains of criticism of the merger and the trend it exemplifies, beginning with columns by reporters on the media beat. From the "Arts/ Culture Desk," for example, Walter Goodman mocked the cuisine metaphor, describing Levin as "carried away by a strange image of gobbling up all the information and entertainment" that he foresaw "flooding America, digitally or otherwise." Levin is quoted as saying: "I want to ingest it" and "consume it," to which Goodman responded: "He sounded like a commercial for Pepcid AC."[59] In a "Digital Commerce" column, Denise Caruso burlesqued the courtship metaphor that likened AOL's proposed purchase to "a snapshot of the new economy versus the old." The merger was not, she insisted, "a slightly sordid wedding between a luscious nubile and her tottering trophy husband, shuffling to the altar on his last hormonal surges." Rather, it was "more like two very wealthy old men doing combovers on their balding pates, trying to look hip and zippy but not quite willing to let go of the past" while gaining as much control over the evolving online entertainment distribution system as possible.[60] On the advertising beat, Stuart Elliott cited a CEO of a leading interactive advertising agency who praised the "union" of Time Warner's database and "amazing knowledge of the American consumer" with AOL's "amazing knowledge" of its 20 million members.[61] He acknowledged that some advertising agency executives had concerns about "overconcentration and oligopolistic control" of the media industry, but did not quote them or explain why: Because advertisers would be forced to pay higher rates as a smaller number of companies charge more for access to their growing range of media outlets. Indeed, these concerns were summarily dismissed with a quote from a Saatchi and Saatchi media director: "I don't think those issues pertain here."[62]

## THE BIG MEDIA DEBATE

The *New York Times* ran a lead editorial following the merger announcement, acknowledging anxiety about the potential societal effects of the monopolization of the media market in the hands of a few companies. Finally, however, the editorial suggests that the deal will increase access to high-speed Internet services and lead to "broader choice."[63] For the *New York Times* editors, the more serious threat posed by such economic concentration was to the U.S. political system: the ability of such "corporate behemoths" to "buy political influence." The editors concluded that there was no need to scuttle such mergers but rather to reform campaign finance laws.

### CARTOONISTS AND OTHER CRITICS

Appearing opposite the *New York Times* editorial, a piece of op-art by cartoonist Tom Tomorrow depicts a clueless middle-class U.S. couple celebrating the merger as the world takes "one step closer to the *single source* of news, information and entertainment" and dreaming about the day when AOL Time Warner merges with Microsoft.[64] Below the cartoon is a serious op-ed piece by Robert H. Frank, a Cornell University economist, who argues that the merger is driven by "the technological imperative" to either "dominate or perish." In his view, AOL Time Warner's ability to dominate the market therefore promises to benefit stockholders and consumers alike.[65]

The *State College (Pa.) Centre Daily Times* also relied on syndicated political cartoons to provide its readers with critical views on the merger. One drawing, by Kevin Siers, imagines an outer space view of planet Earth slapped with a label stating: "Contents: Copyright AOL Time Warner."[66] Another, by Tom Toles, envisions a series of morphing computer screens, beginning with the words "Microsoft Inc." and ending with something called "Soft-CBS-Viacom Inc."[67] Both were welcome commentaries on the ramifications of media concentration. The only extended analysis of the deal was a guest editorial written by Henry Giroux, a Pennsylvania State University professor of cultural studies and education. In it, Giroux criticized AOL Time Warner for seeking to harness culture, entertainment, and information "to unfettered consumerism" at the expense of more important noncommercial values necessary for a healthy democracy, such as "a respect for freedom, equality, liberty, cultural differences, constitutional rights and economic justice."[68] This "My View" column, prefaced with an authorial byline and biographical blurb, was carefully placed on the "Viewpoints" page of the paper under the aforementioned morph cartoon—lest readers assume it in any way reflected the opinions of the *Centre Daily Times*.

NO CAUSE FOR ALARM

Nonetheless, there was nothing approaching even this level of critique in the *New York Times*. A concerned reader had to scour the middle pages of the business section to find two articles raising questions about the effects of the deal on media autonomy and democracy. The journalists consulted their Golden Rolodex for critics of Big Media and dutifully cite Ralph Nader (identified as a "consumer advocate"); Ben H. Bagdikian (author of *The Media Monopoly)*; Robert McChesney (communications professor at the University of Illinois); and Jeff Cohen, founder of Fairness and Accuracy in Reporting (FAIR), described as "a liberal-leaning media watch group."[69] These sources made strong arguments concerning the threats posed by media concentration to journalistic independence and information diversity. In a "News Analysis" article, Laurence Zuckerman noted a seeming paradox:

Public debates over media concentration have diminished since the 1980s, even as media concentration has increased. He subtly acknowledged that the lack of public discussion over Big Media is only apparently paradoxical, since the media themselves, as powerful shapers of the public agenda, have conveniently ignored it. He finally suggested that the ambiguities of the issue may simply have "sapped many people's sense of outrage."[70]

Perhaps the sapping of people's outrage is precisely due to the mainstream media's coverage of media mergers. Traditional journalistic practice is to reduce complex issues to two sides. However, when it comes to covering events concerning the media business, journalists seem compelled to discover ambiguities that resist such reduction. Hence, Zuckerman suggests four reasons for why the AOL–Time Warner merger is not as alarming as the critics he quotes warn. First, concentration of media ownership and control is not a problem because of the proliferation of new media outlets, from cable networks to the Internet. Second, Big Media do not crowd out alternative voices; they enhance the diversity of the marketplace because they have the resources to launch new media products and absorb losses generally incurred by such ventures (for example, the millions spent by the Gannett Company before *USA Today* became profitable). Third, concerns that media conglomerates will use their outlets to protect or promote their own interests are overstated; attempts by these companies to stifle embarrassing news coverage in their subsidiaries will eventually come to light when they are "pounced upon by competitors, often owned by rival conglomerates." Additionally, owners and editors committed to editorial integrity will not allow their media outlets to promote personal causes, because, as Zuckerman quotes Norman Pearlstine, the editor in chief of Time Inc., "then you are going to have bad journalism."[71]

Finally, Zuckerman suggests, critics of Big Media may merely be "blinded by nostalgia" for some "golden age 30 or 40 years ago" when broadcast and newspaper companies were independently owned and operated. In fact, he claims, journalists working for such firms were often beholden to advertisers such as car dealers and supermarket and department store chains, or constrained by the interlocking economic and political interests of the company's owners. He concludes that only global media conglomerates have the clout to stand up to threats from advertisers, big business, or national governments.[72] Zuckerman does not allow his sources to provide counterarguments to his claims. Instead, Nader is cast as alarmist for being "extremely critical of the deal" and elitist in his hopes that mainstream media will finally collapse by boring audiences to tears. Bagdikian is cast as the blinded nostalgist. To find such counterclaims, a critical reader had to turn to the alternative media. They have the least to lose for criticizing media concentration and the most to lose as a result of this process.

*The Technology Fix*

The first claim, which holds that media concentration is not a serious problem because of the proliferation of new media outlets, can be countered by the rebuttal that the very purpose of such mergers is to create closed systems in which content and delivery systems are internally linked. Until the AOL–Time Warner merger, AOL supported open systems, since it required access to phone and cable lines to provide its Internet service, reaching 54 percent of U.S. households at the time. By acquiring Time Warner's cable system, with 22 percent of the nation's cable subscribers, the combined companies created a natural incentive to bundle their services and restrict access to their cable systems.[73] AOL promptly dropped its commitment to open access after announcing the merger. So although the combination of the Internet and broadband cable services has the potential to deliver content from millions of sources, it makes more sense for a media monolith to deliver that which it already owns. AOL Time Warner was tapping into a trend pointed out by Joel Bleifuss, editor of *In These Times,* in which Internet traffic was already being routed to fewer and fewer sites. By the year 2000, the 100 most-visited websites accounted for nearly half of all pages viewed.[74] Jupiter Media Metrix reported that between March 1999 and March 2001, the total number of companies controlling half of U.S. user minutes online shrank 64 percent, from eleven to four. Even more drastic was the drop in the number of companies controlling 60 percent of all U.S. minutes spent online during the same period, from 110 to 14, an 87 percent decrease.[75] According to Bleifuss, the average online user in 2000 spent almost 20 percent of his or her time on the 'Net at the top ten websites. AOL Time Warner's goal was to have its sites among them.[76]

In another *In These Times* editorial, Pat Aufderheide described ways this could be done, such as rigging the speed of transmission of favored websites or making sure AOL–Time Warner services pop up first on the computer screen.[77] Hence, rather than giving people greater ability to produce, distribute, and receive information via the Web, the Big Media continue to seek to reproduce a captive consumer audience. This is inherent to the logic of vertical integration and is confirmed by the media's historical record. Each new medium is introduced with high hopes and expectations of increasing diversity and communications democracy. However, existing economic and political forces always seem to undermine these promises. Brian Winston called this recurrent historical pattern the "'law' of the suppression of radical potential,"[78] meaning there is no reason to believe that the future of the Internet will be any different.

*Deep Pockets and Diversity*

This brings up the second claim, that critics of Big Media need not worry since conglomerates have the resources to develop and sustain new media outlets and therefore foster media diversity. This claim is defeatist and concedes to oligopolistic control of the media while buying into AOL–Time Warner executives' claims that they understood the significance of the social and political power they wielded and promises that they would do so with responsibility. However, although it is true that only Big Media can afford the huge losses that often accompany the launching of new media products such as Gannett's *USA Today*, or sustaining existing unprofitable operations such as News Corp.'s conservative *New York Post*, it is impossible to imagine these companies doing the same for genuinely alternative voices and views. If this were the case, more than 1 percent of U.S. communities would have competing newspapers, instead of one-newspaper monopolies, and more than just 1 percent of box office revenues would be generated by foreign movies. These situations were not caused by a lack of audience demand but rather are due to the fact that these markets do not achieve the levels of profitability expected by media investors.

The deep-pockets argument is more often seen by economists as a threat than an opportunity. Large conglomerates are able to engage in predatory pricing, charging prices below actual costs, because their deep pockets allow them to afford the temporary losses that small and mid-sized firms cannot. Additionally, predatory pricing is usually accompanied by large advertising budgets that cannot be matched by smaller competitors. As smaller firms are forced to leave the business, further concentration of the economy occurs, leading to higher prices and less variety. Although predatory pricing practices are harder to find in the media business, since audiences tend to choose media based on taste rather than price, the large media conglomerates nonetheless maintain significant advantages in the marketplace. They can cultivate tastes for their own products with their enormous advertising and marketing power.

The arguments that new media technologies or socially responsible media conglomerates should mitigate concerns about merger mania are both essentially flawed since they confuse what British communications scholar Graham Murdock has called "multiplicity" with genuine diversity. "More does not necessarily mean different."[79] In its editorial comment on the AOL–Time Warner merger, *The Nation* feared that the rush of media mergers and joint ventures had already "created the worrisome prospect" that the Internet would go the way of television: "500 channels and nothing worth watching; while the cacophony of independent voices that makes for vibrant public discourse will be pushed to the margins, where hardly anyone will even know to look for them."[80]

*Fear of Exposure*

The third reason that critics of the AOL–Time Warner merger were cast as alarmists focused on their supposedly undue concerns about the effects of conglomeration and concentration on media content, particularly journalism. In fact, critics have compiled a long list of episodes in which Big Media have tried to suppress news and information detrimental to their corporate interests.[81] The usual response is that concerns are unwarranted precisely because such a list could be produced. The oligopolistic competition among the Big Media offers assurances that such episodes eventually come to light, embarrassing any company caught violating journalistic ideals. Yet, as Zuckerman subtly admits, "It is impossible to know how many articles have not been pursued because journalists felt it could limit their careers to challenge their corporate parents."[82] Actually, surveys of news professionals suggest that they routinely take such factors into consideration. Bagdikian cites a 1980 survey in which 33 percent of editors working for newspaper chains admitted they would not run stories reflecting negatively on their parent firm.[83] A 2000 poll conducted by the Pew Research Center for the People and the Press along with the *Columbia Journalism Review* found that 35 percent of the nearly 300 reporters and news executives surveyed said that news stories that would hurt the financial interests of a news organization often or sometimes go unreported. More importantly, nearly 80 percent of those surveyed claimed market pressures led to the avoidance of stories deemed newsworthy but seen as too boring, while over half claimed avoidance of stories considered too complicated for their audiences.[84] Such studies reveal the institutionalization of self-censorship, demonstrating that the media are not fulfilling their essential role in keeping the public fully informed.

Critics of Big Media have also compiled a long list of incidents in which media owners have used their outlets to promote their political and economic interests. The counterargument here is that audiences see such self-promotion as poor journalism and reject it. Accordingly, Time Inc.'s Pearlstine points out that *Forbes* magazine never openly supported the presidential candidacy of its owner, Steven Forbes, since the magazine's readers were more interested in the mindsets of CEOs than those of presidential candidates.[85] Although *Forbes* may not have directly plugged its publisher, this self-proclaimed "capitalist tool" did help to legitimize his radically conservative economic policies for a significant percentage of the voting population. Similarly, Rupert Murdoch's repurchase of the money-losing *New York Post* is evidence not of some altruistic effort to preserve another editorial voice, but rather an expansionary move to combine the property with his local television station, even though this was against FCC regulations, and increase his political clout in New York City.

Clearly, Big Media critics can make a solid case demonstrating that media owners routinely find ways to promote and protect their economic and political interests. However, as Robert H. Lande, professor of law at the University of Baltimore, explained in *The Nation,* "These problems could exist without any improper intent on the part of the media barons."[86] Therefore, the critique becomes stronger when the focus is shifted from how the behavior of individual corporations and their owners affect media content to the institutional level of how media are used to protect and promote the political and economic interests of the capitalist class as a whole. Once again the historical record shows that the communications system has generally served the dominant classes since the origins of class-divided societies. Although force and coercion have always been central to class domination, gaining the consent of the dominated has generally proven more efficient in maintaining the status quo.

Despite whatever oligopolistic competition exists among the Big Media, they continue to serve their historical function of maintaining the wealth and power of the current ruling class. As our parenthetical references to the *Forbes 400* are designed to suggest, media owners are among the richest individuals in the United States. According to the 2001 *Forbes 400,* sixty of the richest people in the United States made most of their fortune from media industries.[87] Another thirty-nine members, including Steve Case, made most of their money from new communications technologies that provide the hardware and software for the delivery of information and entertainment products.[88] Additionally, several members of the list who earned their wealth from assets other than media have since made large investments in the communications sector as they diversified their portfolios. For example, Warren Buffett, the second-richest individual on the 2001 *Forbes* list with $33.2 billion, had investments in both the Washington Post Company and the Walt Disney Company.[89]

Big Media and Big Business are also intertwined with one another via stock ownership, joint ventures, and interlocking boards of directors. At the time of the AOL–Time Warner merger, AT&T/Liberty Media owned stock in Time Warner, News Corp., and Sprint PCS. AT&T's largest stock holder was John C. Malone (ninetieth on the 2001 *Forbes* list, worth $2.1 billion), who sold TCI Inc. to AT&T for $54 billion in 1999.[90] The day before the merger was announced, AT&T declared its intent to acquire the cable company MediaOne for $58 billion. AT&T, already the nation's largest cable operator, was set to acquire a 25 percent stake in Time Warner's cable systems.[91] In addition, US West, a regional Bell telephone company, already owned 25 percent of Time Warner's film, television, and cable assets.

Along with Janus Capital, a number of other institutional investors held significant shares of stock in the two companies when the merger was announced. Among AOL's largest stockholders in 1998 were mutual fund managers such as Fidelity Management & Research, Putnam Investment Management, and American Century Investment; and banks including J. P. Morgan, Barclays, and Bankers Trust. Time Warner's second-largest shareholder in 1998, behind Ted Turner, was the Capital Group, a holding company that handles accounts for individual and institutional investors. Its third-largest was Fidelity Management & Research.[92] Other major institutional investors in the two companies in 1998 included American Express Financial, Equitable Companies, Mellon Bank, Travelers, and Wellington Management.[93] Benjamin M. Compaine rightly concluded that financial networks such as these are most concerned with a company's long-term profits and do not concern themselves "with the controversial—or lack of controversial—content of movies or books or television shows."[94] Big Media critics do not claim otherwise. Indeed, as Thomas Guback concluded after examining the ownership and control of the filmed entertainment industry, institutional investors are most concerned with "sound financial results." However, Guback pointed out that there *are* indirect and structural influences in content, since media owners "share a class interest that shapes their posture toward social resources: how they are used, by whom, for what purpose and in whose interest."[95]

Joint ventures in place at the announcement of the merger included the Tribune Company's 25 percent stake in Time Warner's WB network. The Tribune Company, publisher of the *Chicago Tribune* and owner of eighteen television stations as well as the Chicago Cubs, was also an early investor in America Online for a stake that totaled roughly 22 million shares. Times

Mirror, publisher of the *Los Angeles Times,* had invested early on in Netscape, for which it received stock when AOL bought the Internet browser company in 1998.[96] In March 2000, the Tribune Company announced plans to purchase Times Mirror in an $8 billion deal bringing together newspapers, television stations, and Internet services in the nation's three largest markets—Los Angeles, New York, and Chicago. In May 1999, Microsoft agreed to invest $5 billion in AT&T in exchange for use of its software for digital television settop cable boxes.[97] America Online announced agreements in 1999 with Bell Atlantic and SBC Communications Inc. to market the Bell companies' high-speed digital phone service.[98] AOL also partnered with Bertelsman to operate AOL Europe in local languages across the Continent.

The merger required a reshuffling of the boards of directors of both companies. Thomas Middelhoff, then CEO and chairman of Bertelsman, announced his resignation from the board of America Online the day after the merger became public. He insisted that Bertelsman would maintain its partnership in AOL Europe, but said he had to resign because Bertelsman, with stakes in music and books, and as the largest shareholder in Barnesandnoble.com, was now a major competitor of AOL Time Warner and probably in violation of Security and Exchange Commission rules preventing direct interlocks between boards of competing companies.[99] Even without direct interlocks, the membership of both companies' boards was linked via what sociologist G. William Domhoff has called the "power elite," by which he means the leadership arm of the ruling class.[100] As Domhoff explains, the role of the power elite is to promote the short-term specific interests of individual capitalists, companies, or industry sectors.

More important, though, is the role of the power elite in promoting the long-term stability and goals of the ruling class as a whole. Interlocking boards of directors provide a site where such interests can be pursued. Outside board members, those not involved in day-to-day operations, serve precisely that purpose. Thus, AOL's board at the time of the merger included General Alexander M. Haig, Jr., President Ronald Reagan's former Secretary of State; General Colin Powell, the former Chair of the Joint Chiefs of Staff under President George Bush; Franklin Raines, chair and CEO of Fannie Mae; and Marjorie M. Scardino, CEO of Pearson PLC, one of the world's largest publishing companies.[101] Time Warner's board also included outsiders from finance, big business, government, and arts and entertainment. Ties to finance included East-West Capital Associates, an investment banking boutique helping Time Warner find acquisitions, and the Bank of New York Company. Big business links included Hilton Hotels Corporation, UAL Corporation (United Airlines), Colgate-Palmolive Company, and

Philip Morris Companies. Former U.S. Senator John C. Danforth and former U.S. Trade Representative Carla Hills provided the company with access to government. Representing arts and entertainment were Beverly Sills Greenough, chair of the Lincoln Center for the Performing Arts; and Francis T. Vincent, Jr., former commissioner of Major League Baseball.[102]

Like institutional investors, members of boards of directors are expected to protect the interests of stockholders. As Matt Carlson explained in *Extra!*, their presence alone can make media executives think carefully about running stories that may offend certain economic interests.[103] More important is the power directors have to hire, fire, and discipline upper-level management. In January 2002, for example, Viacom's board of directors intervened when quarrels between CEO Redstone and COO Karmazin threatened the company's stock value (see chapter 3). Eighteen months after the AOL–Time Warner merger was completed, Gerald Levin and Robert Pittman were forced out, casualties of collapsing stock market prices. When the merger was announced in January 2000, Time Warner shares traded as high as $100 each and AOL shares as high as $80. By July 2002, shares of the combined company had dropped to as low as $12.

Boards of directors also advise stockholders on how to vote on shareholder proposals—and control the proxy vote of those who don't. For example, in Disney's 2002 *Notice of Annual Meeting of Shareholders,* the board of directors advised shareholders to vote "AGAINST" proposals that would: prevent the company's accountants from also serving as consultants, compel the company to follow a set of widely accepted human and labor rights standards for its operations in China, require the company to disclose its policies on amusement park safety and fully report all injuries, and limit the stock options received by individual executive officers.[104] A "NO" vote on these proposals was virtually predetermined, given the millions of Disney stockholders who own only a handful of shares and the handful of Disney stockholders who own millions of shares and control the proxy vote by default. Disney eventually did adopt the proposal to sever its accounting and consulting services—but only in response to threats by labor unions to drop the company's stock from their pension fund portfolios. In the wake of the Enron, WorldCom, and Global Crossing accounting scandals that came to light in 2001–2002, boards of directors were forced to become even more active in company oversight and even more independent of company management.

The most important function of boards of directors, however, is the role their institutional connections play in forging the unification of the capitalist class around its common stake in preserving the existing unequal distribution of wealth and power. Accordingly, unlike the textbook version of capitalism, nominally competitive and independent firms are formally linked into a "network of relationships that makes cousins of entire broods of economic giants,"[105] including the Big Media, which play a central role in protecting and promoting the family business. Such a critique of the effects of Big Media on news and information runs the risk of being seen as a conspiracy. However, as Bagdikian explained, "in modern times actual conspiracy may not be necessary," since large media corporations "have shared values" that "are reflected in the emphasis of their news and popular culture. They are the primary shapers of American public opinion about events and their meaning."[106]

*False Nostalgia*

Ironically enough, Bagdikian's reference to "modern times" leads to a fourth way in which critics of Big Media have been summarily dismissed. The argument is that contemporary media critics harbor a false nostalgia for some "golden era" when independently owned newspapers put public service before profit. Jon Katz, writing for *The Netizen,* epitomizes this nostalgia in his "Media Rant": "What a truly amazing transformation of American journalism, founded by raggedy outcasts, misfits, idealists, and quarrelsome colonial pamphleteers, none of whom would be allowed to drive Michael Eisner's limousine today."[107] The 2001 *Forbes 400* listed Eisner, chair and CEO of the Walt Disney Company, at number 359, worth an estimated $720 million.

Defenders of Big Media counter that there never really was a golden era. Family-owned newspapers and broadcasting companies often stifled news that would offend major advertisers. Editors and reporters learned not to pursue stories that might embarrass their companies' owners or the owners' friends. Indeed, the apologia goes, as large chains began to gobble up independents in the 1960s, publishers and editors gained greater autonomy, since distant parent companies had less concern about the actual content of the news, provided profit plans were being met. With big parent companies behind them, little papers in news media chains could supposedly stand up to advertisers, business interests, and government officials, serving their communities with stronger local reporting. Compaine dismisses so-called nostalgists with academic research supporting defenders of chain-owned newspapers. Based on "snapshots taken over several decades," Compaine finds that the "overwhelming weight of the research has shown that . . . corporately owned newspapers and 'monopoly' newspapers are, overall, either indistinguishable from family-owned newspapers or, by some accounts, superior."[108]

In fact, critics of Big Media are well aware of the dangers of romanticizing market competition.[109] There are inherent problems in a system in which news is produced to sell audiences to advertisers and produce profits for their owners. Yes, journalists have always faced constraints generated by the system, whether working for family-owned operations or large national newspaper chains. However, McChesney sees a substantial change as a result of concentrated media ownership. Whatever autonomy journalists once had, which was not used very effectively for the most part anyway, has diminished significantly, resulting in "a softening of news stories and a reluctance now to attack major advertisers."[110] For Katz, the problem is that the Big Media have turned editorial content over to mass-marketers. "They have to avoid content that's controversial, idiosyncratic, or too brainy. In the 1990s, the people running the media ape one another in the most important ways: They value market research, profits, status, and expansion."[111] Ultimately, Bagdikian continues, if Big Media do have a record of improvement in service to the public or independence from government, it is "not sufficiently impressive to counter the dangers of tightening control of public information."[112]

Consumer and public interest advocates such as the Consumers Union, Consumer Federation of America, the Media Access Project, and the Center for Media Education opposed the AOL–Time Warner merger on precisely such grounds. Internet service providers (ISPs), regional Bell telephone companies, AT&T, NBC, and the Walt Disney Company also opposed the deal, but due to concerns about market power rather than media democracy. The primary site of intervention for opponents of the merger was in front of the Federal Trade Commission (FTC). In one of its last major decisions under the Clinton administration, the FTC approved the merger in December 2000 after requiring America Online and Time Warner to sign a five-year consent decree promising access to its cable systems to competing ISPs, including the nation's second-largest ISP, Earthlink Inc. This guarantee, as well as the promise that AOL Time Warner would not favor its own content or discriminate against others' when transmitting content over its cable systems, including interactive television services, assuaged opponents of the deal. Without such concessions it is unlikely the merger would have been approved, but by making them, the two companies signaled their belief that cross-marketing opportunities produced by the combination were more important. While the deal was pending, a test of this assumption proved successful when AOL's promotion of Time Inc.'s magazines resulted in 600,000 new subscriptions in just six months.[113] Demonstrating its same belief in the power of branding, the Disney Company issued a statement approving the FTC agreement as a "huge victory for consumers and for competition."[114]

The final site of resistance to the merger was before the FCC. Consumer advocates, media access advocates, and competing firms had petitioned the commission to block the deal. Among the five commissioners was Michael Powell, who refused to recuse himself from the deliberations even though his father served on the AOL board. A year and one day after America Online and Time Warner announced their union, the FCC approved the merger, subject to conditions, and rejected all petitions to deny.[115] The FCC's order required AOL to open its instant messaging service to Internet rivals once the companies began integrating the service with Time Warner's high-speed cable systems. The *New York Times* reported that "consumer groups hailed" the FCC's decision but only Gene Kimmelman, codirector of the Washington, D.C., office of the Consumers Union, is quoted.[116] In his view, the combined actions of the FTC and FCC had averted "enormous dangers to consumers" and "transformed a merger that threatened competition into one that could actually expand consumers' choices for high-speed Internet and interactive TV services." A Time Warner spokesman called the FCC's order "a tremendous win for consumers . . . worldwide."[117]

## CONCLUSION

The fact that both consumer advocates and Big Media approved FTC and FCC conditions on the merger actions suggests that government intervention can appear to strike a balance between the contradictory roles the media play in serving the public while making a profit. However, the historical record suggests otherwise. For example, after reviewing the history of the broadcast reform movement of the 1960s to the mid-1970s, Willard D. Rowland, Jr., concluded that efforts to open broadcast and cable media to diverse voices had merely resulted in an "illusion of fulfillment."[118] One reason is that media reformers have inherited "a continuing set of paradoxes" from U.S. progressivism that is represented by their "yearning for a certain set of myths about the nature of the past, the possibilities of returning to it, and the role of the electronic media in effecting its return."[119] Another reason is that the movement had been co-opted by broadcasters, which, like the FCC, had indeed "become captured by the theater's rules, with little hope of affecting the ending of the play."[120] The reform movement thus became caught up in a ritualistic regulatory and policymaking process that actually served "as a legitimization or ratification of prior governmental and industrial views and structural arrangements."[121] It is precisely these views and arrangements that must be challenged.

Radical critics of Big Media have brought this challenge to the forefront. Writing in *The People,* Ken Boettcher argued that for any "real student of the media it should come as no surprise that new media are being commercialized just like older means of communication." Nor is it a surprise that "the capitalist-owned media are subject to the same laws of competition that lead to greater and greater concentration of capital—and control—in every industry." Furthermore, it doesn't seem to really matter "whether few capitalists or many own and control the mass media," since the so-called information they convey has "not brought the working class one inch closer to knowing what to do about the dire problems capitalism creates." Therefore, Boettcher recommends leaving the antitrust reforms to competing elements of the capitalist class and turning our energy and support to alternative media.[122]

## NOTES

1. *Time,* 27 June 1994, cover page.

2. Edward S. Herman and Noam Chomsky, *Manufacturing Consent: The Political Economy of Mass Media* (New York: Pantheon Books, 1988), 26–8.

3. Ronald V. Bettig, "Who Owns Prime Time? Industrial and Institutional Conflict over Television Programming and Broadcast Rights," in *Framing Friction: Media and Social Conflict,* ed. Mary S. Mander (Urbana: University of Illinois Press, 1999), 125–60.

4. Douglas Gomery, "Radio Broadcasting and Music Industry," in *Who Owns the Media? Competition and Concentration in the Mass Media Industry,* 3rd ed., ed. Benjamin M. Compaine and Douglas Gomery (Mahwah, N.J.: Lawrence Erlbaum Associates, 2000), 285–358.

5. Stuart Elliot, "A Combined Viacom-CBS Would Cast an Awfully Large Shadow Across a Wide Range of Ad Media," *New York Times,* 8 September 1999, sec. C8.

6. Lawrie Mifflin, "Viacom to Buy CBS, Forming 2nd Largest Media Company," *New York Times,* 8 September 1999, sec. A1, C15.

7. Elliot, "Viacom-CBS," sec. C8.

8. Seth Sutel, "Giants of Media Join at the Hip" (Associated Press), *State College (Pa.) Centre Daily Times,* 8 September 1999, sec. 1A, 7A.

9. Sutel, "Giants of Media," sec. 1A.

10. "The 400 Richest People in America," *Forbes,* 8 October 2001, 127–298.

11. Sutel, "Giants of Media," sec. 1A.

12. Charles Haddad, "CBS, Viacom Follow Trail Blazed by Disney, Time Warner" (Knight Ridder Tribune), *State College (Pa.) Centre Daily Times,* 12 September 1999, sec. 15B.

13. Haddad, "CBS, Viacom Follow Trail," sec. 15B.

14. Charles Haddad, "CBS-Viacom Merger Further Narrows Media," *Atlanta Journal-Constitution,* 9 September 1999, sec. F1, F3.

15. *NBC Nightly News with Tom Brokaw,* National Broadcasting Company, 7 September 1999.

16. Edward Herman, "Media Mega-Mergers," *Dollars & Sense,* May 1996, 8–13.

17. Alex Kuczynski, "CBS Chief Wanted His MTV," *New York Times,* 8 September 1999, sec. C1, C14; and Floyd Norris, "The New, Improved Redstone Still Knows How to Get His Way," *New York Times,* 8 September 1999, sec. C1, C13.

18. Felicity Barringer, "CBS News May Face More Cuts," *New York Times,* 9 September 1999, sec. C8.

19. Lawrie Mifflin, "CBS-Viacom Deal Raises Competition Questions," *New York Times,* 9 September 1999, sec. C1, C8.

20. Matt Richtel, "A New Force in Distributing Music across the Internet," *New York Times,* 8 September 1999, sec. 14C.

21. Elliot, "Viacom-CBS," sec. C8.

22. Verlyn Klinkenborg, "The Vision behind the CBS-Viacom Merger," *New York Times,* 9 September 1999, sec. A28.

23. Stephen Labaton, "Wide Belief U.S. Will Let a Vast Deal Go Through," *New York Times,* 8 September 1999, sec. C14.

24. Labaton, "Wide Belief," sec. C14.

25. Stephen Labaton, "Federal Regulators Give Approval to Viacom's Buyout of CBS," *New York Times,* 4 May 2000, sec. C1.

26. "The 400 Richest," 158, 170.

27. Frank Ahrens, "The Great Deregulator: Five Months into His Tenure as FCC Chairman, Michael Powell is Coming through Loud and Clear," *Washington Post,* 18 June 2001, sec. C1.

28. Stephen Labaton, "Court Weighs Easing Limits on Big Media," *New York Times,* 8 September 2001, sec. A1.

29. Stephen Labaton, "Appellate Court Eases Limitations for Media Giants: Rejects Longtime Rules," *New York Times,* 20 February 2002, sec. A1, C6.

30. Labaton, "Appellate Court Eases Limitations," sec. A1, C6.

31. "The 400 Richest," 168.

32. Brett Pulley, "The Cable Capitalist," *Forbes,* 8 October 2001, 42–54.

33. Bill Carter, "Media Talk: An Executive with Synergistic Vision," *New York Times,* 11 September 2000, sec. C17.

34. Frances Katz, "AOL, Time Warner Deal Sets the Tone" (Knight Ridder Tribune), *State College (Pa.) Centre Daily Times,* 11 January 2000, sec. 1A, 7A.

35. Katz, "AOL, Time Warner Deal," sec. 1A.

36. "The 400 Richest," 148.

37. Chris O'Brien, "AOL Merger May Fuel Silicon Valley Growth" (Knight Ridder Newspapers), *State College (Pa.) Centre Daily Times,* 13 January 2000, sec. 6B.

38. *NewsHour with Jim Lehrer,* Public Broadcasting System, 10 January 2000.

39. Walter Goodman, "When Corporate Synergy Becomes Manifest Destiny," *New York Times,* 19 January 2000, sec. E10.

40. Saul Hansell, "America Online Agrees to Buy Time Warner for $165 Billion; Media Deal Is Richest Merger," *New York Times,* 11 January 2000, sec. A1, C11.

41. Amy Harmon, "Exceptions Made for Dress Code, But Never for His Internet Vision," *New York Times,* 11 January 2000, sec. A1, C12.

42. Steve Lohr, "Medium for Main Street," *New York Times,* 11 January 2000, sec. A1, C10.

43. Amy Harmon and Alex Kuczynski, "A Bridge Builder for Corporate Culture," *New York Times,* 12 January 2000, sec. C1, C7.

44. Harmon and Kuczynski, "A Bridge Builder," sec. C4.

45. Lohr, "Medium for Main Street," sec. A1.

46. Harmon and Kuczynski, "A Bridge Builder," sec. C4.

47. Harmon, "Exceptions," sec. A1.

48. Harmon and Kuczynski, "A Bridge Builder," sec. C4.

49. Harmon and Kuczynski, "A Bridge Builder," sec. C4.

50. Saul Hansell, "Not-So-Subtle Engine Drives AOL Profit Forecasts," *New York Times,* 31 January 2000, sec. C1, C12.

51. Harmon and Kuczynski, "A Bridge Builder," sec. C7.

52. Harmon and Kuczynski, "A Bridge Builder," sec. C4.

53. Laura M. Holson, "The Online Generation Courts the Old Guard," *New York Times,* 11 January 2000, sec. C1, C13.

54. Holson, "The Online Generation," sec. C13.

55. Lohr, "Medium for Main Street," sec. C10.

56. Alex Berenson, "Investors Seem to Want to Keep AOL-Time Warner Asunder," *New York Times,* 13 January 2000, sec. C1, C6.

57. Berenson, "Investors," sec. C1.

58. Goodman, "When Corporate Synergy," sec. E10.

59. Goodman, "When Corporate Synergy," sec. E10.

60. Denise Caruso, "Digital Commerce: If the AOL-Time Warner Deal Is about Proprietary Content, Where Does That Leave a Noncommercial Directory It Will Own?" *New York Times,* 17 January 2000, sec. C5.

61. Stuart Elliott, "Advertising: The AOL-Time Warner Deal Changes Everything for Those Who Move, and Buy, in Media Circles," *New York Times,* 11 January 2000, sec. C8.

62. Elliott, "Advertising," sec. C8.

63. "The Biggest Media Merger Yet," *New York Times,* 11 January 2000, sec. A30.

64. Dan Perkins, a.k.a. Tom Tomorrow, op-art, *New York Times,* 11 January 2000, sec. A31.

65. Robert H. Frank, "A Merger's Message: Dominate or Die," *New York Times,* 11 January 2000, sec. A31.

66. Kevin Siers, "Contents: Copyright AOL Time Warner" (Charlotte Observer), *State College (Pa.) Centre Daily Times,* 16 January 2000, sec. 9A.

67. Tom Toles, "Coming to a Screen Near You" (Buffalo News, Universal Press Syndicate), *State College (Pa.) Centre Daily Times,* 13 February 2000, sec. 13A.

68. Henry Giroux, "Merger Mania Dazzles Eyes, But Imprisons You and Me," *State College (Pa.) Centre Daily Times,* 13 February 2000, sec. 13A.

69. Felicity Barringer, "Does Deal Signal Lessening of Media Independence?" *New York Times,* 11 January 2000, sec. C12; and Laurence Zuckerman, "As Media Influence Grows for Handful, Can That Be a Good Thing?" *New York Times,* 13 January 2000, sec. C6.

70. Zuckerman, "As Media Influence Grows," sec. C6.

71. Zuckerman, "As Media Influence Grows," sec. C6.

72. Zuckerman, "As Media Influence Grows," sec. C6.

73. Joel Bleifuss, "Communication Breakdown: AOL Time Warner Threatens Public Interest," *In These Times,* 21 February 2000, 2–3.

74. Bleifuss, "Communication Breakdown," 2.

75. "Rapid Media Consolidation Dramatically Narrows Number of Companies Controlling Time Spent Online," Jupiter Media Metrix, 4 June 2001, <www.iup.com/company/> (accessed 7 January 2002).

76. Bleifuss, "Communication Breakdown," 2.

77. Pat Aufderheide, "Open Access or Else," *In These Times,* 26 June 2000, 2.

78. Brian Winston, *Misunderstanding Media* (Cambridge, Mass.: Harvard University Press, 1986).

79. Graham Murdock, "Programming: Needs and Answers," paper presented at New Dimensions in Television meeting, Venice, Italy, 15 March 1981. Cited in Janet Wasko, *Hollywood in the Information Age* (Austin: University of Texas Press, 1994), 251.

80. "AOL's Big Byte," *The Nation,* 3.

81. Ben Bagdikian, *The Media Monopoly,* 6th ed. (Boston: Beacon Press, 2000); Herman, "Media Mega-Mergers," 11; and James Ledbetter, "Merge Overkill: When Big Media Gets Too Big, What Happens to Open Debate?" *Village Voice,* 16 January 1996, 30–35.

82. Zuckerman, "As Media Influence Grows," sec. C6.

83. "But a Survey," *Special Report: News and Editorial Independence. A Survey of Group and Independent Editors* (Easton, Pa.: Ethics Committee, American Society of Newspaper Editors, 1980). Cited in Bagdikian, *The Media Monopoly,* 30.

84. Pew Research Center for the People and the Press, "Journalists Avoiding the News, Self Censorship: How Often and Why," 30 April 2000, <www.people-press.org/jour00rpt.htm> (accessed 5 January 2000).

85. Zuckerman, "As Media Influence Grows," sec. C6.

86. Robert H. Lande, "Antitrust and the Media—II," *The Nation,* 22 May 2000, 5–6.

87. "The 400 Richest," 158–76.

88. "The 400 Richest," 142–54.

89. "The 400 Richest," 130.

90. "The 400 Richest," 162.

91. Liberty Media split off from AT&T in August 2001 but retained its holdings in both News Corp. and Time Warner.

92. Benjamin M. Compaine, "Who Owns the Media Companies," in *Who Owns the Media? Competition and Concentration in the Mass Media Industry*, 3rd ed., ed. Benjamin M. Compaine and Douglas Gomery (Mahwah, N.J.: Lawrence Erlbaum Associates, 2000), table 8.5.

93. Compaine, *Who Owns the Media?*, 499–502, table 8.6.

94. Compaine, *Who Owns the Media?*, 503.

95. Thomas Guback, "Ownership and Control in the Motion Picture Industry," *Journal of Film and Video* 38, no. 1 (1986): 7–20.

96. Felicity Barringer, "Other Media Companies Assets Tied to Those of Deal's Partners," *New York Times*, 13 January 2000, sec. C6.

97. Andrew Pollack, "Microsoft Makes Another Interactive TV Investment," *New York Times*, 24 January 2000, sec. C4.

98. Seth Schiesel, "A Rush to Provide High-Speed Internet Access," *New York Times*, 12 January 2000, sec. C1, C6.

99. Edmund L. Andrews, "Bertelsman's Chairman to Leave Board of AOL," *New York Times*, 12 January 2000, sec. C7.

100. G. William Domhoff, "State and Ruling Class in Corporate America," *Insurgent Sociologist* 4, no. 3 (1974): 3–16; and G. William Domhoff, *The Power Elite and the State: How Policy Is Made in America* (New York: Aldine de Gruyter, 1990).

101. "America Online Vice Chairman Kenneth J. Novack Elected to Company's Board of Directors," *AOL Corporate*, 25 January 2000, <http://media.aoltimewarner.com/media/> (accessed 5 January 2002).

102. *Time Warner 2000 Annual Report*, 44.

103. Matt Carlson, "Boardroom Brothers: Interlocking Directorates Indicate Media's Corporate Ties," *Extra!*, September 2001, 18–19.

104. *Notice of Annual Meeting of Shareholders*, Walt Disney Company, 4 January 2002, 25–31.

105. Daniel Fusfeld, *Economics: Principles of Political Economy*, 3rd ed. (Glenview, Ill.: Scott, Foresman), 416.

106. Bagdikian, *The Media Monopoly*, 9.

107. Jon Katz, "Invasion of the Billionaire," *The Netizen*, 30 May 1997, <http://hotwired.lycos.com/netizen/97/21/index4a.html> (accessed 21 September 2000); and "The Forbes Richest," 174.

108. Benjamin M. Compaine, "The Newspaper Industry," in Compaine and Gomery, *Who Owns the Media?*, 1–59.

109. David Barsamian, "Monopolies, NPR, and PBS: An Interview with Robert McChesney," *Z Magazine*, February 2000, 40–46.

110. Barsamian, "Monopolies," 42.

111. Katz, "Invasion," 4.

112. Bagdikian, *The Media Monopoly*, 9.

113. Aimee Picchi, "AOL Time Warner Too Optimistic?" (Bloomberg News), *Philadelphia Enquirer,* 15 December 2000, sec. C1, C7.

114. Patricia Horn and Akweli Parker, "AOL Merger Gets Key Approval," *Philadelphia Enquirer,* 15 December 2000, sec. A1, A16.

115. Federal Communications Commission, *Subject to Conditions, Commission Approves Merger between America Online, Inc. and Time Warner, Inc.,* 11 January 2001, <www.fcc.gov/Bureaus/Cable/> (accessed 18 January 2002).

116. Stephen Labaton, "FCC Approves AOL-Time Warner Deal, with Conditions," *New York Times,* 12 January 2001, sec. C1, C11.

117. Labaton, "FCC Approves Deal," sec. C11.

118. Willard D. Rowland Jr., "The Illusion of Fulfillment: The Broadcast Reform Movement," *Journalism Monograph* 79 (1982).

119. Rowland, "Illusion," 35.

120. Rowland, "Illusion," 35.

121. Rowland, "Illusion," 36.

122. Ken Boettcher, "AOL-Time Warner Merger Makes Media Critics Nervous," *The People,* April 2000, 3.

# 3

# MEDIA CONCENTRATION AND CULTURE: THE MOVIE AND MUSIC INDUSTRIES

The effects of media merger mania on culture are most apparent when we examine the structure and output of the oligopolies that dominate the movie and music industries. Douglas Gomery defines oligopoly as "controlled competition with a few players" and notes that oligopoly was "the most common market structure for mass media ownership in the 1990s."[1] The players share common interests, allowing them to more easily agree on standards and practices. They appear competitive on the surface because they allow some entry by independent companies operating on the margins, but their profit-maximizing and risk-minimizing strategies ultimately govern the majority of what gets produced and sold in the so-called media marketplace. Oligopoly continues to characterize the basic structure of the movie and music industries in the twenty-first century. In this chapter, we examine how the economic structure of these culture industries affects what we see and hear.

## MONEY AT THE MOVIES: FILM INDUSTRY STRUCTURE

Most of our news about the movie industry comes from celebrity gossip columns and film reviews. Indeed, in a parasitical way, the various media that cover the film industry are dependent upon its very existence. Much of this coverage lacks any kind of substantive consideration of the movie business, but sometimes there are revealing tidbits that give a glimpse of how things work. For example, the Associated Press syndicates a daily column to newspapers around the nation entitled "People in the News." In May 1999, Sean Connery made the "News" for doubling as both star and "tightfisted producer" of the movie *Entrapment*. The news was that Connery produced the

45

film, budgeted at $68 million due to "complicated stunts" and "exotic locations," for only $66 million. Apparently Connery set the frugal tone "by shunning such usual star perks as private aircraft."[2]

The Academy of Motion Picture Arts and Sciences does not give an annual award for Tightfistedness on the Set of an Important New Action-Adventure Film, but certainly Connery would have been in the running. The point, of course, is that making a movie for under $68 million has somehow become a complicated stunt in Hollywood. Perhaps moviegoers should be grateful for tightfisted producers. The average cost of producing a movie in 2000 was $54.8 million. Marketing expenditures averaged an additional $27.3 million for a total investment of $82.1 million per picture.[3] In 1999, Loews Cineplex Entertainment Inc., controlling half the screens in Manhattan, raised movie ticket prices to $9.50.[4] On the national level, from 1999 to 2000, the average price of a movie ticket rose 6.1 percent to $5.39, more than three times the increase in the Consumer Price Index for recreational expenditures as a whole. That is why box office sales increased to $7.7 billion in 2000 while the number of admissions declined.[5] By 1998, according to the U.S. Bureau of Labor, consumers' average out-of-pocket expenditures for entertainment and reading materials roughly equaled those for health care.[6]

Price inflation is not the only power or privilege of oligopoly. Oligopolies also limit choice. They need not show concern for genuine product diversity, since they control most of the marketplace. Overpriced movie tickets, limited choices, and movies of debatable quality are characteristic of the Hollywood-based film industry. According to *Variety*, seven major producer-distributors shared 88 percent of the 2001 domestic box office.[7] Warner Brothers took the box office crown with 15 percent and, along with New Line's 5 percent share, gave parent company AOL Time Warner a total of 20 percent. Universal, a unit of the French conglomerate Vivendi, finished second with 12 percent of the domestic box office, ahead of Fox (News Corp.), Buena Vista (Disney), and Paramount (Viacom), each with 11 percent. Disney's subsidiary, Miramax, earned the company another 8 percent of the box office for a total 19 percent share. Sony, with 9 percent, and MGM, with 7 percent, rounded out the top seven. MGM was then controlled by Kirk Kerkorian, number twenty-nine on the 2001 *Forbes* list of "The 400 Richest People in America" with $5.3 billion.[8] DreamWorks SKG, founded by producer-director Steven Spielberg (number ninety on the 2001 *Forbes 400* list with $2.1 billion), former Disney executive Jeffrey Katzenberg (number 316 with $820 million), and former record producer David Geffen (number forty-seven with $3.9 billion), accounted for another 5 percent, leaving the "others" with 7 percent of the 2001 box office share.[9] As the list indicates, the top movie companies are controlled by large media conglomerates and the super-rich. Let's look more closely at the ownership and structure of the top six.

## PROFILE OF THE BIG SIX

### WARNER BROTHERS: BIG KID ON THE BLOCK

In 2001, AT&T shared a 25 percent stake in AOL Time Warner's film and video divisions—Warner Brothers, New Line and Fine Line Features, and Warner Home Video (see chapter 2). In addition to the vast Warner Brothers film library, AOL Time Warner also owned rights to MGM and RKO films. Its theater holdings included a 50 percent stake in UCI and WF Cinema Holdings (Mann Theatres) with Viacom sharing the other half.[10] The company's expansive holdings in other sectors of the media provide vehicles to promote its movies, for example celebrity features in magazines such as *Time, People,* and *Entertainment Weekly;* television programming such as *EXTRA,* a syndicated entertainment news show; and entertainment segments on its cable news channels CNN and Headline News. Such synergies in the film, broadcast, and publishing industries raise serious doubts about the integrity of the movie reviewing process. Furthermore, the release of a Warner Brothers "event" film is routinely treated as news in AOL–Time Warner news media outlets.

### DISNEY: THE RECYCLE BIN

Disney's filmed entertainment groups in 2001 included Walt Disney Pictures, Walt Disney Feature Animation, Touchstone Pictures, Hollywood Pictures, Miramax, and Dimension. Disney expanded its range of movie labels in order to protect the child-friendly Disney brand while branching out into more teen- and adult-oriented markets. Disney's recycling of its film library at theaters and on videocassettes and DVDs has been enormously profitable. For example, Disney's 1937 feature animation *Snow White and the Seven Dwarfs* sold 27 million video copies when it was released in 1994. Disney released a restored DVD version of the film in October 2001, loading two discs with the movie plus extras including a newsreel and 30-minute radio broadcast from the world premiere; production timelines; storyboards, clips, and trailers; and a new performance of "Some Day My Prince Will

Come," sung by Barbra Streisand, who is introduced by Disney CEO Michael Eisner (number 359 on the 2001 *Forbes 400* list with $720 million).[11] Disney maximizes the value of its library by creating artificial scarcity for its movies, routinely withdrawing certain titles from distribution for certain periods of time.

Disney can also showcase its feature films on its ABC broadcast network and on its cable networks, including the Disney Channel and the Family Channel. It can plug them on its E! Entertainment 24-hour cable network, with 75 million cable and direct broadcast satellite subscribers in the United States and 400 million in 120 countries worldwide.[12] Touchstone teamed up with Disney's ESPN sports cable network in 2002 to produce the network's first-ever feature film for large format theaters. *Ultimate X* is based on footage from ESPN's 2001 winter and summer "X Games." This is a twist on an earlier Disney project in which life imitated art, when the company formed a National Hockey League team, the Anaheim Mighty Ducks, named after its 1992 movie. Rides in Disney theme parks in California, Florida, Japan, and France are designed to remind visitors of the treasured properties in Disney's vaults. For example, Disneyland in Anaheim, California, features rides with Dumbo's flying elephants and the Mad Hatter's spinning teacups.

FOX: STOP THE PRESSES

Next among *Variety's* 2001 top six box office earners is News Corp. In addition to Twentieth Century Fox, film operations of the Australia-based News Corp. included Fox 2000, Fox Searchlight (categorized as "other" on *Variety's* list),[13] Fox Animation Studios, Fox Studios Australia (a joint venture with Lend Lease Corporation), 20 percent of New Regency, and Fox Home Entertainment. Fox outlets for its valuable film library included the Fox television broadcast network and the FX cable network in addition to extensive global holdings of broadcast, cable, and satellite operations. These operations included BSkyB in Europe and Star TV in Asia. Like AOL Time Warner, News Corp. held many outlets capable of promoting its movies, including newspapers such as the *New York Post* and the *Sun* in Britain, and cable networks such as the Fox News Channel and the TV Guide Channel that feature movie previews and program schedules. News Corp.'s owner Rupert Murdoch, number twenty-one on the 2001 *Forbes 400* with $7.5 billion,[14] has a well-established record of using his media outlets to protect and promote his own business and political interests. For example, in 1999 Fox dropped its film advertising from *The Hollywood Reporter,* an industry trade magazine, in retaliation for negative comments about the studio's movie *Fight Club.*[15]

PARAMOUNT PICTURES: ALL IN THE FAMILY

Fox took its lead from Paramount Pictures, which punished *Spy* magazine in 1991 with an advertising boycott in response to a "snider-than-snide" profile of the head of the Simon & Schuster publishing house. Both the movie studio and book company were units of Paramount Communications Inc.[16] The next year Paramount Pictures threatened to pull its advertisements from *Daily Variety* after the industry trade magazine published a scathing critique of its movie *Patriot Games. Variety's* editors apologized to Paramount for the review, which they conceded was "unprofessional," and promised that the critic would no longer review the company's films.[17] Incidences such as these raise further suspicions about the corruption of the reviewing process.

In addition to Paramount Pictures, Viacom's film division in 2001 included Nickelodeon Movies, BET Arabesque Films, and MTV Films. All three studios capitalize on the company's cable network brands. It also owned Paramount Classics, another "other" on *Variety's* 2001 domestic box office chart.[18] Viacom is part of a larger conglomerate, National Amusements, which controlled 68 percent of the company's voting stock in 2002. National Amusements' holdings included theater chains with over 1,800 screens in eleven countries located in the United States, Canada, Europe, Asia, and South America. In addition, it shared ownership with AOL Time Warner in the theater chains mentioned above. With Vivendi Universal, it ran a joint venture, United Cinemas International, with 104 cinemas on three continents. Another joint venture, Cinema International Corp., also with Universal, served as distributor of home-video products outside North America. Viacom controlled 82 percent of Blockbuster, the largest U.S. video retail chain with over 5,000 stores, and the world's largest renter of videos with stores in twenty-seven countries. Such vertical integration allows the company to profit directly from its retail outlets, from the box office to the video store. Like Disney, Paramount can also promote its movies at its theme parks. In June 2001, Paramount's Kings Island theme park opened a new ride based on its hit movie *Lara Croft: Tomb Raider,* which in turn was based upon a popular video game. Paramount had a sequel in the works at the same time.

Viacom's films can be promoted and shown on its broadcast networks CBS (acquired in 1999; see chapter 2) and UPN and on its cable outlets including Showtime, Comedy Central, TNN, CMT, The Movie Channel, FLIX, and BET. In 2001 it also owned 50 percent of the Sundance Channel (with the rest held by Vivendi Universal and Robert Redford), giving it access to independent films. Its cable networks stretched across the globe, including Europe, Africa, and Asia.[19] Viacom also has become a producer and syndicator of television programming to feed its broadcast and cable networks. Its television production units included CBS Enterprises, King World, Paramount Television, Spelling, Nickelodeon Studios, MTV Productions, and Nicktoons Animation.

In 2001, National Amusements was a wholly-owned company belonging to Sumner Redstone, number fourteen on the 2001 *Forbes 400* list with $10.1 billion.[20] Redstone served as Viacom's CEO and as chairman of the board, which included his son Brent D. Redstone and daughter Shari Redstone, who are director and president of National Amusements, respectively. In January 2002, tensions between Sumner Redstone and Mel Karmazin, president and chief operating officer of Viacom, began to spill into public view. Despite the family ties, the company's outside board of directors intervened. The board requested that the number one and number two men settle their differences because their rift was affecting stock prices and the long-term financial outlook of the company. According to a *New York Times* report, the board's intervention was led by Ivan Seldenberg, president and co-CEO of Verizon. Other outsiders included Verizon's vice chairman and chief financial officer; representatives from finance capital, including private equity firms and the vice chairman of Credit Suisse First Boston; major law firms; big business, including Jan Leschly, former CEO of SmithKline Beecham; and charitable foundations, including William H. Gray III, head of The College Fund/UNCF and former representative to the U.S. House of Congress from Pennsylvania, and Patty Stonesifer, co-director of the Bill and Melinda Gates Foundation.[21] The board's intervention was viewed as highly unusual, but it demonstrated where the real power lies. Even with majority control of Viacom, Redstone could not ignore the way the company was perceived on Wall Street.

UNIVERSAL PICTURES: PARIS COMES TO HOLLYWOOD

Also among *Variety's* top six box office earners in 2001 was Vivendi's Universal Pictures. Additional film operations included stakes in production-distribution units such as StudioCanal, Polygram Films, Gramercy Pictures, and Propaganda. Through Universal, Vivendi owned the world's second-largest filmed entertainment library.[22] With Canal Plus, Vivendi controlled Europe's biggest pay-television service, with thirty channels in fourteen countries. Its U.S. cable television networks included equity stakes in the USA Network, Sci-Fi Channel, and Home Shopping Network. Vivendi also owned theater chains in Europe and theme parks in southern California, Florida, Japan, and Spain.

Vivendi purchased Universal from the Canadian Seagram Company in 2000 as part of its total transformation from a French water-treatment utility to a media conglomerate. The deal was seen as Europe's answer to the AOL–Time Warner merger. Like AOL Time Warner, the combination of Universal with Vivendi's cable systems gave the company control over both media content and the pipes that deliver it. Also like the AOL–Time Warner merger, the Vivendi-Seagram deal attracted the attention of government regulators, in this case the European Commission (EC). The EC set three conditions before allowing the deal to go through. First, it required Vivendi to sell its 23 percent stake in News Corp.'s BSkyB satellite television service. Second, the company had to agree to offer rival pay-television operators access to Universal films while also guaranteeing that its cable service, Canal Plus, would not hold first rights to more than 50 percent of the studio's film output. The third dictate concerned Vivendi's multiaccess Internet portal, Vizzavi, a joint venture with Vodafone Group PLC of Britain. In order to gain the EC's approval, the merged company agreed to offer rival portals access to its music library over the next five years. At the end of 2001, Vivendi announced its intent to acquire full control of USA Networks' film and television units in a complex deal through which John C. Malone, chairman of the Liberty Media Group and number ninety on the 2001 *Forbes 400* list with $2.1 billion, ended up with a 3.6 percent stake in Vivendi.[23] At the beginning of 2002, Liberty also held stakes in AOL Time Warner (4 percent), Viacom (1 percent), and News Corp. (18 percent), giving the company equity interests in four of the top six movie companies.[24]

SONY: FROM CINEMA SCREEN TO HOME THEATER

Last among *Variety's* top six box office earners in 2001 was Sony, which owned Columbia Pictures, Screen Gems, Sony Pictures Classics (also an "other"), and Revolution Films (co-owned with producer Joe Roth, News Corp., and Malone's Starz cable network). Sony charged into the media industry when it bought CBS records in 1988 for $2 billion and Columbia Pictures from the Coca-Cola Company in 1989 for $4.9 billion. In the Columbia deal, Sony acquired the rights to 3,000 movies and 23,000 television episodes. Sony's intention was to use its media software to drive the sale of its consumer electronics hardware. Sony also accelerated a trend toward vertical integration that began when major studios started buying theater outlets in the 1980s. In 1997, Sony merged its Loews Theater Exhibition Group with the Cineplex Odeon theater chain, partially owned by Universal Pictures' parent company Seagram. At the time, the deal created the second-largest theater chain in North America. Sony and Universal sought to recreate the vertical integration of the Studio Era of the 1930s and 1940s, when five companies controlled movie production, distribution, and exhibition. By 1997, according to *Standard & Poor's*, the major movie companies had gained control of 8 percent of U.S. movie screens, with many in prime locations.[25] However, vertical integration did not pay off for Sony and Universal, and in early 2001 Loews filed for bankruptcy. The problem was not with the vertical model but rather a matter of overbuilding theater megaplexes when actual theater admissions failed to increase. Between 1995 and 1999, the number of movie screens increased 34 percent while admissions increased only 16 percent.[26]

In addition to Loews, a number of other large theater chains filed for bankruptcy beginning in 1999, including United Artists Theatre Co., General Cinema Theatres, Carmike Cinemas Inc., and Regal Cinemas. Regal Cinemas was one of the world's largest theater chains in 2002 with 350 theaters and 4,000 screens. Small theater chains filed for bankruptcy as well. These included the nation's oldest family owned-and-operated theater chain, Wehrenberg Theaters, with 199 screens, and the closely held Edwards Theater Circuit Inc. of Newport Beach, California.[27] Commercial developers and their financial backers could take partial blame for the dire straits of the theater business. Before loaning money to developers of large suburban shopping malls, bankers required guaranteed tenants, including national retail stores and movie chains. While the movie chains went on a building spree, many of their older urban theaters went into decline and were closed to cut costs and pay off creditors. Vivendi Universal cut its ties to Loews in 2001 when it sold all of its 25.6 percent stake (15 million common shares) for a nominal payment of one dollar to the Goldman Sachs Group Inc., a Wall Street investment firm. For a dollar, Vivendi qualified for a tax write-off that it used to offset some of its capital gains for the year.[28]

As the theater chains came out of bankruptcy, ownership and control of the industry shifted to finance capital. In late 2001, Canada's Onex Corp., a publicly traded buyout firm based in Toronto, and Oaktree Capital Management LLC, a "distressed-debt specialist" based in Los Angeles, announced their intent to acquire General Cinema Theatres as it came out of bankruptcy.[29] The most striking development involved the fire-sale acquisitions of Edwards Theater Circuit, United Artists, and Regal Cinemas by Philip Anschutz, chairman of Quest Communications International Inc. and number sixteen on the 2001 *Forbes 400* list with $9.6 billion.[30] When the dust from bankruptcy proceedings began to settle at the beginning of 2002, Anschutz had parlayed his oil, rail, and fiber-optic wealth into ownership of 20 percent of U.S. theater screens. Anschutz also owned the Los Angeles Kings National Hockey League team, part of the Los Angeles Lakers National Basketball Association franchise, the Staples Center in which the teams play, and a concert promotion company. He also founded two movie production companies, Crusader and Walden Media, to produce "films with a family bent."[31] With 20 percent of the nation's theaters poised to screen them, these films had a better chance of being seen, and Anschutz had an opportunity to show Hollywood the kinds of films he believed *should* be produced.

Although Sony continued to hold onto its 39.5 percent stake in Loews as the bankruptcy filing proceeded into 2002 (with Onex Corp. and Oaktree Capital nipping at its heels), its primary focus was not on the theater but the home. At the dawn of the new millennium, Sony shunned the merger mania of its competitors who sought to merge content with distribution systems. Sony's strategy was to bypass conventional distribution channels by hooking up directly to owners of its various brands of digital devices, such as PlayStation 2, palm-held personal organizers, PCs, and television set-top receivers.[32] Sony's goal to capture the synergy between its software and hardware operations has remained elusive since the company entered the movie and music business in the late 1980s. However, its entry into distribution of movies over the Internet might produce the windfall it has been seeking.

In August 2001, five of Hollywood's major studios announced a joint venture to deliver movies over the Internet. A front-page article in the *San Diego Union-Tribune* cited studio executives predicting that this was the "first step to the coming world of true video-on-demand when consumers will be able to watch any movie they want, whenever they want."[33] The players included Paramount, Warner Brothers, Universal Pictures, MGM, and Sony Pictures. Sony's Moviefly subsidiary, an Internet movies-on-demand service, would provide the platform for the new venture. The studios planned to release a hundred or so recent movies from their libraries for computer users with broadband connections to download and view "at their leisure." The system was designed so that a downloaded movie would stay on the computer hard drive for thirty days or until the file was opened. Then the clock would start ticking. Within twenty-four hours of opening the file, viewers could watch the film as often as they pleased and reverse, pause, or fast-forward at will. Twenty-four hours after the initial download, the film would erase itself.

The release of such a small number of titles from studio vaults holding thousands of movies betrayed the consortium's concern about the security of online film distribution. Yet the studios had no choice, since piracy of movies on the Internet was beginning to proliferate. In July 2001, Media-Force, a digital copyright enforcement firm, listed its Top Ten movies pirated online, including films that had yet to be released in home video formats, such as *Dude, Where's My Car?* from Fox and *Crouching Tiger, Hidden Dragon* from Sony Pictures Classics.[34] The studios hoped that by offering easy access and high-speed delivery of their own movies they could preempt the still-infant digital piracy industry.

Hollywood's response to movie pirates—undercutting the market for pirated films with lower-priced, higher-quality products—is a well-rehearsed strategy that also includes litigation and legislation aimed at outlawing the theft of intellectual property. The strategy can be traced back to the early 1970s, when the International Federation of Phonographic Industries attempted to stop music cassette piracy in Hong Kong. Faced with increasing videocassette piracy in the early 1980s, Hollywood also targeted Hong Kong in an effort to protect its copyrights. The studios, along with other major copyright owners, worked with the Hong Kong legislature to secure increased criminal penalties for videocassette piracy, and then with local enforcement agencies (police, customs, and tax agents) to crack down on duplicating labs and exporters of illegal videos. Disney supplemented these efforts with its own investigative force, leading to dozens of copyright infringement lawsuits against Hong Kong's video pirates. At the same time, Hollywood sought to undercut videocassette piracy by establishing "legitimate" relations with video producers and dealers, and by cutting prices on prerecorded videocassettes to reduce the differential between pirated and studio-released copies.[35]

Sony extended its efforts to subvert digital piracy a week after the Moviefly deal was announced by striking another deal with the New York-based inDemand, a cable pay-per-view network then owned by four of the largest cable companies in the United States (AT&T Broadband, AOL Time Warner, Comcast, and Cox Communications.). The service was designed to allow subscribers to choose from a selected list of movies to watch at their convenience. In the deal, Sony sold rights to movies such as *Crouching Tiger, Hidden Dragon* and *The Wedding Planner* to inDemand, which had already obtained rights to Universal Pictures films including *The Mummy Returns* and *The Sting*, as well as *The Blair Witch Project*, distributed by Artisan Entertainment.[36]

In September 2001 the two remaining major movie companies, Disney and Fox, unveiled Movies.com, a joint venture for delivering movies on demand to computers and television sets via broadband connections. Unlike the Moviefly-based venture, Movies.com arranged for exclusive rights to Disney and Fox movies for a limited period of time before making them available to other outlets, such as inDemand. Both the Sony-led venture and Disney-Fox's Movies.com caught the attention of federal regulators but studio heads acted unconcerned on the grounds that they were fighting digital piracy and history was on their side. Hollywood had seen these threats before with the introduction of broadcast television, cable television, and the videocassette recorder.[37] Though each new medium posed a threat to the filmed entertainment oligopoly, each has become a major ancillary outlet for the movie companies. By 2000, the studios were earning over 45 percent of their revenues from home video, nearly 29 percent from television, and only about 25 percent from the box office.[38] Although the new digital delivery systems pose a new challenge to the major Hollywood film companies, the companies are poised to close in for the capture.

## MORE MONEY AT THE MOVIES: FILM INDUSTRY PERFORMANCE

The core Hollywood filmed entertainment companies have several advantages over would-be competitors. In addition to financing and distributing their own movies, they also serve as the primary financiers and distributors of coproductions. Movies financed and distributed by the core firms are hardly independent. Their budgets, talent lists, and story ideas must meet the approval of those who hope to profit from the film. In addition, the major distributors charge a 30–35 percent fee for getting the movies into theaters. Usually, these deals are designed so the studio will not lose money, or will at least minimize its exposure by taking its share of the gross revenues first. For example, Disney strong-armed *Pearl Harbor's* producer Jerry Bruckheimer and director Michael Bay into a "backend" deal in which the producer and director would not earn a cent until Disney recovered its production costs.[39] In exchange for financing and distributing a movie, the majors can also insist on obtaining ancillary rights, such as home video, pay cable, broadcast television, and foreign distribution. As Gomery concluded, for the Hollywood oligopoly "distribution has always been a key to corporate longevity" and worldwide distribution has been the basis for its power.[40]

To get a movie financed and distributed by a Hollywood major typically requires pulling talent together, including star directors and actors. As the level of stardom for directors has increased, so has the price for their services. Star actors increase the budget of a film according to their box office value. In the 1980s and 1990s, the triumvirate of action–adventure film stars, Arnold Schwarzenegger, Sylvester Stallone, and Bruce Willis, were among the first stars able to demand as much as $20 million for appearing in a movie. In the late 1990s Jim Carrey and Julia Roberts joined the $20 million club. Star budgets also increase the chance of a big payback. Between 1986 and early August 1997, of the 104 movies that topped $100 million at the domestic box office, 35 percent starred one or more of just seven performers (the five just noted plus Tom Cruise and Robin Williams).[41]

By 2000, the value of star power seemed to be declining with the same seven stars accounting for only 30 percent of 149 films earning $100 million or more between 1990 and 2000.[42] Nevertheless, in December 2001, Schwarzenegger signed a $30 million contract to star in *Terminator 3*.[43] This can be explained by Hollywood's increasing dependence on the global box office and foreign home video and television sales to earn back the high costs of production and marketing. Indeed, only 20 percent of a film's total gross revenues are generated by the U.S. domestic box office.[44] The simplistic dialogue and intensive use of extravagant special effects make the action–adventure movie a genre that easily transcends cultural and linguistic boundaries. Hence, although the big action stars were no longer breaking U.S. domestic box office records by 2002, their global exchange value made the high star salaries and production costs well worth the expense. Even a film such as *Godzilla,* trashed by critics and earning only $136 million at the domestic box office, finished as the fourth-biggest worldwide hit in 1998, earning an additional $248 million in overseas markets.[45]

Hollywood's core film companies also maintain their market power through exploitation of their film libraries. Movie rights represent valuable assets. They can be used as collateral to finance new projects. They can also be split in a variety of ways and used to generate cash or support the growth of new media outlets. A case of the latter occurred in 1986, when Ted Turner bought broadcast and videocassette rights to MGM movies from Kirk Kerkorian for $1.5 billion to provide programming for his growing cable network operations. The deal included classic movies such as *Gone With the Wind, Casablanca, 2001: A Space Odyssey, The Wizard of Oz*, and *Singin' in the Rain*. Recognizing the exchange value of old movies and famous movie stars, Turner remarked, "We've got Spencer Tracy and Jimmy Cagney working for us from the grave."[46] In 1990, Turner acquired broadcast rights for an additional 800 MGM movies as MGM sought to raise cash for its big comeback. MGM regained control of the rights to most of these movies in 1999 in hopes of rebuilding the MGM library and launching its own cable television network. In March 1999, MGM paid $225 million to Warner Brothers to repurchase video rights to the movies it once produced and owned.[47] By rebuilding its filmed entertainment library, MGM hoped to rejoin the Hollywood oligopoly and regain the status it enjoyed in the Studio Era.

In addition to using star actors and directors to attract and retain moviegoers, Hollywood has a long tradition of exploiting star authors. The studios can bank on a bestselling author's fans to show up at the theater. For example, in 1993 both Michael Crichton's *Jurassic Park,* produced by Universal and directed by Steven Spielberg, and John Grisham's *The Firm,* produced by Paramount and directed by Sydney Pollack, became blockbusters. In 2001, the adaptation of books to movies drove the box office to new heights with Warner Brother's *Harry Potter and the Sorcerer's Stone,* written by J. K. Rowling, and New Line's *Lord of the Rings,* written by J. R. R. Tolkien. Both film companies were subsidiaries of AOL Time Warner, but the parent company put much more of its money and effort behind the Harry Potter franchise while leaving New Line to set up its own global distribution, marketing, and merchandising network for *Lord of the Rings.* Warner Brothers recognized the broad appeal of the Harry Potter children's books to readers of all ages. The four *Harry Potter* books in print had already produced sales of 116 million copies in 200 countries and had been translated into forty-seven languages.[48] Warner Brothers transformed the literary work into what its executives described to *Variety* as "a prime example of corporate synergy [in] the brave new world of vertical integration, in which a film becomes 'product' and every department works itself into a crosspromotional frenzy."[49]

The frenzy involving *Harry Potter and the Sorcerer's Stone* was fueled by the widest North American theatrical release of any movie ever. The movie premiered in November 2001 at 3,672 theaters on 8,200 screens, nearly one out of every four screens in the United States and Canada. The film, with an estimated $120 million budget, broke the box office record for a weekend opener with $93 million in its first three days.[50] Hoping not to overexpose the brand or alienate Harry Potter fans, the studio decided to skip fast-food tie-ins, but did sign an exclusive $150 million deal with the Coca-Cola Company on the condition that characters in the movie would not be shown actually using the product. Following the wishes of J. K. Rowling, Warner Brothers further insisted that Coca-Cola promote literacy in its ads.[51] The number of licensees for the movie and book series totaled eighty-five, much less than the 150 licensees signed up for Warner Brothers' *Batman* movie series a decade before. Nonetheless, merchandising was expected to generate as much as $150 million.[52] The merchandise included dozens of toys from Mattel including a Levitating Game and science kit for potion-making, a 682-piece version of the

Hogwarts Castle ($89.00 listed retail price), sheets and pillowcases, collectible dolls and trading cards, action figures, and computer and Gameboy games.[53] To further fuel frenzy for the theatrical release, AOL–Time Warner subsidiaries HBO, TBS, Cartoon Network, the WB network, and the Warner Music record division promoted the movie through ads and special promotions. Its Internet subscribers were deluged with interactive ads for the film.[54] By February 2002, *Harry Potter's* global box office revenues approached $1 billion, of which $313 million came from the North American market.[55]

For the release of *Harry Potter* on videocassette and DVD in May 2002, Warner Brothers Home video mounted its largest marketing campaign ever with a $25 million blitz seeking to make more than 12 billion "impressions" on potential consumers through television, magazines, websites, billboards, and instore displays.[56] AOL Time Warner sold the network broadcast rights for the first two *Harry Potter* films to its competitor, Disney, for $130 million, in the most expensive deal of its kind to date. *Lord of the Rings* stayed in-house when New Line sold the rights to the trilogy for $160 million to AOL–Time Warner's WB network and sister cable networks TNT and TBS.[57] The broadcast window for the first movie was set for fall 2004, after the movie's pay-cable television run on Liberty Media's Starz!/Encore. The sequels were scheduled to air in 2005 and 2006, respectively.

Sequels have long been a Hollywood staple. Studios rely on them to attract a preexisting audience generated by the original film. However, the Hollywood movie oligopoly's reliance on the exploitation of sequels and franchise pictures increased dramatically at the turn of the twenty-first century. Between 1990 and 2000, nine of the top fifty box office hits were sequels (or so-called prequels, such as *Star Wars I: The Phantom Menace,* released in 1999). The majors' 2002 releases were dominated by sequels including the next *Harry Potter, Lord of the Rings,* and *Star Wars* installments, plus *Stuart Little 2* and *Men in Black 2.* Under conglomerate ownership, movie companies have become increasingly compelled to exploit their brands in order to minimize risks.[58] Disney is the master of the movie franchise and has made piles of money from cheaply produced video sequels to its classic films aimed at small children, including *Cinderella II: Dreams Come True, Atlantis: The Lost Empire II, The Hunchback of Notre Dame II,* and *The Lion King II: Simba's Pride. The Little Mermaid II: Return to the Sea* and *Lady and the Tramp II: Scamp's Adventure* were near the top of video sales charts in 2000–2001.[59]

In addition to sequels, the studios hedge their bets with remakes of classical Hollywood films as well as movie versions of hit television shows. Hollywood's obsession with sequels and remakes is perhaps best epitomized by its recycling of Alfred Hitchcock's legendary thriller *Psycho* (1960). Universal produced two sequels, *Psycho II* in 1983 and *Psycho III* in 1986, before signing up star director Gus Van Sant to make what *Variety* referred to as a "faithful-unto-slavish" remake of the original in 1998. A small sampling of other movie remakes includes *King Kong* (1933 RKO, 1976 Paramount), *D.O.A.* (1950 United Artists, 1998 Touchstone/Disney), *Angels in the Outfield* (1951 MGM, 1994 Disney), and *Cape Fear* (1962 and 1991, both Universal).[60] Movies spun off from television shows in the 1990s included *The Brady Bunch, The Flintstones, George of the Jungle, Lost in Space, The Mod Squad, Mission Impossible,* and *South Park.* Sequels of television spinoffs included *Mission Impossible II, Addams Family Values,* and *Rugrats in Paris.* All of these films were designed to capitalize on preexisting audiences while creating enough buzz to attract new fans.

The advantages enjoyed by the dominant filmed entertainment companies make for nearly impenetrable market barriers for potential competitors. Meanwhile, the Hollywood oligopoly hypes event movies to such an extent that they instill a social obligation to participate. Writing in the 1940s, Frankfurt School scholars Max Horkheimer and Theodor Adorno observed that the universal criterion of a movie's cultural merit had become equated with how much was spent on it; what they called "conspicuous production." As they recognized, and as audiences sometimes do also, "The varying budgets in the culture industry do not bear the slightest relation to factual values, to the meaning of the products themselves."[61] They meant that moviegoers had become used to the formulas of movie spectacles because the content of the films themselves did not require any kind of real thought. Since movies are produced as commodities, Horkheimer and Adorno argued that they could no longer be art. In their view, art challenges its audiences to question the status quo and the things they tend to take for granted. However, the products of the movie oligopoly provide no room for independent thinking. In Horkheimer and Adorno's view, if movie theaters were shut down tomorrow there would be no great loss. Once the movie hype disappeared, people would no longer feel obligated to go. Then, the enormous resources, time, and energy spent producing, distributing, and consuming films could be used to do something capitalism has been unable to do: abolish hunger.[62]

## LISTEN TO THE MUSIC: TUNING IN TO THE BIG FIVE

The music recording industry resembles the movie industry in both structure and performance. In fact, some of the same players are involved in both sectors. In this section, we provide a brief review of the structure of the music industry in the early twenty-first century and then conclude with a discussion about the effects of online music distribution on the way music is produced and distributed.

Five music distribution companies accounted for 83.3 percent of the total sales of record albums in the U.S. market in 2001.[63] Vivendi's Universal Music unit led the way with 26.4 percent of total record sales. Universal Music topped the 2001 charts for the third straight year since its acquisition of Polygram Music in 1998. At the time, the Universal Music Group was owned by the Canadian liquor firm Seagram Co., in turn controlled by the Bronfman family (led by patriarch Edgar Bronfman, Sr., who ranked twenty-fourth on the 2001 *Forbes 400* list with $6.8 billion).[64] Seagram acquired Polygram Music from Philips Electronics, a Netherlands-based manufacturer of electronics for military, industrial, and consumer use. Polygram's labels included many formerly independent labels such as A&M, Motown, and Island. Its major labels included Decca, Mercury, Polydor, and Deutsche Grammophon. It was the third-largest music publisher with 375,000 copyrights, along with a 30 percent stake in Really Useful Holdings, which owned the copyrights to the Andrew Lloyd Weber catalog. Polygram also owned music clubs in Britain and France.[65] After the merger, thousands of employees were terminated, a number of bands found themselves without contracts, and some artists were required to buy back their own music.

The Universal Music group's holdings included MCA and full or partial ownership of nearly forty additional record labels. Universal also distributed music for a number of independent labels including Chess (Muddy Waters, Chuck Berry), Margaritaville (Jimmy Buffett), and Nothing (Nine Inch Nails, Marilyn Manson). Its music publishing division, MCA Music Publishing, generated roughly $250 million a year from 155,000 copyrighted songs, including "I Want to Hold Your Hand," "Hound Dog," and "Strangers in the Night."[66] Universal also owned a concert promotion company and several concert halls including the Universal Amphitheater in Los Angeles. Vivendi's takeover of Seagram in 2000 launched Universal Music to the top of the record charts. To gain the EC's approval of the deal, Vivendi agreed to license its online music catalog to competitors of its Vizzavi multiaccess Internet portal service.

Next on *Billboard's* 2001 list of top music distributors was AOL Time Warner's record division, the Warner Music Group, with 15.9 percent of total U.S. album sales.[67] The Warner Group owned more than forty labels, including Atlantic, with artists such as Tori Amos, Brandy, Phil Collins, matchbox20, and Tim McGraw; Elektra, with Jackson Browne, Tracy Chapman,

Metallica, and Phish; and Warner Brothers Records, with Eric Clapton, Madonna, R.E.M., Red Hot Chili Peppers, Paul Simon, Steely Dan, and Neil Young.[68] Like Universal Music, the Warner Music Group held labels spanning a range of music genres, including rock, pop, rap, country, rhythm and blues, jazz, classical, and gospel. With such a stable of music labels, the company can hedge its bets from year to year. So, for example, when rap music sales are down, gospel music sales may be up. AOL Time Warner's music group was a fully vertically integrated operation. Its holdings included a division that manufactures the tapes, CDs, and DVDs for its labels. The company owned or controlled the copyrights to more than 1 million songs through its Warner/Chappel Music publishing house and subsidiaries. On the retail level, the music division shared a 50 percent stake in the Columbia House record club with Sony.

Sony Music Distribution ranked third on *Billboard*'s 2001 list of total U.S. album sales with 15.9 percent.[69] As mentioned above, Sony entered the music business in the 1980s when it bought CBS Records in hopes of finding synergies between music software and hardware. Sony's major labels included Columbia (Bruce Springsteen, Neil Diamond), Epic (Oasis, Pearl Jam), Crescent Moon (Gloria Estefan), and Associated (Rage Against the Machine). Sony Music Independent Labels included MJJ Music, co-owned with Michael Jackson.[70] Sony also manufactured tapes and discs and owned music copyrights through its publishing division. A separate label, Soundtrax, produced the soundtrack for the movie *Men in Black*. The label highlights the synergy between Sony's movie and music divisions and suggests the ways in which movie soundtracks have become vehicles for a company's other interests. A movie soundtrack must now promote a company's contract artists rather than carry the tunes by artists that a filmmaker might have wanted.

Bertelsman's BMG Distribution ranked fourth in 2001 with 14.7 percent of the total U.S. album market share.[71] The German-based company generated revenues of $16.5 billion that year, putting it among the Big Ten of global media conglomerates.[72] Bertelsman was Europe's biggest broadcaster, with stakes in twenty-two television channels. It was also the largest U.S. book publisher, including imprints such as Random House, Knopf, Vintage, The Modern Library, Bantam Doubleday Dell, and Delacorte, as well as one of the world's largest magazine publishers with eighty titles. Its music division controlled over 200 labels, including RCA and Arista, distributed in fifty-four countries. These labels produced and distributed music by artists such as 'N Sync, Britney Spears, Dave Matthews Band, and the Grateful Dead. BMG also distributed records for a number of other labels and controlled the rights to 700,000 songs, including 100,000 Famous Music copyrights co-owned with Viacom's Paramount Pictures. Finally, Bertelsman owned the BMG Music Service with record clubs serving the United States and Canada, giving it direct access to the retail market.

The last of the Big Five recording companies is EMI Music Distribution, which finished fifth in total album sales in 2001 with 10.6 percent.[73] EMI, based in England, owned major labels including Capitol (Beastie Boys, Bonnie Raitt), Chrysalis, Grand Royal, Virgin (Rolling Stones, Smashing Pumpkins), and Pointblank (John Lee Hooker, Isaac Hayes). Additional labels covered the rap, country, R&B/blues/jazz, classical, gospel, and Latin categories. EMI also served as distributor for Apple records. Its bestselling titles in 2001 included *Beatles I*, Janet Jackson's *All For You,* and Garth Brooks's *Scarecrow.* From the recycle bin, EMI scored bestsellers in 2001 with *Now That's What I Call Music 7* and *Now That's What I Call Music 8.*[74] EMI's music division was a fully vertically integrated operation: It owned the world's largest music catalog, with over 1 million titles; it manufactured compact discs, with plants in Britain, Holland, and Japan; and it controlled 231 retail outlets in Britain and the United States, including the Virgin Megastores in New York and Philadelphia.[75] Although it was a major player in the music business, EMI's other media holdings were minuscule compared to those of the rest of the Big Five. This made the company a prime target for takeover.

Such was the case in January 2000, when Time Warner announced its intent to acquire the EMI Group to create the world's largest record company, soon after the announcement of its intended merger with America Online. The combined music divisions would have owned the rights to nearly 2 million songs.[76] In October Time Warner and EMI withdrew the proposed merger after the EC raised concerns about concentrated control over music copyrights, which it feared could be extended into domination of the online music delivery business. America Online already had a distribution agreement with BMG to deliver its music online. Time Warner improved its chances of gaining the EC's approval of its pending merger with America Online by forgoing the EMI acquisition. EMI therefore remained a major music force and also an enticing acquisition for a global media conglomerate.

Another major player in the music industry is Viacom by virtue of its control over the dominant cable television music networks: MTV, VH1, BET, and CMT (Country Music Channel). Music videos are basically ads for music recordings. Music video channels such as MTV serve the same role as radio stations: They sell audiences to advertisers while their programming promotes sales of music. MTV can influence the sale of a recording simply by putting the video into high rotation. An album that might have sold only 100,000 copies might make gold (500,000 copies) with enough exposure on MTV.[77] For established stars, MTV can help sell millions.[78] Despite its hip image, however, MTV's division of standards and practices takes a hard look at each video. From 1989 to 1994, every single winner in the Best Video category of MTV's Video Music Awards was initially rejected for cable play and sent back to its director for re-editing.[79] Similarly, MTV refused to play Madonna's "Justify My Love" video released in the mid-1980s because it found the nudity and images of bisexuality too extreme. MTV's impact on the music marketplace therefore is twofold: What it promotes sells, and what it fails or refuses to promote generally does not (although Madonna took her video directly to retail and opened a new market for music video singles).

Concentration in the music recording industry is matched by concentration at the retail level. Chain music stores accounted for 53 percent of total U.S. album sales in 2001.[80] Mass merchants, including department stores such as Wal-Mart, Kmart, and Target, and consumer electronics outlets such as Best Buy and Circuit City accounted for another 30.2 percent of 2001 album sales. Independent retailers continued to see their share of record sales decline in 2001 to 13.4 percent, a 10.4 percent drop from 2000. Concert, television, and online outlets accounted for another 3 percent of record sales in 2001. The decline of independent retailers reflects a larger trend that includes the demise of independent video outlets and bookstores. Independents generally guarantee a more eclectic stock as well as more personal service. Chains and mass marketers rely on central buyers and employees who have little influence over what appears on their store shelves.

Music, video, and bookstore chains and mass merchants rely on heavy sales of blockbuster titles and rapid turnover of inventory. A CD, video, or book that sits on the shelf represents unsold product and costly space. This results in the massive hype of bestsellers that take up most of the shelf space. The large discount electronics retailers often use CDs as a loss leader, selling them below cost to draw customers into their stores and tempt them with more expensive items. The large retail chains, department stores, and video dealers such as Wal-Mart, Kmart, and Blockbuster have also taken it upon themselves to monitor the content of the products they sell. Wal-Mart alone accounted for somewhere between 7 and 10 percent of annual record sales in the late 1990s. The monster retailer has been able to require record labels and bands to change album design covers and inserts, delete songs from their albums, electronically alter objectionable words, and even change lyrics.[81]

Wal-Mart rejected a 1996 Sheryl Crow recording because it objected to lyrics suggesting that the company sold guns to children. Wal-Mart asked Crow and her label A&M records to change the lyrics on *all* copies of the album, not just those meant for its own retail outlets. Crow refused and forwent 10 percent of her potential record sales. For Crow fans in Murphy, North Carolina, Wal-Mart was the only record outlet around at the time. The nearest record stores were 50 to 150 miles away in Atlanta and Gainesville, Georgia.[82] The effects of the concentrated structure of music production, distribution, and retail made many music fans and musicians hopeful that the Internet would break up the music oligopoly.

I WANT MY MP3 . . .

The history of new media technologies is colored by a spectrum of hopes and fears concerning their impact on society. From the early days of the printing press, new communications technologies have been greeted with some suspicion, but those who develop and deploy them always promise that new media technologies will bring new opportunities for improving the human condition. The technological inventions and innovations that made possible the telegraph, wireless radio, motion picture, telephone, television, cable, VCR, personal computer, and World Wide Web have all been heralded as "revolutionary," as if the very fact of their existence guaranteed a better quality of life for all. The pervasive notion that "progress" might be realized through the development of new technologies themselves—with little or no regard for who controls them or even who has access to them—is problematic to say the least. The latest manifestation of this utopian technological determinism can be seen in the widespread belief that the Internet would set music makers and music lovers free from the five major companies that controlled the world's recorded music industry at the turn of the twenty-first century.

In the late 1990s, the Big Five record labels suddenly became very nervous about MP3, a digital compression format enabling audio files to be stored and exchanged from one computer to another. With its introduction, it seemed that the new technology actually threatened to enhance diversity in the music industry while nibbling at a tiny slice of the Big Five's share of the pie. As *Rolling Stone* reported after surfing the Web: "[I]t has never been easier to find free music on the Web. And thanks to MP3, there were literally millions of near-CD quality songs that music fans could download in a matter of minutes."[83] Accordingly, one *New York Times* report claimed in 1999 that MP3 had "spawned an explosion of web sites" and "frightened the nation's $13.5 billion recording industry with the specter of mass distribution of pirated music over the Internet."[84] Another stated that "frustrated record companies have watched helplessly as millions of illegally copied songs circulate on the Internet."[85]

Of course there were doubts about how helpless the industry really was and how seriously the MP3 format would affect its record sales, not to mention how much it would benefit music makers and record consumers. As these fears and hopes played out in the press, four common myths surrounding MP3 emerged: that it would liberate established recording artists, that it would usher in a renaissance for independent musicians, that its primary beneficiaries would be music consumers, and that it posed a serious threat to the music oligopoly.

The first myth was that MP3 would liberate established musicians from the artistic and commercial constraints imposed by their record labels. This myth is perhaps best expressed by a somewhat dubious *Rolling Stone* reporter who wrote: "Flag wavers of the MP3 revolution, such as Ken Hertz, a powerful music-industry lawyer whose clients include Alanis Morissette and Will Smith, will tell you that we are about to see the beginning of a new era in which artists will seize control of their careers once again and reconnect with fans, while the moguls who have dominated the industry for so long will finally get their comeuppance."[86] Actually, Morissette probably *did* feel liberated, given the deal she cut with MP3.com Inc. to sponsor her 1999 tour. Morissette signed a three-year promotional contract in exchange for 658,653 shares of MP3.com. stock at 33 cents per share. The payoff looked good as the company went public and its stock hit $63 per share on the first day of trading, raising Morissette's stake in MP3.com to $42 million. As *Spin* magazine mused, "[T]he singer would have to sell nearly 30 million copies of *Supposed Former Infatuation Junkie* to get the profit she netted in one *afternoon*. Maybe Internet entrepreneurs really *are* the new rock stars. Why dodge bottles at Woodstock when you can simply sit at home, think, and grow rich?"[87] Of course, after MP3.com's court battles ended and the dot.com bubble burst, Morissette was faced with the prospect of once again actually performing in front of her audiences.

Then there is the case of Tom Petty, who had the temerity to post his new single, "Free Girl Now," on MP3.com in March 1999 as a goodwill gesture toward fans and a way to boost the buzz on his upcoming album release. "It was a bold move," according to *Rolling Stone*, "considering the unspoken agreement among major labels not to allow acts to post MP3 files, particularly for new songs, until there is a way to contain the technology."[88] Just two days after "Free Girl Now" was offered online—and 150,000 people had downloaded it—the song was abruptly yanked from the site. Representatives for Petty and Warner Music refused to comment, but *Rolling Stone* surmised that "Petty and his camp realized that the time to antagonize your label is not weeks before it releases one of your albums."[89] Like Petty, the Beastie Boys initially fought the demands of their label, Capitol Records, to remove MP3 files of their music from their own websites. The Beastie Boys and the label finally reached a compromise: EMI's Capitol artists were allowed to post certain songs on the Capitol website provided they obtain prior approval from the label. The band went on to sign a new deal with Capitol with an estimated $30 million to $40 million advance rather than find another label or go independent. As Hilary Rosen, president and chief executive of the Recording Industry Association of America, commented, "They found that the existing system had a lot of advantages for them."[90] Not only does "the existing system" pay up front, but it also provides the marketing power that is essential for making a musical group visible.

The second myth was that MP3 would bring about a renaissance for garage bands and independent musicians by enabling them to distribute their own music and establish their own fan bases. It was such a hopeful moment that it was painful to call this myth into question, and here Tom Petty's upstart idealism and implicit pitch for MP3 in *Rolling Stone* was particularly poignant: "[T]here's a whole lot of artists that exist beyond the periphery of the corporate music business who suddenly have the power to make this stuff available. It gives these artists a huge outlet—you can have a little band and just get on the computer and sell your stuff and build all these fan bases for things that are completely outside the music industry. I love the fear it strikes into the hearts of these moguls who have shit on us all."[91] Despite the MP3 hype, garage bands remained anonymous on the service and MP3.com had yet to find a way to support them in their efforts. The works of most musicians who posted their works remained lost in cyberspace.

The third myth was the one that scared the music industry the most: that music should and would be free, literally. This myth was based on actual practice and held revolutionary potential to the extent that it challenged the very structure of intellectual property rights. The music industry's counterattack required putting MP3.com, along with Napster, out of business and turning back the ease with which music could be copied and downloaded. The Big Five soon began offering their own "pirate-proof" versions of online music and joined the Secure Digital Music Initiative (SDMI), an antipiracy organization backed by the consumer electronics and technology industries. The record companies also worked the media to counter the growing sentiment that music should be free. Accordingly, the *New York Times* announced in October 1999 that "a crackdown on digital piracy that will have a wide-ranging impact on consumers is about to begin" and warned consumers that some CD burners already add a digital serial number to every CD they make so copyright owners can trace any recording to the machine that made it. The industry also announced new software for digitally watermarking CDs that would prevent SDMI-compliant devices from playing "ripped" disks. Even if a disk were legitimate, the watermark would only allow its owner to make four copies, each of which contains information that allows it to be played on only one machine. So to listen to music on a home stereo, office PC, and car stereo would require separate copies for each, with all the time, inconvenience, and expense involved.[92]

The fourth myth, that online music distribution posed a serious threat to the major record labels, is probably the biggest myth of all. As *Rolling Stone* noted, "While the record industry has always been good at profiting from anthems of revolution, it has never undergone a revolution itself."[93] The point, of course, is that although new technologies may be used for revolutionary purposes, technology itself is never revolutionary. In a music industry driven by the logic of capitalism, he who pays the piper still calls the tune. Within a couple of years of the predicted revolutionary restructuring of the music industry, MP3.com and Napster had been effectively shut down.

... BUT YOU CAN'T ALWAYS GET WHAT YOU WANT

After losing its battles in court, MP3.com agreed in late fall 2000 to settle its legal disputes with the last of the Big Five, the Universal Music Group. MP3.com gave Universal Music a stake in the company as part of the settlement. Universal officials knew that the large settlement claims imposed by the courts would bankrupt MP3.com anyway and that the company had no choice but to settle. Napster found itself in the same boat. After several legal setbacks, the company began final settlements with the Big Five in early 2002, since it was about to run out of money. MP3.com and Napster were victims of both the deep pockets the music oligopoly used to finance the pursuit of litigation and legislation to stifle the threat to their control of the industry. The two upstarts also were doomed by the logic of capitalism. Under capitalism, music compositions and performances belong to the copyright owner (which is not necessarily the actual creator of the work). The role of the government is to protect these rights and their market value. Laws passed by the legislature and enforced by the courts must, out of structural necessity, consistently uphold the rights of intellectual property owners. New means of distributing intellectual and artistic works have inevitably been integrated into the existing market structure since they enter an economic system in which private property rights prevail. The state simply cannot undermine these rights for the sheer convenience of consumers, and any attempts to argue for access to information and entertainment on the basis of the public good cannot hold weight against property claims.

After vanquishing MP3.com and Napster, the Big Five still faced a number of services using peer-to-peer computer networks, such as Morpheus, Kazaa, and Aimster. While pursuing the new predators through litigation, the record companies launched their own online music services to undermine them. These services promised to be more convenient for the casual computer user, but of course would not be free. In April 2001, three of the Big Five—Warner, BMG, and EMI—announced a new online music subscription platform called MusicNet. Shortly thereafter, Universal and Sony announced their joint online digital subscription service called Pressplay. Like the film industry, the Big Five also began hedging their bets on the online music business by licensing their music catalogs to upstarts. By July 2002, Listen.com had secured rights to music from all five of the major labels for its subscription-based streamlining service. In another deal, Warner Music sold rights to 25,000 songs, a small fraction of its music library, to Full Audio. Full Audio intended to charge consumers 99 cents for the right to download and burn a copy of any of the 25,000 tracks.

The convergence toward a single site for retrieving music online, like a video store, was then foreseeable, with some version of the music oligopoly providing the product and the hype.[94] This means, with apologies to Mick Jagger and Keith Richards, that when it comes to musical culture, the music industry will be telling us what we want but not necessarily giving us what we need.

## NOTES

1. Douglas Gomery, "Interpreting Media Ownership," in *Who Owns the Media? Competition and Concentration in the Mass Media Industry*, ed. Benjamin Compaine and Douglas Gomery (Mahwah, N.J.: Lawrence Erlbaum Associates), 507–35, especially 515.

2. "People in the News," Associate Press, 7 May 1999, AM cycle.

3. Lorenza Munoz, "Company Town; Movie Industry Ready to Stage a Comeback, Valenti Says," *Los Angeles Times,* 7 March 2001, sec. C6.

4. Barbara Stewart, "$9.50 for a Movie Ticket? Who's Up for a Protest?" *New York Times,* 2 March 1999, sec. A20.

5. Tom Graves, "Movies and Home Entertainment: Current Environment," *Standard and Poor's Industry Surveys,* 10 May 2001, <www.netadvantage.standardandpoors/netahtml/IndSur/mhe/mhe_05001htm> (accessed 19 November 2001); and U.S. Bureau of Labor Statistics, *Consumer Price Index Summary,* December 2001, <www.bls.gov/news.release/cpi.nr0.htm> (accessed 2 February 2002).

6. U.S. Bureau of Labor Statistics, *Consumer Expenditures 1998,* cited in U.S. Census Bureau, *Statistical Abstract of the United States: 2000,* 120th ed. (Washington, D.C.: 2000), 463.

7. Carl DiOrio, "*Potter* Plants WB on Top of Market," *Variety,* 24 December 2001, 12. Box office estimates based on ticket sales through 16 December 2001.

8. "The 400 Richest People in America," *Forbes,* 8 October 2001, 127–298, especially 179.

9. "The 400 Richest," 160, 162, 174; and DiOrio, "*Potter* Plants," 12.

10. "The Big Ten," *The Nation,* 7 January 2002, 27–30.

11. Bruce Westbrook, "*Snow White* to Make Digital Debut; Disney DVD Set Packed With Extras," *Houston Chronicle,* 7 October 2001, 8; "The 400 Richest," 174.

12. Walt Disney Company. *Notice of Annual Meeting of Shareholders.* 4 January 2002, 42.

13. DiOrio, "*Potter* Plants," 12.

14. "The 400 Richest," 158.

15. Bernard Weinraub, "A Strained Relationship Turns Sour," *New York Times,* 18 October 1999, sec. C18.

16. "Freedom of the Press, Advertising Division," *In These Times,* 24 July 1991, 21.

17. Weinraub, "Strained Relationship," sec. C18.

18. DiOrio, "*Potter* Plants," 12.

19. "The Big Ten," *The Nation,* 7 January 2002, 27–30, especially 29.

20. "The 400 Richest," 158.

21. Bill Carter and Geraldine Fabrikant, "Board Dashes Cold Water on Feud at Viacom Between Top Executives," *New York Times,* 31 January 2002, sec. C1, C7.

22. "The Big Ten," 28.

23. "The 400 Richest," 162; and Seth Schiesel, "Vivendi Is Said to Have Deal for Expansion in U.S. Media," *New York Times,* 17 December 2001, sec. A16.

24. "The Big Ten," 28.

25. "Movies and Home Entertainment," *Standard & Poor's Industry Surveys,* 2 October 1997, 7.

26. Graves, "Movies and Home Entertainment: Current Environment," 2.

27. Claudia Eller and James Bates, "Hollywood Box Office Is Boffo," *Los Angeles Times,* 11 November 2001, 1–4, <www.latimes.com> (accessed 3 February 2002); and Paul M. Sherer, "Loews Cineplex to be Acquired by Onex Group," *Wall Street Journal,* 16 February 2001, sec. A4.

28. Carl DiOrio, "U Dumps Its Loews Shares," *Daily Variety,* 29 June 2001, 6.

29. "Onex Aiming to Acquire Loews Theatre Chain" (Reuters News Agency), *Toronto Star,* 14 November 2001, sec. E11.

30. "The 400 Richest," 142.

31. "The 400 Richest," 142.

32. Claudia Eller and Sallie Hofmeister, "Company Town; The Biz; Sony Still Bets on Gizmos, Not Mergers," *Los Angeles Times,* 3 November 2000, sec. C1.

33. Rick Lyman, "Coming to a Computer Near You: Movie Rentals Direct from Five Studios" (New York Times News Service), *San Diego Union-Tribune,* 17 August 2001, sec. A1, A26.

34. "MediaForce Announces Top Ten Pirated Movies for July; Pirates Using Internet to Grow Personal Bootlegged Movies Collections," *PR Newswire,* 16 August 2001.

35. Ronald V. Bettig, *Copyrighting Culture: The Political Economy of Intellectual Property* (Boulder, Colo.: Westview Press, 1996), 217.

36. "TriStar Strikes Deal with iN-DEMAND," *AP Online,* 28 August 2001.

37. Bettig, *Copyrighting Culture.*

38. Sallie Hofmeister, "Lights, Camera, Download? Studios Focus on the Web," *Los Angeles Times,* 30 November 2000, sec. A1.

39. Tom King, "Hollywood Journal: Mickey Mouse vs. *Pearl Harbor*—Hoping to Avoid a Costly Bomb," *Wall Street Journal,* 6 April 2001, sec. W1.

40. Douglas Gomery, "The Hollywood Film Industry: Theatrical Exhibition, Pay TV, and Home Video," in *Who Owns the Media? Competition and Concentration in the Mass Media Industry,* ed. Benjamin Compaine and Douglas Gomery (Mahwah, N.J.: Lawrence Erlbaum Associates, 2000), 359–439, especially 375.

41. "Movies and Home Entertainment," 1997, 14.

42. Tom Graves, "Movies and Home Entertainment: Industry Trends," *Standard and Poor's,* 10 May 2001, <www.netadvantage.standardandpoors.com/netahtml/IndSur/mhe20501.htm> (accessed 19 November 2001).

43. "Star News and Gossip," *TV Guide Live,* 11 December 2001, <www.tvguidelive.com/newsgossip-archives/01-dec/12-11-01.html> (accessed 28 January 2002).

44. Richard Natale, "Company Town Film Profit Report," *Los Angeles Times,* 30 January 2001, sec. C10.

45. Thomas Schatz, "Show Me the Money: In Search of Hits, The Industry May Go Broke," *The Nation,* 26–31.

46. Stratford P. Sherman, "Ted Turner: Back from the Brink," *Fortune,* 7 July 1986, 25–31, 28.

47. Phyllis Furman, "MGM Buys Back Movie Rights to Launch TV Cable Channel" (Knight Ridder Tribune), *State College (Pa.) Centre Daily Times,* 16 September 1999, sec. 8C; and "MGM Regains Rights to Films" (Reuters), *New York Times,* 16 September 1999, sec. C23.

48. Rick Lyman, "Coming Soon: *Harry Potter* and Hollywood's Cash Cow," *New York Times,* 4 November 2001, sec. A1, A31.

49. Don Groves and Adam Dawtrey, "Hogwarts and Hobbits in Global Grab," *Variety,* 11 February 2002, 1.

50. Rick Lyman, "*Harry Potter* and the Box Office of Gold," *New York Times,* 19 November 2001, sec. E1.

51. Lyman, "Coming Soon," sec. A1.

52. Lyman, "Coming Soon," sec. A1.

53. Phil Kloer, "Poof! Harry Potter Is Visible; Movie, Hype Make Wizard Hard to Miss," *Atlanta Journal and Constitution,* 26 October 2001, sec. 1A.

54. "*Potter* Proves Power of Cross-Marketing," *Investor's Business Daily,* 23 November 2001, sec. A6.

55. "$25 Million Ad Blitz Planned for *Potter* Video," *Milwaukee Journal Sentinel,* 7 February 2002, sec. 6B, wire reports.

56. Jennifer Netherby and Scott Hettrick, "Warner Wild About Harry; Studio Reaches for Stratosphere," *Video Business,* 11 February 2002, 1.

57. "*Rings* Goes to WB for $160 Million," *St. Petersburg Times,* 5 February 2002, sec. 5D.

58. Sharon Waxman, "Hollywood's Great Escapism; 2001 Box Office Receipts Set Record," *Washington Post,* 4 January 2002, sec. A1.

59. Anthony Breznican, "Happily Ever After? Not Everyone Enjoys Disney Sequels" (Associated Press), *State College (Pa.) Centre Daily Times,* 17 February 2002, sec. C6.

60. *Variety Portable Movie Guide* (New York: Berkeley Boulevard Books, 1999), 979.

61. Max Horkheimer and Theodor W. Adorno, *Dialectic of Enlightenment,* trans. John Cumming (New York: Seabury, 1972), 124. Originally published in 1944.

62. Horkheimer and Adorno, *Dialectic,* 139.

63. Ed Christman, "UMVD Marks 3rd Straight Year as Top U.S. Music Distributor," *Billboard,* 26 January 2002, 51.

64. "The 400 Richest," 235.

65. "The Media Nation: Music," *The Nation,* 25 August 1997, centerfold.

66. "The Media Nation," centerfold.

67. Christman, "UMVD Marks," 51.

68. *Time Warner 2000 Annual Report,* 48.

69. Christman, "UMVD Marks," 51.

70. "The Media Nation," centerfold.

71. Christman, "UMVD Marks," 51.

72. "The Big Ten," 27–28.

73. Christman, "UMVD Marks," 51.

74. Christman, "UMVD Marks," 51.

75. "The Media Nation," centerfold.

76. Andrew Pollack and Andrew Ross Sorkin, "Time Warner to Acquire Control of EMI Music," *New York Times,* 24 January 2000, sec. C1, C12.

77. Robert G. Woletz, "A New Formula: Into the 'Bin,' Out Comes a Hit," *New York Times,* 2 August 1992, sec. D1.

78. Michael Goldberg, "MTV's Sharper Picture," *Rolling Stone,* 8 February 1990, 61–64, 118.

79. Neil Strauss, "MTV Winner: Neither Rejected Nor Censored," *New York Times,* 7 September 1995, sec. C15.

80. Ed Christman, "U.S. Music Sales Hit a Wall," *Billboard,* 26 January 2002, 1, 76.

81. Neil Strauss, "Wal-Mart's CD Standards Are Changing Pop Music," *New York Times,* 12 November 1996, sec. A1, C12.

82. Strauss, "Wal-Mart's CD Standards," sec. A1.

83. Tom Samiljan, "I Want My MP3," *Rolling Stone,* 18 March 1999, 69.

84. John Markoff, "Bridging Two Worlds to Make On-Line Digital Music Profitable," *New York Times,* 13 September 1999, sec. C1.

85. Sara Robinson, "Recording Industry Escalates Crackdown on Digital Piracy," *New York Times,* 4 October 1999, sec. C5.

86. Jeff Goodell, "World War MP3," *Rolling Stone,* 8 July 1999, 43.

87. Eric Hellweg, "Down with MP3," *Spin,* October 1999, 57.

88. Eric Boehlert, "MP3.mess: Petty Single Pulled From Net," *Rolling Stone,* 29 April 1999, 40.

89. Boehlert, "MP3.mess," 40.

90. Sue Cummings, "The Flux in Pop Music Has a Distinctly Download Beat to It," *New York Times,* 22 September 1999, sec. G60.

91. Fred Schruers, "Tom Petty: The *Rolling Stone* Interview," *Rolling Stone,* 8–22 July 1999, 88–94, 92.

92. Robinson, "Recording Industry," sec. C5.

93. Goodell, "World War MP3," 43.

94. Graves, "Movies and Home Entertainment: Current Environment," 3.

# 4

# ALL THE NEWS THAT FITS: THE NEWS AND ADVERTISING INDUSTRIES

The motto of the newspaper of record in the United States, the *New York Times,* is "All the news that's fit to print." When Adolph Ochs purchased this "failing and demoralized" operation in 1896, he spoke of "a sincere desire to conduct a high standard newspaper, clean, dignified and trustworthy, [with] honesty, watchfulness, earnestness, industry and practical knowledge applied with common sense."[1] Ochs spoke of his readers as "thoughtful, pure-minded people," and promised that the *Times* would "not soil the breakfast cloth" with sensationalism or scandal as its "esteemed freak contemporaries" were wont to do.[2] "To be seen reading the *New York Times,*" an early self-advertisement aimed at school teachers and college professors proclaimed, "is a stamp of respectability."[3] In 1897, the *Journalist* praised the *Times,* taking special note of the economic incentives for distinguishing a paper on the basis of its propriety in an age of yellow journalism: "It has lived up to its motto of 'All the news that's fit to Print,' and the great cultivated well-to-do class do not want anything beyond that. As an advertising medium for good goods it is steadily growing in value. It may not have so large a number of readers as some of its less conservative contemporaries, but its readers represent more dollars, which, after all, is what the advertiser is after."[4] Early advertisers in the *New York Times* included makers of designer fashions and fine musical instruments, in addition to manufacturers of dry goods and patent medicines.[5]

Nearly three-quarters of a century later, *Rolling Stone* announced its arrival on the San Francisco music scene with a roguish play on the famous appeal of the *New York Times'* to decency and decorum, declaring its motto to be: "All the news that fits."[6] As aware of the sensibilities of his intended readership as Ochs, founding editor Jann Wenner set out to produce "sort of a newspaper and sort of a magazine . . . for the artists and the industry, and every person who 'believes in the magic that can set you free.'"[7] The first issue of Rolling Stone featured an interview with Donovan Leitch, an article about Jimi Hendrix, and a "photographic look at a rock and roll group after a drug bust" (the Grateful Dead on the front porch of their Haight-Ashbury home brandishing clenched fists and rifles).[8] Early issues openly invited submissions from amateur music reviewers: "We'll read it; maybe we'll print it; maybe we'll pay you."[9] In 1989, Tom Wolfe praised the young Rolling Stone for capturing the impudence, gaudiness, and "slightly mad freedom" of a time when "the notion of glamour began to involve a calculated disdain for propriety."[10] Wolfe didn't comment on the magazine's calculated appeals to advertisers, but early issues of Rolling Stone featured ads for psychedelic posters, alternative theater productions, rock concerts, record labels, and stereo equipment. Early subscription drives offered marijuana paraphernalia as an enticement.

Rolling Stone's parody of the New York Times motto hinges on two different meanings of the word "fit": fit as in having enough pages or column inches to squeeze in the necessary material, and fit as in being suitable or appropriate for a particular audience. Both definitions, we argue, are equally important to the business of selling news as a commodity: the practice of gathering and packaging information as a product for distribution to readers and viewers, whose attention (and presumably patronage) is then sold to advertisers for profit. First, the news industry's reliance on advertising is such that the space left over after a newspaper has filled its pages with ads is known as "the news hole." The issues and events of the day, it seems, must finally be shoveled in. In the magazine industry, noncommercial material is referred to as "the editorial well," suggesting that it must be drawn out in small amounts as needed. Second, the advertising industry's concern not only for audience size but also for demographics necessitates that information be selected and shaped so as to attract the most desirable clientele, be it the "great cultivated well-to-do class" of the 1890s or the counterculture youth market of the 1960s. All of this, of course, raises the question of news that either doesn't or isn't "fit to print." That is the subject of this chapter.

We begin with a brief history of news as a commodity: its emergence as a service for merchant capitalists in the late fifteenth century, its transformation into a mass industry in the late nineteenth century, and its consolidation into a multibillion dollar sector of commerce controlled by a handful of media conglomerates today. Our review of these milestones in journalism history is meant to underscore the intricate links between the news and advertising industries as they have evolved under capitalism. We then turn to advertising and journalism as ideological institutions, which function to support and negate certain ways of thinking. We examine a number of widely held beliefs about the functions and effects of both enterprises in a democratic society. Finally, we offer specific examples of advertising as an economic institution that has direct and indirect influence on both the structure and content of the news. We argue that the symbiotic relationship between news and advertising frequently renders them functionally equivalent, despite the dubious claims of advertisers and the best intentions of journalists to inform and educate the public.

## YOU SAW IT HERE FIRST: A BRIEF HISTORY OF NEWS AS A COMMODITY

The news business first emerged in the Italian city-states of the late fifteenth century with the rise of capitalism and the development of the modern printing press. At that time, Venice was a center of commerce, banking, finance, and textile production. It was also the first city in Italy, and practically the first in Europe, in which the business of printing and publishing became important. The Venetian city government sought to encourage the importation of new industrial techniques and stimulate the growth of local commerce by granting certain printers exclusive publishing rights, laying the foundations for later copyright laws.[11] Early printers found that there were tidy profits to be made in providing merchant capitalists with current information about markets and political conditions. The news business thus developed throughout Europe and in many countries around the world as a business aimed primarily at political and mercantile elites.

### THE INFORMATION INDUSTRY

The industrialization of the news business in the nineteenth century resulted in the transformation of news into a mass-produced commodity. The extension of the circulation of newspapers beyond the realm of an educated elite or business class is a familiar feature of press histories in many countries. In the United States, as Michael Schudson notes, this shift can be seen reflected in changes in newspaper names and prices, as well as advertising and editorial content. In the 1830s, conservative names such as the *Chronicle, Patriot, Republican,* and *Telegraph* gave way to more flamboyant ones such as the *Sun, Star, Herald,* and *Tribune.* Penny papers hawked by newsboys on street corners replaced six-cent papers sold exclusively through annual subscriptions. Advertising, "which heretofore addressed the reader only insofar as he was a businessman interested in shipping and public sales or a lawyer interested in legal notices, increasingly addressed the newspaper reader as a human being with mortal needs."[12] With this development, the range and scope of news content expanded to cover a wider range of human events and social behaviors. Human interest stories and melodramatic descriptions of events replaced political argument and analysis. As Calvin F. Exoo aptly summarizes: "Stories of rapes, robberies, suicides, abandoned children left in baskets and the brawling of drunken sailors were the common fare of most penny papers."[13]

Ironically, most newspapers were hostile to advertisers at this time, believing that "large ads wasted space and were 'unfair' to the small advertisers who were the foundation of advertising revenue."[14] According to Schudson, many early editors felt that advertising should command only a limited amount of column inches, and often confined ads to agate-size type. James Gordon Bennett, who founded the *New York Herald* in 1835 and remained its editor until his death in 1872, is a good example. Bennett believed that "the advertiser should gain advantage from what he said, but not from how the advertisement was printed or displayed."[15] Advertisers would not have to put up with such dictates for long.

In 1848, a group of New York newspapers took advantage of the newly invented telegraph and organized the Associated Press (AP). The AP was designed to gather news for a variety of different papers with widely different political allegiances. It could only succeed by making its reporting "objective" enough to be acceptable to its motley crew of subscribers. Here we see the seeds of the journalistic norm of objectivity—the belief that one can and should separate facts from values—which took root in the 1920s and remains prevalent today. The journalistic norm of objectivity was actually invented to help sell wire service stories across the land: to keep reporters in check so as to ease owners' fears of alienating audiences and, increasingly, advertisers. By the late nineteenth century, as Schudson notes, AP dispatches were markedly more free from editorial comment than most stories written for local newspapers.[16]

The relationship between newspapers and advertisers changed dramatically in the 1880s and 1890s. Advertising textbooks like to naturalize the history of advertising by tracing its roots to prehistoric times ("Some of the earliest cave drawings refer to the makers of primitive objects"[17]), but most rather grudgingly admit that advertising as we know it today emerged in the late nineteenth century along with transportation, urbanization, and industrialization.[18] Thanks in part to the growth of department stores and the development of brand names and trademarks by national manufacturing concerns, business demand for advertising space accelerated. The ratio of editorial matter to advertising changed significantly at this time, from about 70:30 to 50:50. Advertising revenues rose from 44 percent of total newspaper income in 1880 to 55 percent by 1900.[19] In the first few decades of the twentieth century, big brand advertisers began to use national magazines to spread the virtues of consumption, not only through the ads themselves but also through editorial content.

Entrepreneurs like William Randolph Hearst (*New York Journal*) and Joseph Pulitzer (*New York World*) seized the day with "lurid, multi-column headlines; seductive portraits of the lives of the rich and famous; 'women's' pages displaying the allure of being a fashionable consumer; and especially, sensational, often prevaricated 'news' of crimes, accidents, scandals, and bizarre or sentimental 'human interest.'"[20] Pulitzer initiated the practice of selling advertising space on the basis of actual circulation and selling it at fixed prices. He also abandoned the traditional penalties for advertisers who used illustrations or broke column rules. Pulitzer's most enduring legacy— far more profound and wide-reaching than the prize bearing his name—is to have helped rationalize newspaper business practices, especially the relationship between newspapers and advertisers.

THE MEDIA MONOPOLY

Today, the shift from "telling the people to selling the people" is a given.[21] Newspapers are owned by multinational corporations, "mammoth entities that answer to stockholders who expect big profits and constant growth."[22] The major broadcast television news operations are all owned by international conglomerates as well. CNN is owned by AOL Time Warner, ABC News by Walt Disney, CBS News by Viacom, and NBC News by General Electric. The cards may change hands even as this book goes to press, but the concentration of the news industry nationally, and its domination of news coverage internationally, is indisputable.

A century after Adolph Ochs scooped up the "failing and demoralized" *New York Times,* the business of the news has flourished. In the early 1980s, Ben H. Bagdikian reported that the U.S. newspaper industry was "fabulously profitable," with a 17 percent return on stockholders' equity.[23] In 2000, Benjamin M. Compaine noted that the "rapid rate with which newspapers have been bought at increasingly higher multiples of dollars per reader or earnings is a sign of a prosperous industry."[24] According to Compaine, the U.S. newspaper industry was worth $37.225 billion in 1996, accounting for 0.5 percent of the gross domestic product (GDP). Daily circulation of newspapers in 1998 was 56.2 million. In 1997, revenues for Gannett alone were $4.73 billion, and profits were $713 million, representing a 15.1 percent return on revenue.[25]

The *New York Times* has evolved into the New York Times Co., ranked number 468 on the 2001 *Fortune 500* list of "America's Largest Corporations."[26] Standard & Poor's described the company as a "diversified media company including newspapers, television and radio stations, magazines, electronic information and publishing, Internet businesses, and forest products investments [logging and paper mills]."[27] The New York Times Co. had revenues of nearly $3.5 billion and profits of nearly $400 million in 2000.[28] Revenues from advertising alone in 2000 were more than $2.5 billion.[29] *Rolling Stone,* the would-be antithesis of the *Times,* has evolved into a glossy music industry magazine filled with ads for expensive cars and designer fragrances. In 2002, *Rolling Stone* was owned by Wenner Media LLC, which also published the slick *Men's Journal* and gossipy *US* magazine. In February 2001, Wenner and Walt Disney Company CEO Michael Eisner (number 359 on the 2001 *Forbes 400* with $720 million) announced a partnership "to make *US Weekly* a mainstay in the celebrity journalism business."[30] Eisner said he "appreciated the soft-shoe approach that *US* takes in its celebrity coverage."[31] Industry analysts noted that "*US Weekly* provides Disney a chance to control a media outlet catering to consumers hungry for news about celebrities and entertainment. It also opens *US Weekly's* subscriber list, allowing Disney to directly market to likely consumers."[32] Disney said it planned to promote the magazine's content and its writers in "*US Weekly*–branded segments" on its ABC television shows.[33] A spokesman for Wenner promised that *US Weekly*—hardly a paragon of journalistic integrity in the first place—would "retain its independence and not display favoritism toward Disney films or programs."[34]

Although some media have traditionally relied on direct consumer sales—the price of a record album or movie ticket—the newspaper, magazine, and broadcast industries are dependent upon advertisers. The news media derive significant revenues from advertising: around 50–60 percent for magazines, 80 percent for newspapers, and 100 percent for radio and television broadcasters. Thus, the sources from which we gain much of our knowledge about the world around us are beholden to companies with a vested interest in how that world is (or is not) represented. Global spending on advertising totaled $463.9 billion in 2000. The United States is home to the largest advertising market and the largest advertising industry in the world, an estimated 53 percent of advertising expenditures worldwide.[35] U.S. advertisers spend about $850 a year for every man, woman, and child in the nation. Newspapers account for 21.8 percent of all U.S. advertising expenditures.[36]

It is worth noting in this light that in 1999, the leading national advertisers had fifteen directors sitting comfortably on the boards of six major media companies. Cigarette manufacturer Philip Morris, the third-leading advertiser and number eleven on the 2001 *Fortune 500* list, had two directors on the board of News Corp. Pharmaceutical giant Pfizer, fourth among U.S. advertisers and number fifty-three on the *Fortune 500*, had directors on the boards of Viacom, AOL Time Warner, and Dow Jones. DaimlerChrysler had a director on the board of Viacom, and Ford Motor Co. had one with the New York Times Co. and another with Dow Jones. Sears, Roebuck & Co. had representatives on the boards of AOL Time Warner, the Tribune Co. and the New York Times Co. PepsiCo had directors on the boards of the New York Times Co. and AOL Time Warner.[37] The symbiotic relationship between the news and advertising industries should now be apparent. It is therefore worth digging a little deeper to examine the ideologies underpinning each institution.

## THE IDEOLOGY OF ADVERTISING

Before it could be an industry, career, or college major, advertising was an ideology. That is, advertising is not only an economic institution operating for the benefit of a few major corporations and their owners; it is also an ideological institution that supports and negates certain ways of thinking. The purpose of a particular ad might be to convince us that life is richer for those whose teeth are whiter or hips are slimmer, or to assure us that "buying a Bud" is the same thing as making a friend. But the overarching purpose of advertising as an institution is to promote capitalism itself.

### SELLING CAPITALISM

The values and practices associated with capitalism include private ownership of the means of production, the pursuit of profit by self-interested entrepreneurs, and the right to unlimited gain through economic effort. "In its 'ideal' formulation," as Exoo writes, "capitalism also stresses competition among producers, a substantial measure of laissez-faire, and market determination of production, distribution, and economic reward. Certain notions from individualist doctrine and the so-called Protestant ethic, such as an emphasis on achievement and hard work, are also widely held as part of the capitalist creed."[38]

Studies have shown an overwhelming support for capitalist ideology in the United States.[39] For example, 68 percent of Americans believe that the most important factor in determining who gets ahead is hard work (over luck and family background), and 70 percent believe that America is the land of opportunity where everyone who works hard gets ahead. Eighty-five percent of Americans believe that incomes cannot be made more equal since people's abilities and talents are unequal, and 95 percent agree with the statement, "There is nothing wrong with a man trying to make as much money as he honestly can." Eighty-seven percent of Americans believe that private ownership of property is as important to a good society as freedom.[40] Such studies, like the ideology of capitalism itself, are fraught with contradictions. Americans also tell pollsters that, in their opinion, "Some have too little, others too much." They agree that "life's road is harder for some—for women, for blacks, for working- and lower-class people—than for others." And they feel that government is run on behalf of "a few big interests."[41] Finally, however, it seems that most Americans have come to associate the ideal of freedom with free enterprise, free markets, and free trade. Advertisers have sold them on the idea.

If capitalism is our national religion, consumption is its ritual sacrament. The Center for the Study of Commercialism defines consumerism as "ubiquitous product marketing that leads to a preoccupation with individual consumption to the detriment of oneself and society."[42] Conspicuous consumption is not so much the accumulation of wealth as the acquisition of stuff. The American ideal of consumerism is epitomized in a 1999 television ad for Levi's jeans in which an androgynous adolescent waif declares: "If you work hard you should have nice clothes." The problem, of course, is that lots of folks who work hard don't have nice stuff, and lots of folks who don't work hard do. In this consumerist worldview, success, happiness, and even love are measured by one's ability and inclination to consume. The good life means a good lifestyle. Goals are material rather than spiritual, sensual, social, or political. Advertising is designed to make people ascribe to such a worldview, and to promote respect, admiration, and envy for those who have achieved success according to its doctrines, the members of the capitalist class.

Consumerism did not become the American way of life without a struggle.[43] Other ways of life stood in its way, "like Indians on the frontiers of . . . development," as Stuart Ewen reminds us in *Captains of Consciousness.*[44] One need only consider all the negative connotations accorded to the pursuit of fortune and the trappings of wealth in U.S. popular culture. Classical Hollywood films, for example, rarely attempt to glamorize bankers, industrialists, or stock speculators. After the stock market crash of 1929, as John Belton notes, capitalist figures tended to be identified with the fiscal mismanagement that brought about the Great Depression—"but their villainy is more often seen in terms of individual greed than of class oppression."[45] Common sayings such as "Money isn't everything," "You can't take it with you," "Money can't buy happiness or love," and "Money is the root of all evil" attest to the resonance of the Protestant work ethic and the Catholic vow of poverty in U.S. society. The Bible tells us that it is easier for a camel to pass through the eye of a needle than for a rich man to enter the kingdom of heaven. "All of this asceticism and humility," as Exoo quips, "was, of course, bad for business."[46]

So advertising had to work to combat negative images of consumption and to perpetuate popular myths of classlessness or positive images of upward mobility. The hero of the Horatio Alger stories is "Ragged Dick," an honest lad of cheerful perseverance who, with luck and pluck, achieves his just reward (in most versions of the tale, a middle management position rather than fabulous wealth). Dick is a self-made man who pulls himself up by his own bootstraps. Since, however, "the key to great wealth in America is still choosing wealthy parents,"[47] luck remains a powerful element of the equation. Contests, lotteries, and chances to win free prizes (often with the hollow disclaimer "no purchase necessary") lure shoppers, and game shows such as "Who Wants to be a Millionaire?" attract viewers. Consuming (rather than, say, saving or sharing) is widely regarded as the appropriate reward for hard work. Indeed, to do otherwise—in other words, *not* to go shopping—is often depicted as downright un-American. The business pages of the newspapers constantly remind us that consumer spending makes up two-thirds of the U.S. economy. Recent U.S. presidents have done everything from making a media event out of buying a pair of socks to urging Americans to take a trip to Disney World in the name of patriotism.

MANUFACTURING DEMAND

If the overarching purpose of advertising is the promotion of consumption, its immediate goal is the creation of needs. Newspaper owners often justify the number of column inches devoted to ads by insisting that advertising informs consumers. In fact, it is inherently *against* the interests of advertisers to make us truly informed consumers, since then they would have to meet our genuine needs rather than those they attempt to create. Ironically, as Exoo argues, much advertising prescribes the products created by capitalism as therapy for the injuries wrought by capitalism: consumption as a remedy for the loss of community, autonomy, craftsmanship, and nature.[48] A credit card promises to buy intimacy with family, friends, and lovers. As a turn of the twenty-first-century ad campaign proclaimed, "There are some things money can't buy. For everything else, there's MasterCard." Ads for mass-produced goods stress individual craftsmanship, and ads for processed foods stress homemade flavor. Food and beverage factories are depicted as cozy country kitchens and breweries.

In the latter half of the twentieth century (a period that advertising textbooks euphemistically refer to as "the research era"[49]), the advertising industry entered into what *Business Week* referred to as a "torrid love affair" with the psychology profession.[50] Since then, the ad industry's strategy has been to focus less on the strengths of the product and more on the weaknesses of the consumer.[51] Increasingly, advertisers have suggested that social and personal relations can be improved by purchasing products such as deodorants and mouthwashes. It is easy enough to ridicule ads from the 1960s and 1970s in which a homemaker's worth is measured by the presence or absence of a ring around the collar or yellowing floor wax, but it is also worthwhile to consider the extent to which advertising appeals can come to seem commonsensical in our culture. Having a dry scalp can be made to seem repulsive in order to sell dandruff shampoos. Natural body odors can be made to seem disgusting in order to sell feminine hygiene products. People with straight hair should have it chemically curled, and people with curly hair should have it chemically straightened. Women with body hair must have it removed, and men without hair must have it replaced. As comedian George Carlin commented wryly, "[We're] all being trained to be part of this big circle of goods being pumped out and everyone buying them and everyone going to work to help make more of them for other people to buy." Carlin claims to have given up on the whole human species, even suggesting we let the insects have a go at world power. "You know, I don't think they'll come up with sneakers with lights on them, or Dust Busters, or salad shooters, or snot candy."[52]

People have real needs, of course, in addition to those created for them by capitalism or manufactured for them by advertisers. One of the primary goals of advertising is to differentiate between the scores of virtually indistinguishable products that promise to fulfill our needs: to persuade consumers that products manufactured by large, national companies with famous brands are superior to those made at home or in town. As a 2001 advertising textbook unabashedly explains, "One important function of advertising is to create, or enhance, the gap between the price of a product and the subjective value given it by individual consumers." The greater this "value gap," the better.[53] Keeping consumers uninformed or misinformed makes it easier for advertisers to persuade consumers to make decisions based on emotional bonds with their products. One of the most cynical examples of these emotional appeals, as Naomi Klein notes, is to associate high-end lifestyle product lines with risqué art and progressive politics.[54] We call this tactic "marketing diversity."

MARKETING DIVERSITY

Benetton's sportswear ad campaigns of the late 1980s and early 1990s are perhaps the most notorious examples of this ploy. Writing for *Advertising Age,* Bob Garfield called these "supposedly socially conscious" ads featuring kids of all colors wearing overpriced knits nothing less than "cynical, trite garbage."[55] Later Benetton ads eliminated the clothes altogether, attempting to associate the brand with "provocative" images including mating horses, dying AIDS victims, and teeming refugees.[56] "Flattering itself as courageous, this shockvertising was actually a cowardly assault on the sensibilities of unsuspecting readers, who have no expectation of being confronted with human tragedy by the ready-to-wear industry," as Garfield wrote.[57] A 2000 "Death Row" campaign finally proved disastrous when Sears threatened to remove all Benetton products from its 400 stores. In 2001, the company sought to polish its tarnished image with a return to a kinder, gentler marketing of diversity: "colourful photographs of young black or white people positioned against a white background wearing Benetton T-shirts, jumpers or swimwear."[58]

A number of other corporations, including Denny's and TCI, have also exploited images of racial, ethnic, and sexual diversity to sell their goods and services. In January of 1999, Denny's was hailed as "perhaps the first national advertiser to focus a TV campaign on race."[59] According to the *Atlanta Journal and Constitution,* "The spots feature a young minority spokesperson and end with the words 'Diversity. It's about all of us.' Only the Denny's logo identifies the sponsor."[60] Denny's sought to portray itself as a leading advocate of the golden rule—"do unto others" with an emphasis on "others." In fact, the ads were mandated as part of the $54.4 million settlement of two class-action suits against Denny's brought by thousands of African-American customers who claimed that restaurants in the chain persistently refused to seat or serve them. Despite this slap on the wrist, Denny's remained "a corporate poster child for racial discrimination," a restaurant chain "known as much for bias as for breakfasts."[61] Indeed, the very same day in 1999 that Denny's announced its $2 million diversity ad campaign, a group of South Bay Latino customers filed yet another discrimination lawsuit against the chain.[62] This raised serious doubts about the company's sudden "redemption" in 2000, when Denny's was ranked number 1 on *Fortune's* list of the nation's "Best 50 Companies for Minorities."[63]

In one more example, a 1999 ad for TCI, the multisystem cable operator, celebrated rabid individualism masquerading as multiculturalism by parading a rainbow of racial and ethnic minorities on the TV screen, each proclaiming "*I* will be the one" or "It will be *me.*" The ad reaffirms the myth of the individual rising above the collective, rather than the collective enabling and empowering the individual, which is the way human society really works. It closes with an image of a black man standing at the seashore and a voiceover narrator suggesting that if it weren't for diverse sources of information like those brought to us by TCI, we might still think the world was flat. The unintentional irony, of course, is that the Age of Exploration ushered in colonialism, genocide, and the slave trade.

The ad was part of the company's larger campaign to promote product loyalty to cable television as a superior option to satellite. It aired just as TCI was merging with AT&T in a deal worth nearly $50 billion. The combined company hoped to become a one-stop information store, providing local and long-distance telephone service, cable TV, and Internet access. Wall Street analysts and economists hailed the deal as bringing about a new age of competition in local telecommunications markets. They ignored the threat it posed to information diversity, as the combination involved control over both the information pipelines and programming. TCI already had a reputation for using its list of 19 million subscribers to promote cable networks in which it held an equity stake, while rejecting others on the grounds of limited channel capacity. Media activists blamed TCI's cancellation of The 90s Channel—a one-hour news magazine show with a radical take on political, economic, and social issues—in part on the conservative politics of its owner, John Malone (number ninety on the 2001 *Forbes 400* list with $2.1 billion).[64]

Corporate sponsors of media programs are pleased to promote diversity, but media concentration squashes it and media moguls are happy to exploit it for a buck. Cable television has increased the number of channels and fractured the television audience into niches of race, age, and gender, as in Fox's Boyz and Girlz channels. A 1999 *New York Times* editorial lamented the increasing fragmentation and marginalization of audiences, the emergence of what one producer called "a chitlin circuit on TV." The column nonetheless concluded with the suggestion that anyone worried about losing a sense of national community as television grapples with its recombinant future should "Get a life."[65] The truth is that the capitalist marketplace, in which the advertising industry plays so central a part, *cannot* deliver diversity. Even the *New York Times* was forced to recognize the unlikelihood of media concentration leading to a broader spectrum of programming: "Established networks and cable channels have an enormous advantage, even as they clone themselves, because they already control a stockpile of paid-up shows. That is why when digital channels begin to multiply we will be watching a lot of leftovers. Luckily, Americans are used to that."[66]

Multiplicity doesn't equal diversity any more than concentration equals community, and celebrations of identity and difference often spiral into debates about whether "my oppression is worse than yours." Such fragmentation invites defeat, for it prevents the type of unified struggle against dominant forms of oppression and exploitation that are necessary to produce significant social change, especially when it is really all about selling designer clothing, fast food, and, finally, in the case of TCI, media concentration itself.

## THE IDEOLOGY OF THE NEWS

Like advertising, journalism is an ideological institution that functions to support and negate certain ways of thinking. Among the most important values and practices associated with journalism in the United States are (1) the journalistic norm of maintaining objectivity, or at least fairness and balance, in reporting; (2) the storied tradition of "muckraking" to discover the truth, as in investigative journalism; and (3) the responsibility of a free press to act as a watchdog for society, protecting citizens from government graft and greed. These three journalistic values and practices are closely related to one another and reflect deeply held beliefs about the functions and effects of the news media in a democratic society. It is therefore worthwhile to take a closer look at each.

### TWO SIDES TO EVERY STORY

The notion that journalists can and should separate facts from values has long been cultivated by the U.S. news media and is so pervasive in our culture as to risk being thought of as commonsensical. As noted above, the norm of objectivity was originally invented to help sell wire service stories, but in professional journalism it evolved into a kind of moral philosophy, a declaration about "what kind of thinking and writing one should engage in."[67] Given the obviously subjective nature of journalistic practice—determining what stories are reported, how they are treated, where they are placed—contemporary newsmakers have backed off from claims of objectivity, and more typically purport to seek "balance and fairness" by covering "both sides" of "the issue." This, too, is problematic, for it obscures the broad spectrum of ideas and opinions on any one issue that might emerge in a less rigid format, not to mention the other issues that might arise in a truly democratic media system.

Nonetheless, the belief that there are two sides to every story is embraced by most journalists. A 1998 AP article, for example, took great pains to quote both sides of a story, speculation on voter turnout in light of "fallout from the Lewinsky affair." The first source cited was construction worker John Mason of Louisville: "'I'm so bitter at Republicans, it makes my support of Democrats even stronger,' declared the Democrat, wearing a blue hard hat with a stubby pencil over one ear." A second source was quoted for balance: "'The Democrats are not as likely to be interested in the election, they are less intense about voting and about supporting their candidate,' said Republican pollster Ed Goeas, citing his detailed survey of voter intensity."[68] A "detailed survey" undoubtedly carries more weight than a "stubby pencil" when it comes to the credibility of sources. A more balanced report might have drawn parallel portraits of the two subjects, describing the Republican as "insisting upon the validity of his statistics, wearing a black fedora, with a Cross pen slipped in one pocket." A report covering a broader spectrum of ideas and opinions might have included the thoughts of a Green Party member, or maybe a conscientious nonvoter. In a true media democracy, in which the subjects of public debate are determined by the people whose lives are actually affected by them, "fallout from the Lewinsky affair" would probably not have been a news "issue" in the first place.

Even such simplistic notions as objectivity and balance are routinely disregarded by the mainstream media anyway. Indeed, many newsmakers apparently assume that there is only one side to certain stories. A 1998 story in the State College (Pa.) Centre Daily Times (CDT), prominently placed in the first section under the heading "Local and State" news, provides a good example. The article announced that a regional chain, Uni-Marts Inc., had hired the Kaiser Group, a marketing firm "with a proven track record in the convenience store industry." Kaiser was reported to specialize in merchandizing, store design, and point-of-sale programs.[69] This business story, compiled from staff reports and presented as local news, highlights the procorporate bias of the media, celebrating the efforts of a locally based company to rescue its falling stock prices by selling more Twinkies. If this is news rather than advertising—that is, pertinent information gathered for readers to consider rather than a public relations release reprinted to spur consumption—there ought to be other sides to the story.

A little history would have helped readers put the story into context. A marketing historian, for example, might point out that convenience store chains are filling the retail gap left by the disappearance of neighborhood mom-and-pop grocers. Locally owned stores have been driven out of business by large supermarket chains, which lure consumers with lower prices and the appearance of variety reinforced through large advertising expenditures. A psychologist might note that convenience stores capitalize on impulse buying, allowing them to charge high prices on a limited stock of brand-name snack foods and drinks. Since consumers are "primed" for an impulse buy, point-of-sale displays strengthen the stimulation to consume. A nutritionist might suggest that the Kaiser Group is aiding and abetting Uni-Marts in increasing consumption of nutritionally bereft products. (The *CDT* would never have referred to them as "junk food pushers," although two weeks earlier it did run a Knight Ridder story headlined "Food Police: Teens Consume Too Much Soda," dismissing a study conducted by the Center for Science in the Public Interest" as "unfounded consumer alarm."[70] See chapter 5.) Even a person on the street might have pointed out the downside to the fact that Uni-Marts Inc., newly armed with "the best marketing team in the country," also operates 21 Choice Cigarette Discount Outlets. Providing this kind of context would have been bad for business. It would also have entailed "beating the bushes."

WORKING THE BEAT

Even journalists who are truly committed to "beating the bushes" are routinely relegated to "working the beat." The difference, as noted in chapter 1, is crucial. Searching out stories that aren't advertised or announced requires time, effort, and, crucially, money. Relying on a Golden Rolodex to cover the courthouse, police station, city hall, or Wall Street ensures stories on a predictable timetable and at low costs. The result is that news and public affairs are often defined by authority figures such as politicians, corporate spokespersons, and readily available experts from think tanks and research institutes. Such officials are prone to beating *around* the bushes—to withholding information, spreading half-truths, or just plain lying.

*Meet the Press,* the NBC Sunday morning news show to which the title of chapter 1 alludes, is a good example, although there is no need to single out one network here. CBS's *Face the Nation,* ABC's *This Week,* CNN's *Late Edition,* NBC/PBS's *McLaughlin Group,* and the Fox network's *Fox News Sunday* all serve the same function. They are the sites where Washington's elite meet to set government and media agendas for the week. According to *Extra!*, these programs are watched every week by White House staff and congressional aides "to determine the 'hot' issues confronting the public."[71] No one knows how many other folks tune in, because only Washington, D.C., ratings are measured. Nonetheless, the topics discussed on these Sunday shows invariably become the subjects of national newspaper reports and analyses on Monday. The media thereby become the means by which officials define public issues and set the parameters of policy debates.

Those in power also use the media to determine what is not news and what therefore will not be debated. Important arguments are often left unspoken and significant news is unreported or banished to the last paragraph of a column or final minutes of a broadcast. George Farah and Justin Elga conducted an exhaustive analysis of the transcripts of four Sunday morning news talk shows and concluded decisively that issues of corporate power are not on the mainstream media agenda. None of the four shows surveyed (*Meet the Press, Face the Nation, This Week,* and *McLaughlin Group*) even once mentioned the World Bank, the International Monetary Fund (IMF), or foreign trade during the last seven months of 1999. This is astonishing, considering that massive protests at the World Trade Organization (WTO) meeting in Seattle in late November and early December of 1999 were major news stories (see chapter 6). As Farah and Elga put it: "Instead of addressing consumer issues, environmental matters, corporate crime, the IMF, the WTO, labor rights or the minimum wage, the 1999 shows devoted time to topics like the Women's World Cup soccer victory, a moon landing tribute, Jerry Springer's possible senatorial campaign, Father's Day, a heat wave and Tina Brown's kick-off party for *Talk Magazine*."[72]

WATCHDOG ON A LEASH

There are two popular views of the relationship between the media and the government in the United States, both comforting in the sense of living in a bad neighborhood but having a good security system. The first is that the media function as a watchdog for society, protecting citizens from government graft, greed, and the general abuse of political power. This view is reflected in the notoriety of investigative reporters like Bob Woodward and Carl Bernstein, who uncovered the Watergate scandal, and in the popularity of ethical (if fictional) newspaper editors like television's Lou Grant. The second is that the government serves as a watchdog for society, guarding citizens against economic concentration and market manipulation. This view is bolstered by news coverage of the antitrust suit brought by the U.S. Department of Justice against the Microsoft Corporation in the late 1990s. When Judge Thomas Penfield Jackson handed down his "stinging ruling"[73] finding Microsoft guilty in April 2000, the press could barely conceal its glee. The lead of the top story on the front page of the *New York Times* read: "The Microsoft Corporation violated the nation's antitrust laws through predatory and anticompetitive behavior and kept 'an oppressive thumb on the scale of competitive fortune,' a federal judge ruled today."[74]

Of course, Microsoft's egregious abuse of market power made the company an easy target for the press. More importantly, the Microsoft case exemplifies an enduring value Herbert Gans found in the news, which he called "responsible capitalism."[75] Journalists hold "an optimistic faith that in the good society, businessmen and women will compete with each other in order to create increased prosperity for all." Therefore, Gans explained, "While monopoly is clearly evil, there is little explicit or implicit criticism of the oligopolistic nature of much of today's economy." Journalists expect both government and business officials to be honest and efficient and to see corruption and bureaucratic misbehavior in either as undesirable. They are nonetheless somewhat more tolerant when these norms are violated by business than when they are transgressed by government.[76]

Webster defines "watchdog" singly and specifically as "a dog kept to guard property."[77] Technically, then, both the media and the government are doing their jobs. The essential connection between the government and the capitalist class is that they both seek to protect private property. Since the U.S. media *are* private property controlled by a handful of elites, an essential contradiction emerges: The goals of amassing great profits and informing ordinary citizens are distinctly at odds with one another. So both the media and the government tend to act more as lapdogs for each other than as watchdogs for the people.

The ideal of a free press protected by the First Amendment ignores the role government officials play in setting media agendas, not to mention more direct forms of intervention such as laws and regulations regarding libel and obscenity and the allocation of radio and satellite frequencies. More importantly, it ignores what Edward Herman calls "market system constraints on freedom of expression,"[78] or the ways in which profit-making goals result in the suppression of diversity. If indeed the marketplace of ideas is prone to failure, then the assumption that "the truth" will prevail becomes problematic.

## ALL THE NEWS THAT SELLS:
## THE EFFECTS OF ADVERTISING ON NEWS

Advertisers exert two main influences over the information programming they sponsor. First, they influence the *context* in which news as a commodity is produced, the structure of the entire media industry of which news reporting is only one small part. Second, they influence the *text* of news as it is reported, the actual form and content of information as it is presented to consumers. In this section, we examine some specific examples of direct and indirect influence of advertising on the structure and content of the news.

### ADVERTISING AND NEWS STRUCTURE

Advertisers determine the structure of media industries simply by choosing where to spend their money. They support media outlets that reach the right demographic groups, audiences that consume the most. Media producers seeking to serve "undesirable" audiences cannot count on advertising revenues to finance their operations and therefore remain marginalized. Casualties of advertiser indifference or disdain for unprofitable media markets include the working-class press, competitive newspapers, African-American radio stations, and independent magazines.

### The Working-Class Press

At the turn of the twentieth century, the U.S. labor movement published hundreds of newspapers in dozens of languages. According to Jon Bekken, "These newspapers practiced a journalism very different from that of the capitalist newspapers (produced and sold as commodities by publishers closely tied to social and economic elites), which, they contended, were poisoning the minds of the public."[79] Advertisers had little interest in the vibrant working-class press, not only because working-class audiences had little to spend on manufactured goods, but also because the anticapitalist sentiments these newspapers expressed were obviously contradictory to their goals. Advertisers therefore shunned publications that challenged consumerism as a lifestyle, especially as it became more essential to sustaining the capitalist industrial system. Hearst and Pulitzer, meanwhile, responded to the "New Woman" movement of the period by addressing women as consumers. Thus, although advertisers had no vested interest in women's suffrage, as Schudson remarks, "They must have been favorably impressed by the growing coverage of fashion, etiquette, recipes, beauty culture, and interior decorating" in the mainstream papers.[80]

In England, as Curran and Seaton explain, "Radical newspapers could survive in the new economic environment only if they moved upmarket to attract an audience desired by advertisers or remained in a small working-class ghetto with manageable losses that could be met from donations. Once they moved out of that ghetto and acquired a large working-class audience, they courted disaster."[81] Even nonsocialist newspapers found that controversial editorial policies led to the loss of commercial advertising. As one early advertising handbook warned, "You cannot afford to place your advertisements in a paper which is read by the down-at-heels who buy it to see the 'Situations Vacant' column." Another advised, "A journal that circulates a thousand among the upper or middle classes is a better medium than would be one circulating a hundred thousand among the lower classes."[82]

*The Only Game in Town*

Mainstream newspapers with moderate politics and wide circulation are not immune to the effects of advertising. Bagdikian charts the dramatic decline of towns with competing newspapers in the United States over the last century, and offers Washington, D.C., as a compelling case study of "the process by which competitive papers have been eliminated from the United States for the last three generations."[83] When the *Washington Post* was founded in 1877, the city had a population of 130,000 and five daily newspapers. By 1970, the number of dailies had shrunk to three, even though the metropolitan population had grown to 2.8 million. At that time, the *Post* had a circulation of 500,000, and the other two dailies, the *Star* and the *Daily News,* had about 300,000 and 200,000, respectively. The costs of producing and distributing each paper were roughly the same, but the *Post,* with the highest circulation and lowest cost per unit, could deliver its half-million papers more cheaply than the others. The *Post* could also charge the most for advertising, which it did. If an advertiser could afford the larger investment in a *Post* ad and could use the same ad for the whole geographic area, the *Post* ad actually cost far less per household.

Big advertisers took advantage of the opportunity. "The *Post,* with ever-increasing revenues and profits, could spend more on salespeople, on editorial vigor, and on circulation promotion. The *Star* and the *News,* their revenues and profits shrinking, had less to spend while they were under growing pressure from the *Post*."[84] The rest of the story has become all too familiar. The *News* suspended operations in 1972, and the *Star* followed in 1981, leaving only one newspaper in the nation's capital. In 1920, according to Bagdikian, there were 700 cities with competing dailies.[85] Compaine's research shows that just three years later, in 1923, the number of cities with competing dailies was down to 502. By 1953 it had shrunk to ninety-one. In 1996, only nineteen cities, or 1.3 percent of all cities and towns with daily newspapers, had head-to-head newspaper competition.[86] The "only game in town" newspaper is likely to be owned by a large chain. In 1996, the three largest chains (Gannett, Knight Ridder, and Newhouse) accounted for 22.5 percent of total daily circulation.[87]

The effects of newspaper concentration due to mass advertising are far reaching. For example, monopoly newspapers have hurt small businesses, which do not need mass circulation and cannot afford monopoly advertising rates. Chain newspapers go hand-in-hand with big box chain retail outlets and with the demise of mom-and-pop stores. Of even greater concern is the fact that the concentrated structure of the news media is completely out of sync with the nation's political system. In the United States, most public policy is set at the local level. Local officials govern schools, courts, zoning, water, fire, police, and other vital functions. However, as a smaller number of newspapers grew larger in size, fewer communities had local papers to help them make informed decisions about issues that affect their daily lives. In 1920, there were 2,722 urban places and 2,400 daily papers in the country. By 1980 there were 8,765 urban places and only 1,745 dailies, leaving more than 7,000 American cities with no daily newspaper of their own.[88] As Bagdikian writes, "The inappropriate fit between the country's major media and the country's political system has starved voters of relevant information. . . . It has eroded the central requirement of a democracy that those who are governed give not only their consent but their informed consent."[89]

*Advertising and Minority Media*

Much as early advertisers shunned the working-class press, later advertisers avoided radio stations with largely African-American or Latino audiences. In 1999, the Federal Communications Commission (FCC) released a study conducted by the Civil Rights Forum on Communication Policy investigating practices in the advertising industry that pose potential barriers to competition in the broadcast marketplace. The study focused on two business practices: "no urban/Spanish dictates," the practice of not advertising on stations that target programming at racial and ethnic minorities; and "minority discounts," the practice of paying minority-formatted radio stations less than general market stations with comparable audience size.

An analysis of the data, drawn from 3,745 radio stations in 1996, concluded that advertisers regularly discriminate against minority-owned stations and stations with large African-American or Latino audiences, either excluding them altogether or paying them less. Ninety-one percent of minority broadcasters indicated that they had been subject to nonurban dictates. Survey respondents estimated that 61 percent of the ads purchased on their stations had been discounted by an average of 59 percent. The dictates and discounts were attributed to a variety of factors, including advertisers' assessments of listener income and spending patterns, and racial and ethnic stereotypes that influence the media buying process.[90] "This report's findings are bleak and shameful," as Congresswoman Carolyn C. Kilpatrick (D-MI) said in a press release. "However, they come as no surprise."[91]

When advertisers do choose minority media, they often ghettoize. The magazine industry is a good example. Cigarette advertising in most magazines surged in the 1970s when tobacco companies withdrew from radio and television in order to terminate the FCC-mandated Fairness Doctrine messages of the American Cancer Society and others.[92] By the early 1990s, according to the *Wall Street Journal,* cigarette companies were "turning away from the educated, upscale readers that so many magazines court and targeting their efforts to lower-income women and minorities."[93] The trend may have resulted in a windfall in advertising revenues for some minority magazines, but it was certainly not in the best interests of the health of these communities. When the nonurban dictates study was released, FCC Chairman William Kennard stated, "Minority broadcasters should have a fair opportunity to compete for ad dollars."[94] The problem with this is that advertisers who once shunned minority audiences have proven themselves all too willing to exploit them. Advertising has contributed to the perpetuation of racial and ethnic inequality in the United States by suppressing media diversity and exploiting minority markets, not to mention by perpetuating stereotypes in the ads themselves.

*Magazines without Umbrellas*

Like working-class newspapers and minority radio stations, companies that exist to publish a single magazine lend diversity to an increasingly concentrated and homogenous media environment. They are also, however, vulnerable to the whims of advertisers. The benefits of single-title publishing can include not being bogged down by conflicting agendas, not having to answer to shareholders, and simply not being distracted from the mission of putting out a magazine. Solo publications have been rated as some of the best in quality. *Nylon,* founded in 1998 as "an old-fashioned mom-and-pop operation," was a finalist for a National Magazine Award for general excellence and was named Magazine of the Year by the Society of Publication Designers in 2001. *Outside,* an outdoor lifestyle magazine, had a circulation of 665,000 and was one of only a handful of independently owned magazines among the top moneymakers. In December of 2001, it was feeling the pain of going it alone in an advertising recession. "Unlike magazines owned by media conglomerates like Gruner & Jahr [a subsidiary of Bertelsman, Germany's largest publisher and a giant in U.S. book publishing and music recording], Hearst, or AOL Time Warner, *Outside* does not have any corporate parent to absorb the losses or cash-cow sibling publications to tide it over."[95]

The biggest drawback to solo publication, from a business standpoint, is not being able to sell ads in discounted packages with other media. "It's harder for the independents," Mark Gleason, publisher of *Book* magazine, told the *New York Times.* In an economic downturn, a car manufacturer is more likely to spend its resources on "a multiplatform deal with one of the big guys, with TV, Internet and print. We have to wait and see what budgets are left over."[96] Mass advertising has driven the concentration of the media. Media companies have merged with the express purpose of attracting advertisers. Indeed, according to the *Wall Street Journal,* major advertising packages were precisely the kind of deals that Time Warner executives envisioned when the two media giants, Time Inc. and Warner Inc., joined forces in 1990. Advertisers could not have been more pleased. In 1991, Time Warner signed an $80 million crossmedia advertising deal with General Motors (GM) and announced a $100 million deal with Mazda. As the *Wall Street Journal* reported, "GM executives have said their arrangement will allow the company to market different car models with targeted media. One model, for instance, could be promoted in selected magazines, brochures and videos sent to prospective customers' homes, and ads on cable TV."[97]

While solo magazines struggled to stay alive, Big Media magazines began striking deals with Big Advertisers for solo sponsorship. In 1999, Ford Motor Company marketing executive David Roper told the American Magazine conference, "We still need ad pages, but we need more creative ways to use your pages."[98] The year before, Ford was the lone sponsor of *Time* magazine's "Heroes of the Planet" series focusing on environmental issues. According to *Extra!*, the coverage explicitly excluded any criticism of automobile pollution.[99] With this in mind, we turn to the effects of advertising on news content.

ADVERTISING AND NEWS CONTENT

Advertisers exert direct and indirect influence over news media content. There are many documented cases, and surely many more undocumented ones, of advertisers canceling or threatening to cancel their accounts because of critical reporting. GM, the company that salivated over the cross-media marketing possibilities of the Time Warner merger, has become infamous for withholding advertising dollars as punishment for unfavorable coverage and as warning against future bad publicity. In 1990, for example, GM ordered its advertising agencies not to place commercials on television programs that featured documentary filmmaker Michael Moore.[100] Moore's film *Roger & Me* (1989) is a scathing indictment of GM's cavalier closing of its truck plant in Flint, Michigan, which put 30,000 employees out of work and devastated the city. In 1992, GM sentenced *Automobile* magazine to three months without advertising after the magazine's editor, David E. Davis, criticized the company in a speech at the Washington Automotive Press Association's annual black-tie gala.[101] Expressing dismay at GM's announcement of twenty-one more plant closings eliminating 74,000 more jobs, Davis likened the company's management to "piano players in whorehouses" who knew what was going on upstairs but did not get personally involved. Davis later told the *New York Times* that since *Automobile* sold only about 900 pages of advertising annually, "the 50 or 60 from GM could well be the difference between a profit and a loss for the magazine."[102] Such tales of corporate censorship are damning, but the indirect influence of advertising on news content is more ubiquitous and insidious. It affects the quality and quantity of news reporting on vital topics such as war and healthcare.

*"Not An Upbeat Environment"*

In 1991, the *New York Times* reported that national advertisers were "extremely reluctant" to buy commercial time on special network news programs about the war in the Persian Gulf. Executives at the three major networks said that advertisers' skittishness about war coverage was costing them millions of dollars. Howard Stringer, president of the CBS Broadcast Group, said the news division would be forced to scale back plans for prime-time war specials, despite the fact that they had received high ratings, several attracting more viewers than entertainment programs competing with them on other channels. The specials sold only 20 percent of available commercial time, making them economically unfeasible for the network."[103] Richard Dale, an executive at Deutsch Advertising, explained the ad industry's rationale for not running ads on war news programs: "I just think it's wasted money. Commercials need to be seen in the right environment. A war is just not an upbeat environment."[104]

The projected effects of the news media's dependence on advertising during the Gulf War included the following: First, there would be fewer prime-time news specials on CBS. As Peter Lund, executive vice president of the CBS Broadcast Group, told the *New York Times* in 1991: "In fairness to our shareholders, we can't lose $1 million every time we do one of them, and we are losing an easy million between what we lose in ad revenue and the production costs."[105] Second, there would be less war coverage even on regularly scheduled news programs such as *60 Minutes* and *48 Hours.* An anonymous NBC executive could almost be heard heaving a sigh of relief as he told the *Times,* "The Today Show got back to more normal programming, and the advertisers were happy with that. A lot of them said they wanted us to get back to Gene Shalit's movie reviews and the other light stuff."[106] Finally, war coverage would be "tailored" to provide a better context for commercials. CBS executives admitted that they courted advertisers with assurances that commercials could be inserted into "segments that were specially produced with upbeat images or messages about the war, like patriotic views from the home front."[107] They seemed to have taken heed of another rationale offered by Dale from the Deutsch ad firm: "After a segment about a chemical attack that includes a shot of a disfigured face, it might not be the best time to talk about Oil of Olay skin care."[108]

Ten years later, in 2001, the *New York Times* lamented that "There is never a good time for a war, but for big media and news companies, the timing of the current crisis is especially poor."[109] The *New York Times* reported that the networks lost $500 million in advertising revenues in the days immediately following the September 11, 2001, attacks on New York's World Trade Center and the Pentagon in Washington, as they went on 24-hour news. In October, Wall Street analysts estimated that ABC, NBC and CBS were each incurring $1 million a day in extra costs covering the aftermath. "Most say they are trying to look beyond the short-term financial impact to see the long-term value that extensive coverage can bring to their news 'brands.' They remember that when CNN distinguished itself during the Persian Gulf War, the cable network's halo lasted for years."[110] Like CNN, the major broadcast television news operations are owned by international conglomerates with deep pockets. Because news is just one small part of what each of these companies do, they can better afford to wait and see how long a crisis drags on before deciding whether to let news spending hurt their overall financial results. By contrast, news is the main operation for companies like the *Washington Post* and the *New York Times.* As the *New York Times* admitted, "There may be less leeway for trimming costs—and so less ability to avoid financial pain,"[111] not to mention less information for readers.

*Health and Beauty Aids*

When it comes to the sale of products that affect people's health in one way or another, advertisers usually have one of two missions. The first is to assure consumers that a product rumored to be bad for them really is not (or at least to suggest that those who consume the product will feel so hip and happy that it does not matter if they are healthy anyway). The second is to convince consumers that a product that has not been proven to be good for them really is (or at least to imply that those who use the product will look so young and lovely that everyone else will think they are). The tobacco industry has taken on the first challenge, and the pharmaceutical and cosmetics industries have taken the second. Advertisers for these industries have affected news coverage of health issues related to the products they sell.

In 1988, a California company named Advantage/Quik-Fit attempted to launch a national magazine advertising campaign for its new smoking cessation system, Cigarrest. Donald L. Danks, vice president of sales and marketing, was reportedly stymied by the refusal of *Time, Newsweek, Sports Illustrated, Life,* and *US* magazines to carry the company's ad. Perhaps he should not have been. Earlier the same year, RJR Nabisco removed more than $70 million worth of food advertising from Saatchi & Saatchi after the agency created ads that heralded Northwest Airlines' ban on smoking.[112] In 1992, the *New England Journal of Medicine* published a study proving that magazines that relied heavily on cigarette advertising were far less likely than others to write about the dangers of smoking. The study surveyed nearly 100 magazines over a period of twenty-five years and found that those carrying tobacco ads were 38 percent less likely to discuss smoking risks than those that did not.[113] Women's magazines were the worst offenders; they were 50 percent less likely to cover the health dangers of smoking.[114]

*Time* and *Newsweek* magazines—known for sniping at each other over issues of journalistic integrity—provide textbook examples of the *New*

*England Journal's* findings. In 1985, *Time* carried a special section devoted to health. The American Academy of Family Physicians supplied the informational copy. *Time* provided the editorial expertise that deleted all references to the hazards of smoking—a decision that undoubtedly delighted the tobacco companies that bought seven pages of ads in the same edition. In 1988, *Newsweek* published a cover story entitled "What You Should Know about Heart Attacks." The back cover featured an ad for Malibu cigarettes, while, on the inside, editors deleted any suggestion that smoking contributes to heart attacks.[115]

In 1998, ten years after Cigarrest ads were shunned by mainstream magazines, smoking cessation programs had become far more fashionable as the tobacco industry ended a slew of state-initiated, health-related lawsuits by agreeing to make annual payments to the states worth $246 billion. The following year, according to the Federal Trade Commission (FTC), the five largest cigarette manufacturers spent $8.24 billion on advertising and promotions—a 22 percent increase from 1998.[116] Backed by Big Advertising, the tobacco industry made it clear that it would not go down without a fight.

The pharmaceutical and cosmetics industries are known less for strong-arm tactics than for exploiting the fears and weaknesses of consumers to sell their wares. As a prosperous generation of baby boomers matured in the 1990s, both industries actively promoted products associated with aging. Both industries also significantly affected the ways in which issues of aging were treated as news. A March 2000 issue of *Parade* magazine featured supermodel Lauren Hutton on the cover, promising that she and other celebrities would "share their secrets for looking good—and feeling good too—near or past 50."[117] A small picture of Hutton appears on page 10, at the top of the cover story. She attributes her good health to losing a few pounds and briefly outlines her diet and exercise regimen. "But my No. 1 secret is estrogen," she declares. "It's good for your moods, it's good for your skin. If I had to choose between all my creams and make-up for feeling and looking good, I'd take the estrogen."[118]

A third picture of Hutton, this one full-body and nearly full-page, is featured on page 15, in an ad sponsored by Wyeth-Ayerst Laboratories warning of "the consequences of estrogen loss at menopause."[119] The ad blends perfectly with the celebrity bias and "editorial" content of the magazine. It also perfectly illustrates the findings of a 2000 study conducted by researchers at the University of California, Davis, and published in the *Journal of Family Practice:* "In addition to failing to educate, most [prescription drug ads] don't explain the basics and some cleverly obscure facts about the products they promote."[120] There is no mention of debates among healthcare professionals about the benefits and risks of taking estrogen supplements in this issue of *Parade*.[121]

Meanwhile, newsmakers routinely treat cosmetic matters typically associated with aging as news. In September 1998, the *Centre Daily Times* reported that as "baby boomers fight the war on wrinkles," remedies for "visible signs of aging" rank among the "top ten unmet needs" of contemporary consumers. This "news" was provided by product development managers at Oil of Olay, Mary Kay, Q-Tips, and Vaseline.[122] In March 2000, New York's WCBS-TV carried a news report about a Web ad for laser surgery that featured live video of an elective operation. "Advertisements are not generally considered news," as media watchdogs at *Extra!* pointed out, "but the station seemed to think that the fact that it was placed on WCBS's own website made it more newsworthy." Station managers ordered that the ad be treated as news, angering journalists. The eye center, which paid more than $300,000 for the ad, was delighted. "The funny thing about it," a representative was quoted as saying, was that CBS decided to do a news story on the surgery right after the paid webcast. "That was a bonus. That was free."[123]

*A Real Estate Advertising Disaster*

News content also includes form, which is the way in which information is reported or presented. Although the classified advertising section of a paper is not presented as news in the manner of war coverage or health-care reports, it can certainly be used for information purposes, especially if one is looking to sublet an apartment or buy a used car. In 1990, the *Boca Raton News,* a Knight Ridder paper, began organizing such notices in a grid that allowed readers to compare what was offered more easily. For example, all the Mazda 323s were listed together in descending order by model year and then by price. This innovation was extremely popular with subscribers: A *News* survey showed that 87 percent of readers loved the grids. Unfortunately, however, many advertisers did not. "The grids were a real reader benefit, but a real estate advertising disaster," according to Thomas P. O'Donnell, publisher of the rival *Fort Lauderdale Sun-Sentinel.* O'Donnell reported that advertising in the South Palm Beach edition of the *Sun-Sentinel* had increased 82 percent since the *News* began running the grids. He credited advertiser animosity toward the *News* for his own paper's gains.[124] The *New York Times* reported that the Boca Raton case became the "subject of intense interest throughout the newspaper industry" as the *Boca Raton News* struggled to "resolve whether advertisers or readers have a higher priority."[125] James Gordon Bennett, who argued in the early 1800s that advertisers should gain advantage from the substance of their ads rather than appearance or placement,[126] would surely be dismayed.

*Covering the Capitalist Class*

The biggest void in news content is not caused by the direct or indirect influence of any individual advertiser on any particular newspaper or media company. The real hole in the news is a by-product of advertising as an institution. The primary effect of the ideology of advertising on the practice of news reporting is the coverage (or cover-up) of the capitalist class *as a class*. Most mainstream newspapers have "business" sections, but few devote space to labor and fewer still even acknowledge the existence of capitalism. As noted in chapter 3, snippets of news on media moguls can sometimes be found in syndicated gossip columns such as "People Watch," produced by the Associated Press and featured daily in newspapers around the country. Because so many members of the capitalist class have either made their fortunes in media enterprises or invested their fortunes in media companies, this is a good place to begin searching for news about them.

"The Sundance Kid doesn't have a monopoly on the name," a 1998 People Watch story begins, rather gleefully reporting that Robert Redford had lost a trademark battle with Ed Bass over the right to establish a chain of Sundance Theaters in Texas, where Bass and his brothers already held a chain by that name. Redford is duly identified as the actor "who played the outlaw in *Butch Cassidy and the Sundance Kid*" and as a businessman who founded Sundance Enterprises, the Sundance Institute, and the Sundance Film Festival. A file photo of Redford accompanies the item for readers who may have forgotten what he looks like. The Bass brothers are identified only as brothers, and come off like mom-and-pop theater owners thumbing their noses at a Hollywood movie star in defense of their right to use a common word.

Here is the hole in the news. Robert Redford may be rich and famous, but the Bass brothers are super rich. Ed was the least so, ranked at number 236 on the 2001 *Forbes 400* list, with $1 billion. Brother Lee was number fifty-five, with $3.3 billion. Brothers Sid and Robert were numbers sixty and seventy, with $3 billion and $2.6 billion, respectively, while father Perry came in at 172, with $1.3 billion. The Bass brothers thus had a combined net worth of $11.2 billion. In this context, which People Watch of course fails to provide, it seems less surprising that Redford lost his trademark battle. By taking great pains to identify one of the most visible figures in the entertainment industry, and none at all to identify a family that quietly invested its oil wealth in the media to expand an already great fortune, this story serves to perpetuate a myth of equal opportunity and classlessness in the United States, obscuring who the real controllers of wealth, power, and information really are.

As it turned out, Ed Bass was allowed to keep operating his Sundance theater chain throughout Texas and Redford got permission to use the name anywhere else on the planet he might decide to put up theaters. The issue of whether *anyone* should be entitled to claim the term "sun dance" (which, according to Webster, denotes "a ceremonial dance of North and South American Indians in honor of the sun at the summer solstice"[127]) as private property was never called into question. Texas moviegoers were more likely to see Disney animations than Sundance productions at Ed's theaters in 1998, and not just due to fallout over the trademark rivalry. The entire Bass family—including Perry, who inherited the oil empire, and Sid's ex-wife Anne, described by *Forbes* as "poster dame for the First Wives Club"—held huge stakes in Disney at the time.

## CONCLUSION

Perhaps a celebrity gossip column cannot be expected to raise issues of class structure in the United States. The editors of *Forbes,* who proudly wear the badge of "capitalist tool" and openly fawn over the super rich, can only be expected to celebrate it. But *news* coverage of the business dealings of members of the capitalist class should at the very least attempt to escape the ideology of advertising and embrace the values of journalism. Their mergers and acquisitions affect the quality of our information and culture.

The editors of *Forbes* regularly come up with tortured interpretations of their list of "The 400 Richest People in America" to perpetuate a myth of classlessness. The introduction to their 1996 survey, for example, instructed readers to "Forget America's 50 families. Forget old money. Forget silver spoons. Great fortunes are being created almost monthly in the U.S. today by young entrepreneurs who hadn't a dime when we created this list 14 years ago."[128] Even if that were true, at least half of those on the list started out with $50 million or more—the equivalent of a good leadoff from third base. The editors of *Forbes* bristle at the suggestion, but the key to great wealth in America is still "choosing wealthy parents."[129]

The AP's ritual coverage of the *Forbes 400* list often makes front-page news. In September of 1998, for example, it was featured on page 1 of the *Centre Daily Times.* The bold headline read "Market Woes Lessen Ranks of Billionaires."[130] Apparently, a stock market dive that summer "left empty chairs at the billionaires' club." Bill Gates remained sitting, with $58.4 billion, despite the fact that the Microsoft chief's net worth "plunged" $9 billion that year. Others, like Roy Disney of Walt Disney and David Filo of Yahoo!, "missed the cut to remain mere megamillionaires." A letter to the editor of the *Centre Daily Times* "applauded" the paper for "reprinting the most inane, incomprehensible piece of 'news' in recent memory," noting that it would take him 464 years to clap once for each of Bill Gates's dollars. The editor responded that the paper had also published six stories since April on poverty and homelessness in Centre County.[131]

Buried at the bottom of the column (and cast as a "disturbing trend for parents and teachers"), was the news that fifty-eight members of that year's *Forbes 400* never finished college and yet had amassed an average fortune of $4.8 billion. The message is clear: "Parents, don't bother sacrificing to send your kids to Ivy League schools. Graduates of these prestigious colleges averaged only $2.3 billion." The column suggests that one needn't have a good education or even connections to become super rich; all it takes is "smarts." Bill Gates, perennially number one on the list, is often cited as an example. In fact, Gates started on first base. Son of a professional couple, he attended Harvard, where he met Paul Allen (number three on the 2001 list, with $28.2 billion) before dropping out. His big break came in 1980 when IBM contracted him to develop the operating software system for its first PC. Gates and Allen did not *develop* that software—they merely bought QDOS for $50,000, renamed it MS-DOS, and rode to fortune on the backs of Big Blue. With MS-DOS in more than 90 percent of the world's PCs, Microsoft used its market power to stifle competition. Contrary to popular belief, much of Gates's $54 billion fortune is based on questionable business practices rather than "smarts." Most of it, moreover, is the result of contributions to computer technology produced by scholars and researchers and funded by taxpayer money.

The *Forbes 400* reinforces false notions of upward mobility in what is actually a very rigid U.S. class structure. Again, perhaps we should expect nothing more from the self-proclaimed capitalist tool. In a sense, *Forbes* does us a service by publishing its annual list so that we can see how obscenely wealthy the super rich are, but shouldn't readers expect that rather than simply repeating the *Forbes* line, our "watchdog" media should take the ritual report as an opportunity to put the list into context?

The unequal distribution of wealth and income in the United States is beginning to resemble that of many Third World societies. In 2001, according to the Institute for Policy Studies and United for a Fair Economy, the average chief executive officer of a major American corporation made 531 times as much in pay, bonuses, and stock options as the average factory worker.[132] Wealth is even more concentrated. According to Federal Reserve data, the richest 500,000 U. S. households (out of 100 million) own one-third of the total wealth in the United States (minus home equity, the main repository of most household wealth). The richest 10 percent of the population own a whopping 77.5 percent of the total wealth (again, minus home equity) and they own 84 percent of the stock as well as 90 percent of the bonds.[133]

The absurdly unequal distribution of wealth and income within the United States is magnified globally. More than 1 billion of the world's 6.2 billion people go to bed hungry every night. At the turn of the twenty-first century, 900 million people existed on less than $1 a day in Asia alone.[134] This state of affairs and the discontent it fosters require the rich to use more coercion to protect their fortunes, fueling conditions for increased social conflict internationally. The concentration of the world's wealth in the hands of a few poses a serious threat to democracy, since great wealth gives those who own it inordinate power to dictate public policy and mold public opinion through the media. These are the kinds of data that we need to begin filling the hole in the news—not a handful of features about what a shame it is to be poor, or what a drag it is to be a little less rich.

## NOTES

1. Michael Schudson, *Discovering the News: A Social History of American Newspapers* (New York: Basic Books, Inc., 1978), 110–11.

2. Schudson, *Discovering the News,* 111–12.

3. Schudson, *Discovering the News,* 112–13.

4. *The Journalist,* 4 December 1897, 46, cited in Schudson, *Discovering the News,* 107.

5. Gerald J. Baldasty, "The Rise of News as a Commodity: Business Imperatives and the Press in the Nineteenth Century," in *Ruthless Criticism: Perspectives in U.S. Communication History,* ed. William S. Solomon and Robert W. McChesney (Minneapolis: University of Minnesota Press, 1993), 112–13.

6. *Rolling Stone* officially adopted the motto later, but the antiestablishment tone it embodies is evident from the first issue.

7. Jann Wenner, "A Letter from the Editor," *Rolling Stone,* 9 November 1967, 2.

8. *Rolling Stone,* 9 November 1967, 1–8.

9. "Help!" *Rolling Stone,* 20 January 1968, 3.

10. Tom Wolfe, "Preface," in *Rolling Stone: The Photographs,* ed. Laurie Kratochvil (New York: Simon & Schuster, 1989), ii.

11. Ronald V. Bettig, *Copyrighting Culture: The Political Economy of Intellectual Property* (Boulder, Colo.: Westview Press, 1996), 16.

12. Schudson, *Discovering the News,* 16–19.

13. Calvin F. Exoo, *The Politics of the Mass Media* (New York: West Publishing Company, 1994), 119.

14 Schudson, *Discovering the News,* 93.

15. Schudson, *Discovering the News,* 93.

16. Donald L. Shaw, "News Bias and the Telegraph: A Study of Historical Change," *Journalism Quarterly* 44 (spring 1967): 3–12, 31. Cited in Schudson, *Discovering the News,* 4.

17. W. Ronald Lane and J. Thomas Russell, *Advertising: A Framework* (Upper Saddle River, N.J.: Prentice Hall, 2001), 1–3.

18. Lane and Russell, *Advertising,* 1–3.

19. Schudson, *Discovering the News,* 93.

20. Exoo, *The Politics of the Mass Media,* 120.

21. Exoo, *The Politics of the Mass Media,* 119.

22. Matt Carlson, "Boardroom Brothers: Interlocking Directorates Indicate Media's Corporate Ties," *Extra!,* September/October 2001, 18.

23. Ben H. Bagdikian, *The Media Monopoly,* 6th ed. (Boston: Beacon Press, 2000), 265.

24. Benjamin M. Compaine, "The Newspaper Industry," in *Who Owns the Media? Competition and Concentration in the Mass Media Industry,* ed. Benjamin M. Compaine and Douglas Gomery (Mahwah, N.J.: Lawrence Erlbaum Associates, 2000), 2–6.

25. Compaine, "The Newspaper Industry," 2–6.

26. "The 500 Largest Corporations," *Fortune* (16 April 2001): F19.

27. "New York Times Co.," *Standard & Poor's Corporate Descriptions Plus News,* 29 January 2002, LexisNexis (accessed 1 February 2002).

28. "The 500 Largest Corporations," F19.

29. "New York Times Co.," *Standard & Poor's.*

30. "*Rolling Stone,* Disney Join Forces for *US*" (Associated Press Reports), *State College (Pa.) Centre Daily Times,* 28 February 2001, sec. B9.

31. Alex Kuczynski, "Disney to Take 50% Stake in *Us Weekly* Magazine," *New York Times,* 28 February 2001, sec. C1.

32. Jeff Leeds, "Disney Returns to Publishing with Stake in *US,*" *Los Angeles Times,* 28 February 2001, sec. C1.

33. Leeds, "Disney Returns," sec. C1.

34. Leeds, "Disney Returns," sec. C1.

35. William H. Donald, "Industry Profile: The Spoils Are Concentrated at the Top," <www.netadvantage.standardandpoors.com/netahtml/IndSur/adv/adv11202.htm> (accessed 26 December 2001).

36. Compaine, "The Newspaper Industry," 2–16.

37. Carlson, "Boardroom Brothers," 18.

38. Exoo, *The Politics of the Mass Media,* 24.

39. Exoo, *The Politics of the Mass Media,* 25–27. Exoo draws data from three sources: Herbert McClosky and John Zaller, *The American Ethos* (Cambridge, Mass.: Harvard University Press, 1984); Sidney Verba and Gary R. Owen, *Equality in America* (Cambridge, Mass.: Harvard University Press, 1985); and Kay Schlozman and Sidney Verba, *Injury to Insult* (Cambridge, Mass.: Harvard University Press, 1979).

40. Exoo, *The Politics of the Mass Media,* 25–26.

41. Exoo, *The Politics of the Mass Media,* 26–27.

42. Michael F. Jacobson and Laurie Ann Mazur, *Marketing Madness [A Survival Guide for a Consumer Society]* (Boulder, Colo.: Westview Press, 1995), 12.

43. Exoo, *The Politics of the Mass Media,* 262.

44. Stuart Ewen, *Captains of Consciousness* (New York: McGraw-Hill, 1977), 58.

45. John Belton, *American Cinema/American Culture* (New York: McGraw-Hill, 1994), 234.

46. Exoo, *The Politics of the Mass Media,* 264.

47. Chuck Collins, "Horatio Alger, Where Are You?," *Dollars and Sense,* January/February 1997, 9.

48. Exoo, *The Politics of the Mass Media,* 258.

49. Lane and Russell, *Advertising,* 2.

50. Philip Gold, *Advertising, Politics, and American Culture* (New York: Paragon, 1987): 18.

51. Exoo, *The Politics of the Mass Media,* 266.

52. Marc Cooper, "The *Progressive* Interview: George Carlin," *The Progressive,* July 2001, 32–37.

53. Lane and Russell, *Advertising,* 15.

54. Naomi Klein, *No Logo: Taking Aim at the Brand Bullies* (New York: Picador, 1999), 17.

55. Bob Garfield, "Benetton on Death Row," *Advertising Age,* 10 January 2000, 45.

56. Jade Garrett, "Shock! Horror! New Benetton Ad Shows Clothes," *The Independent* (London), 24 January 2001, 12.

57. Garfield, "Benetton on Death Row," 45.

58. Garrett, "Shock! Horror!," 12.

59. Bob Dart, "Denny's Begins TV Spots on Race Today," *Atlanta Journal and Constitution,* 13 January 1999, sec. E10.

60. Dart, "Denny's Begins TV Spots," sec. E10.

61. Dart, "Denny's Begins TV Spots," sec. E10.

62. Todd Henneman, "Denny's Sued by Bay Area Latinos; Restaurant Announces Anti-Discrimination Ads on TV Same Day," *San Francisco Chronicle,* 13 January 1999, sec. A4.

63. Tannette Johnson-Elie, "Denny's Turnabout Means Fair Play for Minority Employees," *Milwaukee Journal Sentinel,* 31 October 2000, sec. D10.

64. Malone continued to run his programming company, Liberty Media, after the 1999 merger. Liberty split off from AT&T in August 2001, and raised its stake in UnitedGlobalCom Inc., Europe's second-largest cable operator, the following December.

65. Editorial, "Whither the Tube?" *New York Times,* 4 January 1999, sec. 18A.

66. "Whither the Tube?", sec. 18A.

67. Schudson, *Discovering the News,* 8.

68. Will Lester, "Poll: Democratic Voters Still Support Their Candidates" (Staff Reports), *State College (Pa.) Centre Daily Times,* 28 August 1998, sec. 6A.

69. "Uni-Marts Inc. Hires Marketing Firm" (Staff Reports), *State College (Pa.) Centre Daily Times,* 7 November 1998, sec. 5A.

70. Usha Lee McFaring, "Food Police: Teens Consume Too Much Soda" (Knight Ridder), *State College (Pa.) Centre Daily Times,* 22 October 1998, sec. A1.

71. George Farah and Justin Elga, "What's *Not* Talked About on Sunday Morning?" *Extra!,* October 2001, 14–17.

72. Farah and Elga, "What's *Not* Talked About," 14–17.

73. "Microsoft's Illegal Monopoly," *New York Times,* 4 April 2000, sec. A30.

74. Joel Brinkley, "U.S. Judge Says Microsoft Violated Antitrust Laws With Predatory Behavior," *New York Times,* 4 April 2000, sec. A1, C12.

75. Herbert J. Gans, "The Messages Behind the News," *Columbia Journalism Review,* January/February 1979, 40–45.

76. Gans, "The Message," 40–45.

77. *The New Webster's Dictionary and Thesaurus of the English Language* (Danbury, Conn.: Lexicon Publishers, Inc., 1992), 1111.

78. Edward Herman, "Market Constraints on Freedom of Expression," *Journal of Communication Inquiry* 15 (1991): 45–53.

79. Jon Bekken, "The Working-Class Press at the Turn of the Century," in Solomon and McChesney, *Ruthless Criticism,* 151.

80. Schudson, *Discovering the News,* 100.

81. J. Curran and J. Seaton, *Power without Responsibility,* 3rd ed. (London: Fontana, 1988), 39.

82. Curran and Seaton, *Power without Responsibility,* 37–38.

83. Bagdikian, *The Media Monopoly,* 122–23.

84. Bagdikian, *The Media Monopoly,* 122.

85. Bagdikian, *The Media Monopoly,* 124.

86. Compaine, "The Newspaper Industry," 8.

87. Compaine, "The Newspaper Industry," 9–10.

88. Bagdikian, *The Media Monopoly,* 177.

89. Bagdikian, *The Media Monopoly,* 192.

90. "When Being No. 1 Is Not Enough: The Impact of Advertising Practices on Minority-Owned & Minority-Formatted Broadcast Stations," <www.fcc.gov/Breaus/Media> (accessed 29 December 2001).

91. "Kilpatrick Responds to FCC Minority Advertising Study," <www.fcc.gov/Bureaus/Media> (accessed 30 December 2001).

92. Richard W. Pollay, Jung S. Lee, and David Carter-Whitney, "Separate, But Not Equal: Racial Segmentation in Cigarette Advertising," in *Gender, Race and Class in Media*, ed. Gail Dines and Jean M. Humez (Thousand Oaks, Calif.: Sage Publications, 1995), 109–11.

93. Joanne Lipman, "Media Content Is Linked to Cigarette Ads," *Wall Street Journal*, 30 January 1992, sec. B7.

94. "FCC Presented with Advertising Study Which Reveals a Tale of Two Systems: Study Shows Broadcasters Serving Minority Community Earn Less Per Listener," <www.fcc.gov/Bureaus/Media> (accessed 28 December 2001).

95. David Handelman, "Without a Media Umbrella: Solo Magazines Must Scramble in Hard Times," *New York Times*, 10 December 2001, sec. 9C.

96. Handelman, "Without a Media Umbrella," 9C.

97. Thomas R. King, "Time Warner Close to Big Cross-Media Ad Deal for Mazda," *Wall Street Journal*, 28 May 1991, sec. C15.

98. "SoundBites: Ads Are Not Enough," *Extra! Update*, December 1999, 2.

99. "SoundBites: Ads Are Not Enough," 2.

100. "Advertising: G.M.'s Response to *Roger & Me*," *New York Times*, 31 January 1990, sec. D23.

101. Doron P. Levin, "When Car Makers Retaliate against Critical Magazines," *New York Times*, 26 June 1992, sec. D9.

102. Levin, "When Car Makers Retaliate," sec. D9.

103. Bill Carter, "Few Sponsors for TV War News," *New York Times*, 7 February 1991, sec. D1, D20.

104. Carter, "Few Sponsors for TV War News," sec. D1, D20.

105. Carter, "Few Sponsors for TV War News," sec. D1, D20.

106. Carter, "Few Sponsors for TV War News," sec. D1, D20.

107. Carter, "Few Sponsors for TV War News," sec. D1, D20.

108. Carter, "Few Sponsors for TV War News," sec. D1, D20.

109. Seth Schiesel with Felicity Barringer, "News Media Risk Big Losses to Cover War," *New York Times*, 22 October 2001, sec. C1.

110. Schiesel, "News Media Risk," sec. C1.

111. Schiesel, "News Media Risk," sec. C1.

112. "Antismoking Product's Ad Stirs Debate," *New York Times*, 11 November 1988, sec. D17.

113. Lipman, "Media Content," sec. B7.

114. Lipman, "Media Content," sec. B7.

115. *In These Times*, 18–24 March 1992, 5.

116. Nancy Zuckerford, "Study: Ads Have Greater Effects than Anti-Tobacco Efforts," Associated Press, *State College (Pa.) Centre Daily Times*, 12 June 2001, sec. A4.

117. "Live Longer, Better, Wiser," *Parade*, 19 March 2000, 1.

118. Joan Tarshis, "Celebrities Reveal Their Secrets," *Parade*, 19 March 2000, 10.

119. Advertisement, Wyeth-Ayerst Laboratories, *Parade*, 19 March 2000, 10.

120. Sally Squires, "Experts Say Medicine Ads Often Omit Basics" (Washington Post), *State College (Pa.) Centre Daily Times*, 18 December 2000, sec. C1.

121. Breast cancer, for example, is known to be an estrogen-dependent disease. See Tom Monte, *Natural Healing* (New York: The Berkeley Publishing Group, 1997), 60.

122. Connie Lauerman, "Aging Baby Boomers Fight War on Wrinkles" (Knight Ridder Tribune), *State College (Pa.) Centre Daily Times,* 7 September 1998, sec. C3.

123. "SoundBites: Buy One, Get One Free," *Extra! Update,* June 2000, 2.

124. Alex S. Jones, "Knight-Ridder Faces a Newspaper Puzzle," *New York Times,* 18 November 1991, sec. 8D.

125. Jones, "Knight-Ridder Faces," sec. D8.

126. Schudson, *Discovering the News,* 93.

127. *New Webster's Dictionary,* 992.

128. Ann Marsh, "Meet the Class of 1996," *Forbes,* 14 October 1996, 100.

129. Collins, "Horatio Alger, Where Are You?", 9.

130. Eric R. Quinones, "Market Woes Lessen Ranks of Billionaires" (Associated Press), *State College (Pa.) Centre Daily Times,* 28 September 1998, sec. A1.

131. Alex E. Hill, "Letters to the Editor: Who Cares about the Depletion of Billionaires?" and "Editor's Note," *State College (Pa.) Centre Daily Times,* 4 October 1998, sec. A11.

132. R. C. Longworth, "CEO's Average 531 Times the Salary of Workers" (Chicago Tribune), *State College (Pa.) Centre Daily Times,* 28 August 2001, sec. B7.

133. "Measuring Privilege," *Left Business Observer,* July 1997, 3.

134. Barbara Crossette, "Experts Scaling Back Their Estimates of World Population Growth," *New York Times,* 20 August 2002, sec. D8.

# 5

# STUDENTS FOR SALE: THE COMMERCIALIZATION OF EDUCATION

Advertising aimed at children, teens, and young adults reached a new high in sophistication—and sank to a new low in scruples—when corporations began to invade public schools and universities. Although it is well known that the media are in the business of selling audiences to advertisers, most of us like to believe that the classroom is a place for exploration and inspiration rather than exploitation and consumption. We would rather not think of children as commodities whose brand loyalties are being sold off to the highest bidder from the moment they get on the bus. Increasingly, however, this is the case. Elementary education is compulsory in the United States; for kids up to age sixteen, going to school is not just a right but a responsibility. It is the obligation of a democratic society to provide equal educational opportunities for all its citizens. In recent years, however, more and more underfunded school districts have found it difficult to resist corporate sponsorship, so it is in the once-sacred realm of public education that advertisers have found a most lucrative captive audience.

In this chapter, we examine the commercialization and privatization of education in the United States. We start with a look at advertising campaigns aimed at elementary and high school students. These include aggressive marketing of brand-name school supplies; corporate sponsorship and control of school materials and activities; and the subjection of students to advertising in classrooms, hallways, gymnasiums, and cafeterias. Next, we turn to the increasing commercialization of colleges and universities, focusing on exclusive contracts, sponsored research, and endowed centers and chairs. We pay special attention to the corporate world's exploitation of academia's fascination with new information technologies. Finally, we look at some of the conditions that have made it seem necessary for public schools and land-grant universities to seek private funding, and easier for corporations to exploit this perceived need.

## BACK TO SCHOOL WITH THE RIGHT STUFF

One way corporations have wormed their way into the classroom is by suggesting that students will perform better at school (and eventually succeed more in business) if they purchase designer school supplies. A good example of this ploy can be seen in a 1998 Office Depot commercial featuring characters from the popular comic strip *Dilbert*. Dogbert, an evil and cynical business consultant (who is, in a tribute to the military-industrial complex, costumed as General Patton in this ad), informs elementary school children, "Some students will shop at other stores. They will grow up to be your feeble-minded servants." Parents are then assured that Office Depot has the National Parent Teacher Association's official seal of approval, sanctioning the company's conflation of consumerism, power, and greed as "smarts." Children whose families can afford to purchase "the right stuff" (i.e., expensive brand-name products sold at places like Office Depot) are given license to belittle their less privileged classmates as geeky underlings. All because they have loose-leaf binders in shades such as eggplant, ebony, and teal rather than purple, black, and blue.

Actually, it's not all that surprising that a retail chain like Office Depot would attempt to boost sales of high-priced calculators and kiddie date books by threatening students with the prospect of being treated like dimwitted servants by their peers if they don't buy them. Other big chains like Kmart and Wal-Mart routinely do the same. The larger issue here is the extent to which our public schools themselves are being infiltrated and even dominated by corporate interests. As noted in chapter 4, big businesses are eager to create brand loyalty in the 78 million young people born in the United States between 1978 and 1998, 48 million of whom were enrolled in elementary and high schools by 1999.[1] So where better for corporate America to teach children to be good consumers than in the classroom? We thought the pressure on kids to go back to school with the right stuff was bad enough. A generation of "baby boomerangs" is going back to school with the Fortune 500 as well.

## BRANDED FOR LIFE:
## THE COMMERCIALIZATION OF K–12

Although corporate influence in the classroom has increased dramatically recently, it is not a new phenomenon. In *The Media Monopoly*, a classic text now in its fifth edition, Ben Bagdikian argues that corporate materials have long been prominent in our public schools. In the first edition, published in 1983, Bagdikian cited evidence that only 1 percent of already tight public school budgets was being used for instructional materials and that industry had rushed in to fill the gap with largely self-serving publications. Already, free classroom materials were being produced by 64 percent of the 500 largest American corporations, 90 percent of utility companies, and 90 percent of industrial trade associations. Most of these materials concentrated on nutrition, economics, energy, and the environment—and almost all were supplied by industries with a stake in their own solutions to the problems posed.[2]

Bagdikian rightly predicted that the commercialism in the classroom would grow—and, we might add, grow increasingly aggressive and manipulative. For example, in 1998, a public relations consultant advised members of the Independent Petroleum Association of America to develop "a more grass-roots approach to telling industry's story in the nation's public schools" in an effort to "assuage the guilt of Americans concerned about global warming or the dangers of petro-chemicals." The consultant recommended that in addition to supplying schools with free course materials, energy companies should host workshops for teachers "in resorts or campuses in pleasant surroundings."[3]

The 1990s saw a widespread selling-out of U.S. public schools to big business. According to the Center for the Analysis of Commercialism in Education (CACE), "Commercial activities now shape the structure of the school day, influence the content of the school curriculum, and determine whether children have access to a variety of technologies."[4] A CACE study showed significant increases in a number of corporate activities in the classroom between 1990 and 1999, including the following: a 1,875 percent increase in industry sponsorship of educational materials, a 231 percent increase in corporate contests and other incentive programs, a 384 percent increase in exclusive agreements between businesses and schools, and a 539 percent increase in the private appropriation of public school space. The figures themselves are staggering; the actual practices are worth examining.

SPONSORED EDUCATIONAL MATERIALS

Sponsored educational materials are products or services purporting to have instructional content that are supplied directly to schools by corporations or trade associations. Perhaps the most notorious example is Channel One, a twelve-minute news program launched by Primedia Inc. in 1990 and broadcast daily to 8 million students in 12,000 middle and high schools in the

United States by 2000. Primedia installs $25,000 worth of TVs and VCRs in classrooms in each school, and in return the schools agree to require 80 percent of their students to watch Channel One programs on 90 percent of all school days. The catch? Channel One programs are peppered with ads for Fortune 500 companies. Firms such as Reebok and Nintendo pay about $200,000 for each half-minute commercial, and peer pressure to purchase their upscale products is undoubtedly heightened in such a setting. Channel One also tempts impulse snackers with ads for M&Ms, Snickers, Twix, Hostess Cakes, Milky Way, Doritos, Mountain Dew, Nestlé Crunch, and Skittles.[5] CACE figured that Channel One cost taxpayers and their kids $1.8 billion a year in classroom time, including $300 million for the commercials.

Former Channel One President Joel Babbit admitted, "The biggest selling point to advertisers [is that] we are forcing kids to watch two minutes of commercials"—a remark so unabashedly blunt, as one critic noted, that it may explain why Babbit is now the former president.[6] A *Washington Post* reporter who sat in on a Channel One screening observed that only three of the fifteen seventh graders in the class appeared to be paying attention to anything but the ads. Asked what they liked best about the program, the students replied, "The commercials! They're funny."[7]

Textbooks can also be seen as sponsored educational materials, although publishers bristle at the suggestion. One example is a glossy mathematics primer published by McGraw-Hill. The book is graced with what appear to be advertisements for products like Cocoa Frosted Flakes, Gatorade, and M&Ms, as well as Sega and Sony video games. We say "appear" because McGraw-Hill insists that the inclusion of color photos of brand-name products in the textbook cannot be considered advertising since the corporations don't pay for it. A spokesperson for McGraw-Hill claimed that the brand names are used only to give junior high students some examples they can appreciate. In one story problem, budding mathematicians are asked how long a child will need to save his allowance in order to purchase a pair of Nikes.[8]

It is difficult to imagine this textbook asking students to calculate the profit Nike makes on each $120 pair of shoes produced by a southeast Asian girl working in a sweatshop for pennies per hour, or to figure out how long it would take Nike CEO Philip Knight (number thirty-four on the *Forbes 400* list of the richest people in America in 2001[9]) to deplete his $3.9 billion fortune if he spent, say, $100,000 a day on Cocoa Frosted Flakes. Rather than encouraging consumption, such exercises would invite students to contemplate the unequal distribution of wealth in the United States and worldwide.

INCENTIVE PROGRAMS

Incentive programs are arrangements whereby corporations provide awards, goods, or services to students, schools, or school districts in return for their participation in specified activities. Such programs often appear altruistic, but they inevitably benefit the corporations far more than the schools. Students who participate get trinkets splattered with corporate logos, token cash awards, or certificates good toward the purchase of the company's products. Corporations get good publicity, cheap advertising, and easy access to an attractive demographic group. Although these programs often purport to be incentives to learning, many students find that their intellectual curiosity and creativity are limited by corporate dictates.

For example, a 1999 article in the *Centre Daily Times (CDT)* of State College, Pennsylvania, celebrated "the gadgetry of young inventors," putting a hometown spin on a contest administered by the National Science Teachers Association (NSTA). We were delighted to see that two local students were finalists, and especially impressed by a 14-year-old's ingenious "Anti-Squirrel Birdfeeder Defense System." But creative students who envisioned gadgets that didn't run on batteries weren't eligible to enter. Why? Because although the contest was administered by NSTA, it was sponsored by Duracell. All inventions were required to "educate, entertain, make life easier or perform a practical function"—and, crucially, to "be powered by Duracell batteries."[10]

The veneer of the educational value of incentive programs is fading ever thinner. For example, Cape Cod Potato Chips sponsored a contest in which New England middle school students were required to build model ships in honor of the Sail Boston 2000 festival using Cape Cod Potato Chips.[11] Campbell's Soup offered schools a science experiment designed to prove that its Prego spaghetti sauce was thicker than Ragu's.[12] It seems clear that such incentive programs are utilizing public education to cultivate brand loyalty and foster consumption.


EXCLUSIVE AGREEMENTS

Exclusive agreements are contracts drawn up between school districts and businesses whereby the schools agree to sell and advertise one company's products and, of course, not to sell or advertise any competing products. The schools get much-needed cash upon signing, and the corporations get a chance to hook young consumers on their products for life. Some sponsor companies are very protective of what "their" students are exposed to, even prohibiting schools from serving generic fast food. For example, schools that make deals with McDonald's have agreed not to sell ordinary beef patties in their cafeterias, even though students on the federal lunch program cannot use their vouchers to buy Big Macs. Schools that make deals with Pepsi or Coke have been required to remove juice and bottled water machines from their hallways.[13] As one student wrote in a letter to the editors of *Adbusters:* "What ever happened to the good, old-fashioned lunch lady who would slop some mystery meat on your tray and a carton of 2% milk?"[14]

The giant soda manufacturers fought some of the fiercest battles for exclusive contracts with schools in the late 1990s. By 2000, according to CACE, about 175 districts around the nation had arrangements with either Coca-Cola or PepsiCo.[15] The deals varied according to the number of students the schools had to offer and how much brand loyalty they were willing to pledge. Some schools agreed to purchase all cups, carbon dioxide, and related materials from the same vendor. Coke and Pepsi made it hard to resist. One of the biggest payouts went to a Colorado Springs school district: $8.1 million from a Coke bottler for a ten-year deal.

At first, soda manufacturers didn't feel the need to pretend that their products were good for kids. As a spokesman for the National Soft Drink Association put it, "Soft drinks make no nutritious claims."[16] How could they? Studies show that a significant increase in soda consumption among teenagers, along with a decrease in their intake of milk and fruit juices, has left them deprived of calcium and Vitamin C and made them overweight. From 1990 to 1994, the number of clinically obese children ages six to eleven in the United States nearly doubled from 6.5 percent to 11.4 percent. A study published in the medical journal *Lancet* in 2000 found that "an extra soft drink a day gives a child a 60 percent greater chance of becoming obese." The study involved tracking 548 children ages 11–12 from public schools across Massachusetts for two years. The soft drink–obesity link was found to be independent of the food children ate, how much television or videos they watched, and the amount of exercise they got.[17]

Nonetheless, the news media often derided those who objected to sodas being advertised, sold, or given away in public schools. For example, Knight Ridder distributed a story about a congressional bill designed to prohibit the sale of foods of minimal nutritional value during federally funded meals. The story cites a study conducted by the Center for Science in the Public Interest (CPSI), which highlights the negative nutritional effects of soda on young people. The headline reads "Food Police: Teens Consume Too Much Soda," and the sarcastic lead disparages the CPSI: "They warned you about Chinese food, oil-soaked popcorn and cinnamon buns. . . . Now the nation's food police have taken on a new scourge. Soda pop." The report stresses that soda is often "a free treat" for students provided by soft drink companies, and emphasizes that many of the lawmakers supporting the bill "hail from dairy states," suggesting that their motives are purely economic. Concerns raised by the CPSI study are ultimately dismissed as "unfounded consumer alarm."[18]

Mainstream coverage of the cola controversy reflects the probusiness bias of the media, even when the health and welfare of young people are at stake. Nonetheless, protests by physicians, dieticians, parents, teachers, and other activists continued. Finally, in the summer of 2001, Coca-Cola announced that it would end its exclusive beverage contracts with schools, include juice and milk in its vending machines, and "tone down" its advertising aimed at kids. Pepsi promised to follow suit. The announcements came one month after the U.S. Department of Agriculture announced that all food sold in schools should meet nutrition standards. The strategy of the cola companies, as a number of critics noted, was to "give the teacher an apple" so they wouldn't be expelled for good.[19]

PRIVATE APPROPRIATION OF PUBLIC SPACE

Private appropriation of public space refers to any allocation of public school facilities for corporations to display logos, advertisements, or products. Also included under this heading is the use of classroom time or school facilities for commercial activities, such as recruiting students for product testing or market research. In exchange for granting such privileges, the schools are rewarded with cash or supplies and the students are often given free samples. The corporations get rapt audiences and invaluable marketing profiles to inform future ad campaigns. Corporate logos and ads are plastered on scoreboards, basketball backboards, bulletin boards, display cases, and buses. They are commonly placed on school calendars, book covers, assignment books, and sports schedules. They are ubiquitous on computer screens.

Some product displays are school-related, as in the case of school pictures, yearbooks, or class rings, but even these promotions are based on exclusive contracts and designed to create peer pressure to consume. Other examples of commercial use of class time and school facilities are decidedly less justifiable. Hershey, the number one chocolate manufacturer in the United States, gave schools cash for every Peppermint Pattie or Almond Joy wrapper kids brought in. General Mills rewarded young students who collected cereal box tops from Lucky Charms and Frosted Cheerios with a classroom visit from the Trix Bunny. McDonald's gave students cookies, juice, and coupons in exchange for watching a recruitment video and filling out job applications. Clairol gave high school girls shampoo samples for completing a survey with questions like "Was this a good hair day or a bad hair day?"

As a representative for the Citizens Campaign for Commercial-Free Schools put it, "If there is a national problem with funding our schools, then selling off the school environment to corporate interests surely isn't the answer to it."[20] Yet freedom from corporate sponsorship is fast becoming the exception rather than the rule in elementary and secondary education, although some students, parents, teachers, and administrators have resisted it. School boards in State College, Hershey, and Pittsburgh, Pennsylvania, for example, were reported to "weigh," "ponder," "question," and "raise concerns" over exclusive drink contracts.[21] (There were no follow-up reports on whether or not they eventually caved.) The school district of Madison, Wisconsin, which signed a three-year contract with Coke in 1997, declined to renew it in 2000.[22] In 1998, Berkeley High School turned down lucrative offers from both Pepsi and Nike in response to student protests. In 1999, the San Francisco School Board approved the Commercial Free Schools Act, which prohibits the district from signing exclusive beverage contracts or adopting educational materials that contain brand names.[23]

Increasingly, however, public and private school teachers and administrators are defending corporate sponsorships with explanations that sound, well, defensive. For example, when students at Our Lady of Assumption Elementary School in Lynnfield, Massachusetts, spent two days testing cereals and answering opinion polls, their principal, Martha Marie Pooler, compared the exercise to a science experiment: "It's a learning experience," she said. "They had to read, they had to look, they had to compare." The school got $600 for its part in the market research project.[24] As Lisa Seed, an English teacher at Harrison High School in Colorado Springs, Colorado, said of the ZapMe company, which offered schools thousands of dollars' worth of computers, all of which displayed a constant stream of onscreen ads: "They are absolutely using the kids—and I don't like it when my kids are used. On the other hand, I'm happy to be sitting in a room with fifteen computers."[25]

## ACADEMIA, INC.:
## THE CORPORATIZATION OF THE UNIVERSITY

The notion that institutions of higher learning might be impervious to the encroachment of the corporate sphere is, perhaps, naïve. Yet the culture of academia has been likened "more to the ideals of communism than to capitalism," with the supposedly free exchange of artistic and intellectual discoveries.[26] In many ways, as Naomi Klein argues, schools and universities remain our culture's most tangible embodiment of public space and collective responsibility. "University campuses in particular—with their residences, libraries, green spaces and common standards for open and respectful discourse—play a crucial, if now largely symbolic, role: they are the one place left where young people can see a genuine public life being lived."[27] Klein's observations are particularly poignant in light of the tendency—both inside and outside of the academy—to refer to the private, corporate sphere as "the real world." Increasingly, often in the name of preparing students for that world, institutions of higher learning are emulating big business.

Major universities and even smaller, alternative colleges are selling campus facilities and curriculum decisions off to the highest bidder. According to Stanley Aronowitz, "As long as they get the cash, desperate administrators are eager to have their university reflect the whims of individuals and the interests of corporations. They will train corporate America's workers and conduct its research. Small private colleges like Hampshire hire a veritable army of consultants, marketing staff, and fundraisers to attract students, beef up their endowments and organize partnerships with industry."[28] Indeed, corporate spending on academia has risen dramatically in recent years, surging from $850 million in 1985 to $4.25 billion less than a decade later.[29]

As in grades K-12, university partnerships with corporations often involve sponsored materials, incentive programs, exclusive agreements, and the private leasing of public space. Moreover, the stakes are higher and the profits bigger at the college level. In the realm of higher education, sponsored educational materials are likely to be state-of-the-art labs or auditoriums named after corporate donors rather than merely TVs or VCRs. Incentive programs give professors and graduate students large research grants to test experimental drugs. Exclusive agreements bring in millions of dollars in cash and merchandise for universities—and billions of dollars in brand recognition and sales for corporations. Finally, the corporate appropriation of campus space for advertising and sales has transformed student unions into shopping malls.

SPONSORED EDUCATIONAL MATERIALS

Corporations routinely supply universities with educational materials such as film, video, or laboratory equipment; computers and Internet access; and classrooms, labs, or even entire buildings. One marked trend in this area is an increase in industry-endowed chairs, many of which come with strings attached. For example, Kmart has endowed a chair in the management school at West Virginia University that requires its holder to spend up to thirty days a year training assistant store managers. Other endowed chairs are rather obvious attempts at damage control: Freeport-McMoRan, a mining company embroiled in allegations of environmental misconduct in Indonesia, has created a chair in environmental studies at Tulane University. Among the more promotional academic titles are the Yahoo! Chair of Information Systems Technology at Stanford University, the Lego Professorship of Learning Research at the Massachusetts Institute of Technology, and the Taco Bell Distinguished Professor of Hotel and Restaurant Administration at Washington State University.[30]

Why settle for a chair when you can have a whole center? Many universities have sought to attract corporate sponsors by creating research centers bearing their names or serving their interests. The Pennsylvania State University provides a good example. The university established the AT&T Center for Service Leadership in 1994 and the MBNA Career Services Center in 1999. In 2000, General Electric awarded the university $475,000 to bring the schools of engineering and business together in the Center for Product Realization. However euphemistic its name, the purpose of this center is avowedly to "foster entrepreneurship."[31]

In 2000 also, six communications companies—IBM, Xerox, AT&T Wireless, Delphi Ventures, SAP, and Unisys Corp.—pledged $1.85 million to create the Penn State eBusiness Research Center, with faculty and graduate students providing a corporate "think tank." According to a representative for Xerox, "The advantage here at Penn State is knowledge to identify and test new areas that we can consider taking advantage of." Her thoughts were echoed by a representative for Unisys: "If we can get input on where the world is moving, we'll have a greater chance one of our initiatives will be a winner."[32]

In each case, the advantages to big business are obvious and those to academia only apparently so. Corporate sponsorship of educational materials and facilities allows industry to influence the kinds of research projects that are conducted and the kinds of findings that will be rewarded. The mission of the university to advance knowledge is superceded by that of Big Business to increase profits while promoting corporate images.

CORPORATE INCENTIVE PROGRAMS

Corporate incentive programs, which are often administered through endowed centers like those described above, have spawned what Eyal Press and Jennifer Washburn have called "The Kept University."[33] To wit, Penn State's Center for Product Realization is charged with developing "a new four-course sequence for engineering students on the principles and practices of entrepreneurship."[34] Faculty and students who study engineering for more altruistic reasons need not apply. As Aronowitz puts it, "Those who choose to remain aloof from the new regime risk extermination or marginality."[35]

The six companies that pledged nearly $2 million to Penn State's eBusiness Research Center were unabashed about the profit-making impetus for their donation. The *CDT* quotes the vice president of worldwide e-business marketing & strategy for Unisys Corp. as saying, "We're going to the university as a corporation and saying we want to tap its ideas early on." Later in the article, it is revealed that Unisys does product development in-house and is looking to the Penn State center (merely) to test its own e-business ideas. Unisys promises to "submit a number of research proposals to the center." It seems unlikely that these proposals will be scrutinized, criticized, revised, or rejected by faculty and graduate students newly beholden to Unisys and partners, especially since the center is headed by a new faculty member who just happens to be a former IBM executive.[36]

In a deal heralded by the *CDT* as "a unique partnership between business and academia," the Shaner Hotel Group and the University of Delaware announced plans to collaborate in the development and management of an upscale "branded" hotel catering to business and leisure travelers. According to Plato Ginos, the Shaner Group's vice president of development, a member of the university faculty will manage the hotel, and students in the department of hotel, restaurant, and institutional management will "be able to utilize the facility as an active learning environment"[37] (i.e., they'll work there). This partnership is not nearly so unique as the *CDT* would have it. A number of universities have made similar arrangements with the Walt Disney World College Program, billed as "an intensive yet fun internship program that provides students with a chance to live and learn, while becoming a member of the Disney crew." Job categories include park greeting, food service, and custodial work, and the pay is $6.00 per hour. What used to be called a summer job is now an internship, and students can earn up to 18 college credits for participating.[38] The internships include "classes" promoting the Disney business philosophy.

In 1998, the University of California at Berkeley entered into a partnership that makes these deals seem benign by comparison. The corporate sponsor is Novartis, a Swiss pharmaceutical giant and producer of genetically engineered crops. Under the terms of the agreement, Novartis promised to give Berkeley $25 million to fund basic research in the Department of Plant and Microbial Biology, one of four departments within the College of Natural

Resources. In exchange for the cash, Berkeley granted Novartis first rights to negotiate licenses on roughly a third of the department's discoveries—including not only the results of research funded by Novartis but also by state and federal sources. It also granted the company unprecedented representation (two of five seats) on the department's research committee, which determines how the money is spent, and allowed the company to postpone the publication of the university's research findings for up to four months.[39]

The National Institutes of Health recommend that universities allow corporate sponsors to prohibit publication for no more than one or two months, the amount of time ordinarily necessary to apply for a patent. Yet, studies show that a majority of life-science companies require delays of more than six months. Such delays allow not only for exclusive rights, but also for damage control. Not that it is often necessary: A 1996 study published in the *Annals of Internal Medicine* found that 98 percent of papers based on industry-sponsored research reflected favorably on the drugs being examined.[40] Occasionally, however, researchers tell corporate sponsors things they don't want consumers to hear.

For example, four researchers working on a study of calcium channel blockers (used to treat high blood pressure) quit the project in protest when their sponsor, Sandoz, deleted passages from a draft of their report that highlighted the potential dangers of the drugs (including stroke and heart failure). More than a year before the appetite suppressant Fen-Phen was pulled off the shelves, a group of researchers published a study in the *New England Journal of Medicine* warning that drugs like it could have potentially fatal side effects. The same issue contained a commentary written by two academic researchers downplaying the dangers of the drugs. It turned out that the "balance" here was provided by two authors who had served as paid consultants to the manufacturers and distributors of similar drugs—connections that were not mentioned.[41]

As Mildred Cho, a senior research scholar at Stanford's Center for Biomedical Ethics, contends: "When you have so many scientists on boards of companies or doing sponsored research, you start to wonder, How are these studies being designed? What kinds of research questions are being raised? What kinds aren't being raised?"[42] One thing is clear: The answers have more to do with corporate profits than public health or welfare.

EXCLUSIVE AGREEMENTS

Like elementary and high school cafeterias, university campuses have become battlegrounds as the major soft drink companies compete for exclusive access to college students. According to a Coca-Cola spokesperson, campus deals are important because "they help 'brand' students at a point in their lives when they have a lot of years of consuming left to do."[43] Coke and Pepsi pay millions of dollars for sole rights to soda advertising and sales on all university properties—including classrooms, libraries, dorms, cafeterias, offices, sports arenas, performance centers, restaurants, and even golf courses. They also demand benefits such as secrecy clauses and antidisparagement rules that put a lid on cola critics.

Pepsi won out at Penn State and the university has taken its vow of fidelity to this brand of bubbly sugar water quite seriously. In the summer of 2001, a local distributor offered to continue its tradition of donating money and bottled spring water to the Second Mile Golf Classic, a charity event held annually at Penn State. The cash was accepted but the water was not. It seems that a strict interpretation of the university's exclusive agreement with Pepsi prohibited even the donation of "not-for-sale" beverages to private charities using Penn State properties.[44]

Following their leaders in business, many universities have forced manufacturers and retailers big and small to enter into exclusive arrangements with the academy. They use their own registered trademarks, patents, and copyrights to generate revenues. The most obvious example of this is the licensing of athletic logos and mascots, although with so many teams named after common animals, the granting of exclusive rights to such emblems can become absurd in practice. For example, few Penn State fans probably know that the five-toed Nittany Lion paw print—which manufacturers pay the university lavishly to emblazon on everything from t-shirts to refrigerator magnets to shot glasses— is "anatomically incorrect." South Carolina's Clemson University owns the only trademark for a proper four-toed paw print, so no other school in the nation is allowed to use it. Penn State's coordinator for licensing programs instructs all licensees to use either a three- or five-toed design.[45]

University of Tennessee fans can at least get the color of their house paint right. The school has lent its name to a particular shade of orange paint being sold at Home Depot stores in Knoxville. A gallon of Tennessee Orange semigloss sold for $25, about twice the cost of regular orange. A shopper at Nebraska's Husker Authentic minimalls could pick up an Adidas sports bra for $26 and a red Cornhuskers football jersey for $200.[46] The really big money, however, is not in schools selling their logos to businesses; profits from such licensing arrangements are generally limited to the purchases of students, alumni, and loyal locals. More and more universities are cashing in by selling their playing fields and student athletes themselves to be used as advertising billboards for corporate sponsors.

Nationally, more than a dozen schools have sold naming rights to new athletic facilities for fees ranging from $300,000 at Wichita State University to $25 million at the University of Maryland. The University of Nebraska touts its scoreboard in the north end zone of Memorial Stadium as an ideal vehicle for corporate messages (a five-year package includes one fifteen-second electronic message per quarter at a rate of $40,000 per year). The University of Texas has signed deals with American Airlines, Budweiser, and Southwestern Bell. Its annual football game against the University of Oklahoma has been sponsored by Miller Beer, Mercedes Benz, Bank of America, and Dr. Pepper.[47]

In return for millions of dollars in cash and merchandise from Nike, Reebok, or Adidas, college teams have put their names, logos, and storied traditions on the block. Under the terms of its five-year contract with Nike, for example, the University of Florida received more than $1.2 million a year in cash, $400,000 worth of Nike products, and an additional $150,000 in cash and products. Nike, for its part, gained prized marketing opportunities and access to Florida's coaches and facilities. (Coaches were required "to exercise best efforts to wear Nike products while appearing on any television broadcast, show, or special relating to their activities.") A deal between the University of Texas and Nike provided the school with $850,000 in cash annually and more than $1 million in jackets, jerseys, shoes, and other gear.[48] Even Penn State's austere uniforms—with no player, team, or university name—sport the Nike swoosh.

Nike executive Chris Bevilacqua explained the company's strategy like this: "College sports was essential to Nike. It really hits in the sweet spot of the Nike consumer. It gets them at a time in their lives when they are starting to get their disposable income and they start spending money on these kinds of products." Nike is careful not to include the word "advertising" in its contracts, so schools don't have to pay taxes on the revenue. Nonetheless, the company's intent is clear, as this clause from University of Florida's contract illustrates: "UNIVERSITY acknowledges that one of the principal inducements for NIKE's entrance into this agreement is: the accompanying brand exposure . . . and that such continued exposure is of the essence of this agreement." The contract goes on to say that Nike may slash its payment if the size, color, or location of its logo on team uniforms is changed in any way. If an athlete tapes over the Nike logo on his shoes, it could result in a 10 percent cut of the total base compensation (about $120,000) for the first offense and a 15 percent reduction ($180,000) for the second.[49]

With the ramifications of such exclusive agreements under increasing scrutiny, the National Collegiate Athletic Association (NCAA) commissioned an investigation into the commercialization of college sports.[50] The Knight Commission's report, released in 2001, advocated sweeping changes in the structure of college athletics. If the proposed changes were to be adopted, corporate logos would be eliminated from team uniforms, games would be scheduled independently of the wishes of television networks, and programs that fail to graduate at least 50 percent of their student-athletes would be ineligible for postseason competition.[51]

"I think departments will resist [limiting commercialization] because there's big money involved," said former Penn State President Bryce Jordan, a member of the Knight Commission. "But the position of the Commission was simply, we don't think student-athletes ought to be an advertising medium." If Penn State's response to the report is any indication, then Jordan was right to expect resistance. Asked by the *CDT* to comment, head football coach Joe Paterno could not be reached, men's basketball coach Jerry Dunn declined to comment, and women's basketball coach Rene Portland fretted that she would have to spend "a big chunk of change" on shoes and uniforms without support from Nike. In a masterful dodge, Penn State President Graham Spanier remarked, "I think the report is very principled, and I support the principles and the spirit, and the motivation for it is worthy. The actual specifics and the implementations, I think you could have a pretty good discussion about." Spanier reminded readers that he has "religiously defended the NCAA's right to limit the size of the logos." As Jordan predicted, "You're not going to see an explosive change."[52]

PRIVATE APPROPRIATION OF PUBLIC SPACE

Perhaps the most visible evidence of the corporatization of the university is the increasing allocation of university space for businesses to display advertisements, logos, and products. Sometimes products are sold or given away, often with strings attached. Sponsored student activities, whether fun or philanthropic, become grand-scale advertising productions and quickly find their way online. Posters appear in dormitories, cafeterias, auditoriums, stadiums, and even lavatories.

When students at Ontario's Trent University went back to school in the fall of 2000, they found their previously ad-free environment covered with Zoom Media posters. Over the summer break, Trent had granted Zoom exclusive advertising rights on campus in exchange for $18,000. The ads were concentrated in hallways, dining areas, and, predominantly, washrooms. According to a company representative, students would enjoy the idea of ads in washrooms, especially since Zoom ads were "funky, trendy and fun."[53] As it turned out, Trent students were not amused. An imaginative group of culture jammers struck back, retouching and covering Zoom ads. They even pasted thirty-five of them on Trent President Bonnie Patterson's large office windows. The university's security force was ordered to patrol restrooms, and for two consecutive weeks the local Crime Stoppers unit featured Zoom vandalism at Trent as the county's "crime of the week."[54]

In another invasive action, Tommy Hilfiger made an appearance at one of Penn State's most hallowed traditions, the Intrafraternity Council–Panhellenic Dance Marathon. The annual THON, now in its thirtieth year, raises money for children with cancer through the Four Diamonds Fund. Just before the spring 2000 event, Hilfiger representatives conducted a "student casting call" at a local mall. The company's "stylist extraordinaire" and a group of professional dancers worked with the chosen ones to produce a fashion show designed to lift the spirits of the participants, and, of course, to sell designer jeans. The *CDT* reported that Tommy Hilfiger himself would deliver a video address to dancers and spectators, and "offer the THON experience to supporters outside University Park via his Web site, Tommy.com."[55] The THON does rely on corporate sponsors for donations, but few ask for more than an acknowledgment in the program or a banner on the wall in return. Hilfiger used the charity event as background for an online advertisement. The students raised more than $3.5 million for cancer that year, a fraction of what Hilfiger spends on guerrilla ad campaigns notorious for packaging popular youth culture, branding it as a lifestyle, and licensing the name to manufacturers of upscale lifestyle goods.

Students are able to buy such products because they have credit cards. Another striking example of the corporate appropriation of university space is the proliferation of booths, tables, and tents from which vendors hawk credit cards. Most offer free gifts such as t-shirts, phone cards, and water bottles to students who sign up. First USA offered credit cards to University of Tennessee students at the 2000 opening football game, part of a $14 million deal between the bank and the school. According to Robert Manning, a sociologist at the Rochester Institute of Technology, credit card issuers are hungry to hook college students, who often stay with their first card long after graduation. Two recent studies—a joint survey by the Education Resources Institution and Institute for Higher Education Policy, and a survey by the firm Student Monitor—found that nearly two-thirds of all college students have at least one credit card. Between 6 and 13 percent have four or more. Almost half of those students got their first credit card during their freshman year. According to a study conducted by Nellie Mae, the student loan provider, the average undergraduate student credit card debt in 2000 was $2,478. Thirteen percent of the students surveyed had balances between $3,000 and $7,000, and 9 percent had even higher ones. The figures for graduate students are even more alarming, with the average debt near $5,000. Twenty percent of graduate students owed between $6,000 and $15,000.[56] Some students use credit cards to make tuition payments, although the maximum interest rate for most federal government–backed student loans is 8.25 percent, less than half that for most credit cards.[57] In Manning's view, "The unrestricted marketing of credit cards on college campuses is so aggressive that it now poses a greater threat than alcohol or sexually transmitted diseases."[58]

MBNA, the largest independent credit card lender in the world with $62 billion in managed loans, committed $10 million to Penn State to extend and expand its role as exclusive provider of the university's official credit card. Forty percent of the gift was earmarked for an MBNA Career Services Center. The arrangement serves a dual purpose for the bank. First, students become indebted to MBNA, then the career center helps them find jobs so they can make their credit card payments. Students are largely unaware of the high interest rates that come with consumer credit. In a survey conducted by the Public Interest Research Group, students were asked how long it would take to pay off a $1,000 debt at 18 percent interest by making the minimum 3 percent monthly payments. Only 20 percent guessed the correct answer: six years.[59]

Although students may not be fully cognizant of the inflated amount of money they will eventually owe, they are nonetheless aware of their looming credit card and student loan debts. Along with pressure from parents and peers, these debts increase pressure on students to pursue majors that promise to prepare them for high-paying jobs, regardless of their genuine interests and aspirations. The gravitation of students to corporate vocational prep programs diminishes the vitality of liberal arts and humanities programs. The loss for individual students here is also a loss for the university community and society as a whole.

## NO MORE PENCILS, NO MORE BOOKS: HI-TECH/VO-TECH

Manufacturers of new information technologies have been particularly successful at infiltrating public schools and universities. "There's a fervor among educators to embrace the Internet," according to Jeffrey Chester, executive director of the Center for Media Education. "Companies know this, and they've tried to seize control of the technology."[60] The corporate world has skillfully exploited not only the nation's fascination with new technology but also its fear of being without it. A popular metaphor at Penn State likens modern technology to a train. Faculty members are expected to get on the train whether or not it's going their way. This can mean anything from substituting chat rooms for class discussions to offering entire courses online. Those who don't get on the train will be left at the station, and if they try to stand in its way, they'll get run over.

Advertisers have responded to objections to corporate-sponsored technology in the classroom with grim metaphors of their own. In *Adbashing: Surviving the Attacks on Advertising,* for example, marketing executive Jack Myers compares schools without state-of-the-art technology to juvenile detention centers: "The choice we have in this country is for our educational system to join the electronic age and communicate to students in ways they can understand and to which they can relate. Or our schools can continue to use outmoded forms of communications and become the daytime prisons for millions of young people, as they have become in our inner cities."[61]

BUT CAN HE TYPE?

Such reasoning, as Klein points out, baldly equates corporate access to schools with access to modern technology—and, by extension, to the future itself. New information technologies lent a new urgency to problems caused by the chronic underfunding of public education. Just as schools were facing ever-deeper budget cuts, the costs of delivering a modern education were rising steeply, forcing educators to look to alternative sources for help. Swept up by info-tech hype, schools that could barely afford new textbooks were suddenly expected to provide students with audiovisual equipment, classroom computers, and Internet access. In this context, corporate partnerships and sponsorships came to seem not just attractive but essential, especially in poorer school districts.[62]

This is despite the fact that, as many education experts have pointed out, the pedagogical benefits of technology are dubious at best. Indeed, there is mounting evidence that study habits have suffered since pupils began preferring "the chaos of the web to the drudgery of the library."[63] In the fall of 2000, an organization called the Alliance for Childhood issued a statement calling for a moratorium on the further introduction of computers into elementary schools until their effects on young children have been assessed more carefully. The statement was signed by more than 85 experts in fields as varied as psychiatry, education, philosophy, neurology, and nutrition. One of the signers, educational psychologist Jane M. Healy, said she was appalled at the flood of money being allocated to computers in schools at the expense of other programs. "For the sake of technology, schools have cut reading and math specialists, arts, music, phys. Ed., all the things we have clear evidence that prepare kids for the real world."[64] Even some classroom technology advocates have qualified their claims. John Bosco, a professor at Western Michigan University and chairman of the Consortium for School Networking (a nonprofit group that promotes technology in schools), admitted: "We're beginning to see that it is not magic, and that there are things done in the name of information technology which are either foolish or wasteful."[65]

Teachers and administrators have nonetheless been pressured into believing that they need wireless bells and whistles, and the technology giants have been only too willing to oblige. For example, the *CDT* reported, "Students in the Governor's School for Information Technology at Penn State this summer [2000] are experimenting with the newest hand-held computers, thanks to donations by two corporations." Palm, Inc. and 3Com donated 100 handheld computers for a group of high-achieving high school juniors to play with during the month-long program, probably just long enough for most of them to want one of their own—at $450 a shot— when the school reclaimed them to lend to the next batch of students.[66] The following year, Palm awarded eighty similar grants nationwide, awards that included a week for teachers at the company's technology training center in San Francisco.[67]

Such corporate donations, endowments, and awards are almost always uncritically reported by local news media. "Penn Staters Tinker with Computers" and "State High Teacher Awarded Palm Grant" are two typical story headlines. The unqualified celebration of corporate gifts of technology to schools often leads to sins of omission in the press. For example, a *CDT* article entitled "Raytheon Grant Helps Endow State High Award" reported that the Raytheon Company's Matching Gifts for Education program awarded $10,000 to the State College Area School District to endow the Superintendent's Award for Educational Innovation. The recipient of the first grant was Bill Hughes, who teaches a technology education class in which sixth graders design, build, and engineer air-power rockets. "The grant was for a timer so we could accurately time the speeds of these [rockets] and take the information and add math lessons to calculate velocity and acceleration," explained Hughes.[68] No mention is made of the fact that Raytheon is a major U.S. defense contractor, or that the goals of the class project parallel those of the National Missile Defense System.

## NEW INFORMATION TECHNOLOGIES AND
## THE NEW GLOBAL ECONOMY

The symbiotic relationship between the government and big business in creating and serving the technological needs of education is exemplified by the ninety-second annual meeting of the National Governors Association, held in State College in the summer of 2000. The official theme of the conference was "Strengthening the American States in a New Global Economy," and the focus was on new information technologies. Pennsylvania was touted as one of the top eight "cyberstates" in the nation, an honor bestowed by the American Electronics Association. Penn State used the opportunity to introduce its new $41 million School of Information Sciences and Technology.

Town and gown rolled out the red carpet for the governors and their entourages with a gala reception showcasing interactive displays of Pennsylvania's technology initiatives, including the distinction of being the first state to put its World Wide Web address on its license plates. The life of the party was a robotic poodle named Aibo ("pal" in Japanese). The *CDT* noted that the $3,000 pet "has its own personality and can be trained like a real dog" thanks to "advanced chip technology." The story was accompanied by a photo of a young female representative of the Sony Corporation presenting the "mechanical mutt" to a beaming then-Governor Tom Ridge.[69]

The focus of the NGA conference on the "New Global Economy," along with the host committee's emphasis on new technologies, points up two poignant ironies. First, the new information technologies that serve as the nerve system of the new global economy have been primarily developed and deployed to serve the needs of big business. Global telecommunications systems have allowed multinational corporations to extend their access to cheaper raw materials and labor while maintaining centralized control over production and distribution. These same technologies distribute entertainment programming and advertising designed to promote the consumption of mass-produced, brand-name goods—in short, the same old stuff.

Second, although the vendors of new information technologies often purport to be "freeing" us, we are, in fact, increasingly enslaved by their machines. As *Boston Globe* columnist Ellen Goodman writes: "The ability to work anywhere means that you work everywhere. The cell phone that allows you to connect makes it impossible to disconnect. The equipment that makes it possible to do the job at home turns home life into moonlighting."[70] An ad in a United Airlines on-flight magazine even suggests that a good time to listen to your e-mail might be while sitting on the toilet. It is no surprise that manufacturers of new information technologies have fueled the fear that not being hooked up or plugged in means missing out. Their advertising campaigns seek to cultivate this fear and to establish brand loyalty to the products that assuage it.

In his speech at the NGA meeting, Federal Reserve Chairman Alan Greenspan challenged the nation's governors to "develop an American work force with lifelong conceptual skills as well as technical expertise and to devise public-private partnerships to meaningfully integrate technology into schools."[71] According to the *CDT,* Greenspan's message was simple: Those who commit to training workers, supporting innovation, and having a flexible labor market will be prime locations for firms at the cutting edge of technology. In other words, the successful twenty-first-century university will attend to the business of producing information technologists at the behest of global capitalists, with little or no concern for the nature of the information they are processing.

TECHNOLOGY, TEACHING, AND TAXES

Both the government and big business have worked to foster the high-tech aspirations of school administrators, teachers, students, and parents—and both have fueled their fears of being left at the virtual station or locked behind bars in the unwired classroom. In the 1990s, a growing number of politicians made "a computer on every desk" a rallying cry. Toward the end of his presidency, Bill Clinton trumpeted his goal of "connecting every classroom in America to the Internet by the year 2000."[72] However, technology in the classroom is meaningless if schools don't have the human resources to utilize it effectively. First and foremost, this means the ability to hire teachers who are trained not only to operate new information technologies but also to think with them. The difference is crucial. Most often students in poorer school districts are taught data processing, while their peers in richer school districts are taught data programming.

Education funding shortages have long been a problem in the United States due to the unequal distribution of tax money for school systems and the contradictory way the public thinks about taxes. The largest portion of public school revenues is generated from local property and income taxes. This naturally creates large gaps between rich and poor school districts that are based on where the students live. Although everyone wants their children to have access to new technologies and the skills to work creatively with them, those living in poor neighborhoods cannot afford it and those living in richer neighborhoods don't want to pay for it. Both groups tend to view taxes as an infringement upon their right to consume rather than as a way of sharing resources to provide services and build communities.

The broader issue here is whether the tax system is fair and just in its collection and redistribution of tax revenues. This requires informed citizens who can see beyond the bottom line on their checkbooks and credit card statements each month. How we allocate our tax dollars has long-term ramifications. In the late 1970s, few Californians probably realized that they were setting into motion the decline of the best state university system in the country when they voted to cap annual increases in property taxes with the passage of Proposition 13. Voters in Colorado Springs stopped approving tax increases for education in the mid-1970s. By 1989, the school district was $12 million in debt, and, in 1993, it became the first in the nation to "sell for cash something we always had, but never knew we had," as Superintendent Kenneth Burnley put it: access to students.[73] Voters in the state of Washington failed to pass a tax increase for Seattle's schools in 1999—just months after the approval of $336 million for a new baseball stadium for the Mariners. Seattle education funding advocates argued that "continued public spending on stadiums—combined with populist-styled initiatives to roll back car registration fees and other state taxes—could have a ripple effect on education."[74] In Pennsylvania in 2002, both the Republican and Democrat gubernatorial candidates advocated the installation of slot machines at the state's racetracks to fund education.

In a democracy, the education of all children is the responsibility of all citizens, but tax dollars earmarked for education need not be spent on new information technologies. Indeed, they might better be used to revive devastated music and art programs. In a 1995 essay, Neil Postman marveled at our blind worship of technology. He likened it to a religion in that we believe in it, rely on it, feel bereft when denied access to it, and alter our lifestyles, schedules, habits, and relationships to accommodate it—even though, for most people, it works in mysterious ways. "It is strange," Postman wrote, "indeed shocking—that with the twenty-first century so close, we can still talk of new technologies as if they were unmixed blessings—gifts, as it were, from the gods."[75]

Steven Manning has likened sponsored technology to a "digital Trojan horse," a beguiling gift that brings with it a corporate invasion.[76] Educators and administrators in beleaguered public schools, as well as those in wealthier districts, accept such gifts from information technology firms all too readily. In exchange, school officials offer up captive students to corporations seeking to develop lifelong loyalties to expensive and instantly outmoded products in a new group of consumers. At the same time, they give corporations the right to determine what kinds of intellectual and creative endeavors are encouraged and rewarded in the classroom.

## CONCLUSION

At the turn of the twentieth century, institutional economist Thorstein Veblen argued that far from engaging in disinterested higher learning, American universities were constituted to serve corporations and other vested interests. The claim seemed heretical at the time. At the turn of the twenty-first century, what was once a hidden curriculum, the subordination of higher education to the needs of capital, has become an open, frank policy of public and private education. Today, as Aronowitz writes, "Leaders of higher education wear the badge of corporate servants proudly."[77]

In 1952, historian Richard Hofstadter wrote: "It has been the fate of American higher education to develop in a pre-eminently businesslike culture. . . . Education is justified apologetically as a useful instrument in attaining *other* ends: it is good for business or professional careers. Rarely, however, does anyone presume to say that it is good for man."[78] Half a century later, Hofstadter's observations seem truer than ever. Successful business dealings have become not only the means with which education is provided, but the end as well. The idea that the ultimate goal of education is to train students to serve and succeed in business has been taken to its logical extreme in the form of elementary charter business schools designed to turn out junior MBAs. In these recently proposed schools, according to the *Utne Reader*, kids would wear office attire and sport business-style haircuts. Reading material would consist of resumes, memos, and business reports. Students would be encouraged to carry briefcases rather than backpacks.

These critics focus on the crucial role education plays in reproducing the labor force by giving students the skills necessary to become good workers. Now, with the commercialization of schools and the commodification of students as audiences, the educational system itself is being transformed into a profit-making industry. This makes it necessary for school administrators to choose between the fundamental principles of education and the logic of business. Some have already made that choice. As University of Florida President John V. Lombardi declared, "We have taken the great leap forward. . . . 'Let's pretend we're a corporation.'"[79] Rather than a makeover, Wall Street would prefer a takeover. Writing for the *New York Times*, Arthur Levine, president of Teachers College at Columbia University, recounts the following warning, issued to him by a corporate entrepreneur: "You know, you're in an industry which is worth hundreds of billions of dollars, and you have a reputation for low productivity, high cost, bad management and no use of technology. You're going to be the next health care: a poorly managed nonprofit industry which was overtaken by the profit-making sector."[80] One could argue that education need only be seen as a failed industry if educators insist on seeing it as an industry in the first place. Perhaps the point is that under capitalism, it can be nothing else. The barbarians have already crashed the gates of the ivory tower.

## NOTES

1. Cynthia Peters, "Marketing to Teens," *Z Magazine,* April 1999, 23.

2. Ben Bagdikian, *The Media Monopoly,* 5th ed. (Boston: Beacon Press, 1997), 51.

3. Wayne Grytting, "Teach the Kids," *Z Magazine* (citing a *Clear View* story), May 1999, 6.

4. Alex Molnar and Jennifer Morales, "Commercialism@Schools," *Educational Leadership,* October 2000, 43.

5. "Marketing of Junk Food to School Children," *Commercial Alert,* <www.essential.org/alert/junkfood/> (accessed 8 November 2001).

6. Ken Schroeder, "One-derful Channel One," *The Education Digest* 66, no. 1 (September 2000): 72.

7. Mark Francis Cohen, "Must-See TV," *Washington Post,* 9 April 2000, sec. 20W.

8. Wayne Grytting, "The New Math," *Z Magazine* (citing an Associated Press story), 27 March 1999, 5.

9. "The 400 Richest People in America," *Forbes,* 8 October 2001, 34.

10. Caroline Terenzini, "Productive Tinkering," *State College (Pa.) Centre Daily Times,* 18 May 1999, sec. C1.

11. Molnar and Morales, "Commercialism@Schools," 40.

12. Andrew Stark, "Taste: Let's Make a Deal—Commerce," *Wall Street Journal,* 31 March 2000, sec. W17.

13. Ryan Doherty, "State College Schools Weigh Soft-Drink Deal," *State College (Pa.) Centre Daily Times,* 5 May 2001, sec. A5.

14. Mark Little, letter to the editor, *Adbusters,* no. 34, March/April 2001, 6.

15. Constance L. Hayes, "District Rethinks a Soda-Pop Strategy," *New York Times,* 19 April 2000, sec. A19.

16. Usha Lee McFarling, "Food Police: Teens Consume Too Much Soda" (Knight Ridder), *State College (Pa.) Centre Daily Times,* 22 October 1998, sec. A6.

17. Gina Kolata, "While Children Grow Fatter, Experts Search for Solutions," *New York Times,* 19 October 2000, sec. A1.

18. McFarling, "Food Police," sec. A6.

19. "Corporate Spotlight," *Adbusters,* no. 35, May/June 2001, 93.

20. "TV News in Schools Costs $1.8 Billion in Class Time," *New York Times,* 1 April 1998, sec. B11.

21. "School Questions Pepsi Contract," *State College (Pa.) Centre Daily Times,* 6 June 2001, sec. A2; and "School District Ponders Deal for Coke Products," *State College (Pa.) Centre Daily Times,* 2 July 1999, sec. A11.

22. Hayes, "District Rethinks," sec. A19.

23. Steve Manning, "Students for Sale," *The Nation,* 27 September 1999, 15.

24. Mary B. W. Tabor, "Schools Profit from Offering Students for Market Research," *New York Times,* 5 April 1999, sec. A1.

25. Steve Manning, "Zapped," *The Nation,* 27 September 1999, 13.

26. Eyal Press and Jennifer Washburn, "The Kept University," *Atlantic Monthly* 285, no. 3 (March 2000): 41.

27. Naomi Klein, *No Logo: Taking Aim at the Brand Bullies* (New York: Picador USA, 1999), 105.

28. Stanley Aronowitz, "The New Corporate University: Higher Education Becomes Higher Training," *Dollars & Sense,* no. 216, March 1998, 32–35.

29. Press and Washburn, "The Kept University," 41.

30. Klein, *No Logo,* 98–101.

31. "GE Fund Awards Two Grants to Penn State," *State College (Pa.) Centre Daily Times,* 18 December 2000, sec. A5.

32. Margaret Hopkins, "Six Companies Pledge $1.85 Million for e-Business Center," *State College (Pa.) Centre Daily Times,* 14 December 2000, sec. B10.

33. Press and Washburn, "The Kept University," 41.

34. "GE Fund Awards Two Grants to Penn State," sec. A5.

35. Aronowitz, "The New Corporate University," 32.

36. Hopkins, "Six Companies Pledge $1.85 Million," sec. B10.

37. Local Hotel Group to Build on Delaware Campus," *State College (Pa.) Centre Daily Times,* 24 May 2001, sec. A5.

38. Megan Novack, "Program Provides Disney Experience," *Daily Collegian,* 26 September 2000, 2.

39. Press and Washburn, "The Kept University," 39–40.

40. Press and Washburn, "The Kept University," 41–5.

41. Press and Washburn, "The Kept University," 42. Figure is compared to 79 percent of papers based on research not funded by industry.

42. Press and Washburn, "The Kept University," 42.

43. "Newsflashes," *Adbusters,* no. 30, June/July 2000, 17.

44. Dick Cooper, "Saying 'No' to a Gift of Water," letter to the editor, *State College (Pa.) Centre Daily Times,* 5 July 2001, sec. A6.

45. David Smith, "Nittany Lion Print Foots Too Many Toes," *Daily Collegian,* 29 January 1999, 8.

46. Gilbert M. Gaul and Frank Fitzpatrick, "What Was Sacred Is Now Up for Sale," *Philadelphia Inquirer,* 14 September 2001, sec. A1.

47. Gaul and Fitzpatrick, "What Was Sacred," sec. A1.

48. Gaul and Fitzpatrick, "What Was Sacred," sec. A1.

49. Gaul and Fitzpatrick, "What Was Sacred," sec. A1.

50. National Collegiate Athletic Association (NCAA). "A Call to Action: Reconnecting College Sports to Higher Education," <www.ncaa.org/databases/knight_commission/2001_report/2001_knight_report.html> (accessed June 2001).

51. Douglas Braunsdorf, "Knight Commission Report Sparks Debate," *State College (Pa.) Centre Daily Times,* 29 June 2001, sec. B1.

52. Braunsdorf, "Knight Commission Report," sec. B1.

53. Darryl Leroux, "Who's Zooming Who?" *Adbusters,* no. 34, March/April 2001, 47.

54. Leroux, "Who's Zooming Who?" 47.

55. "THON to Showcase Hilfiger Wear," *State College (Pa.) Centre Daily Times,* 12 February 2000, sec. A5.

56. "Credit Card Usage Analysis," <www.nelliemae.com/shared/ccstat.htm> (accessed December 2000).

57. W. A. Lee, "Student Loan GSE Slams Card Company Marketing," *American Banker* 166, no. 42 (2 March 2001): 8.

58. Betty Lin-Fisher, "Credit Cards for Students Mean Big Business" (Knight-Ridder Tribune) *State College (Pa.) Centre Daily Times,* 26 August 2001, sec. C8.

59. "Students Binge on Credit," *USA Today,* 14 September 2000, sec. A26.

60. Manning, "Zapped," 13.

61. Jack Myers, *Adbashing: Surviving the Attacks on Advertising* (Parsippany, N.J.: American Media Council, 1993), 151.

62. Klein, *No Logo,* 88.

63. Lori Leibovich, "Choosing Quick Hits over the Card Catalog," *New York Times,* 10 August 2000, sec. G1.

64. Katie Hafner, "Schools and Computers: Debate Heats Up," *New York Times,* 5 October 2001, E8.

65. Tom Zeller, "Amid Clamor for Computer in Every Classroom, Some Dissenting Voices," *New York Times,* 17 March 2001, sec. A3.

66. "Penn Staters Tinker with Computers" (Staff Reports), *State College (Pa.) Centre Daily Times,* 25 July 2000, sec. A5.

67. "State High Teacher Awarded Palm Grant," *State College (Pa.) Centre Daily Times,* 10 September 2001, sec. A5.

68. "Raytheon Grant Helps Endow State High Award," *State College (Pa.) Centre Daily Times,* 24 September 2001, sec. A5.

69. Barbara Brueggebors, "'A Taste of Pennsylvania' Gives Governors a Flavor of High-Tech," *State College (Pa.) Centre Daily Times,* 11 July 2000, sec. A7; and Yuri Kageyama, "Mechanical Mutt: Sony Puppy Robot Good for Laughs, Still Far Call from Lovable Pet," *State College (Pa.) Centre Daily Times,* 24 December 2000, sec. E3.

70. Ellen Goodman, "Technology Sets You Free . . . To Work All The Time," *State College (Pa.) Centre Daily Times,* 25 July 2000, sec. A6.

71. Margaret Hopkins, "Greenspan Visit Caps NGA Event: Fed Chief Challenges States to Provide Training for Workers," *State College (Pa.) Centre Daily Times,* 12 July 2000, sec. A1.

72. Zeller, "Amid Clamor for Computer," sec. A3.

73. Manning, "Students for Sale," 12.

74. Christopher Carey, "Lisa MacFarlane's Story," *St. Louis Post-Dispatch,* 11 July 1999, sec. B1.

75. Neil Postman, "Virtual Students, Digital Classrooms," *The Nation,* 9 October 1995, 377.

76. Manning, "Zapped," 13.

77. Aronowitz, "The New Corporate University," 32.

78. Press and Washburn, "The Kept University," 54.

79. *Business Week,* 22 December 1997, quoted in Klein, *No Logo,* 101.

80. Arthur Levine, "The Soul of a New University," *New York Times,* 13 March 2000, sec. A25.

# 6

# CONCLUSION:
# TAKING IT TO THE STREETS

When we began writing this book at the turn of the twenty-first century, millennium hyperbole and hysteria dominated the headlines. The mainstream news media issued dire warnings of a "Y2K bug," a glitch in computer time-keeping systems that threatened to shut down everything from Main Street to Wall Street at the stroke of midnight on New Year's Eve 1999. Apocalyptic predictions of retail shortages invariably featured good consumers as smart survivalists, stocking up on bottled water and flashlight batteries. The turn of the twenty-first century also witnessed an extraordinary surge of impassioned protests against global capitalism—demonstrations that were staged and struggled and sometimes squashed but never silenced at meetings of the rich and powerful around the world. It didn't get as many sound bites as the Y2K bug, yet it proved to be far more real and long lasting. The movement was inspired in part by what has come to be known as the "Battle of Seattle."

It is fair to compare the massive protests against the World Trade Organization (WTO) meeting in Seattle in the early winter of 1999 to the shot heard 'round the world, or at least the Boston Tea Party. More than 70,000 people gathered in the rainy city and marched through the streets, protesting the WTO's attempts to advance global capitalism by "lowering trade barriers." The protesters came under a number of different organizational umbrellas but were unified in their conviction that the policies of the WTO enable the super rich and powerful to exploit workers, ignore human rights, squeeze Third World countries, and destroy the environment—all in pursuit of profits. The 1999 WTO talks shut down as thousands of police and National Guard troops arrested hundreds of protesters amid vague reports of black-masked anarchist provocateurs. Peaceful protesters were showered with pepper spray and pummeled with rubber bullets. Seattle's chief of police resigned amid charges of incompetence and brutality.[1]

137

The mainstream media quickly christened the events the Battle of Seattle. The lead story in the *New York Times* the following day cynically reported that "what was planned as the biggest American demonstration yet against global trade . . . turned into a burst of window-breaking and looting," a "surge of violence that ended in a civil emergency. . . . It died out with the image of a grinning young man in a Gap sweatshirt trying to cart off a satellite dish from a Radio Shack store."[2] Meanwhile, alternative news sources denounced the mainstream media's "Prattle on Seattle." As one participant observer told *Z Magazine,* "Most of what has been written is so inaccurate that I can't decide if the reporters in question should be charged with conspiracy or simply incompetence. . . . The police, in defending their 'mishandling' of the situation, have said they were 'not prepared for the violence.' In reality, they were unprepared for the nonviolence."[3]

Over the next two years, scores of protests against global capitalism were mounted at similar meetings in the United States and abroad, including Washington, D.C.; New York; State College and Philadelphia, Pennsylvania; Porto Alegre, Brazil; Madrid and Barcelona; London; Paris; Genoa, Italy; Salzburg, Austria; Davos, Switzerland; and Göteborg, Sweden. Many participants credited Seattle with tapping into a widely held and deeply felt sense of outrage at "a grotesque and dangerous polarization and inequality around the world."[4] In 2001, the *Irish Times* reported, "Ever since antiglobalization groups staged protests at a meeting of the World Trade Organization in Seattle in 1999, major gatherings of world leaders have become targets for increasingly violent demonstrations."[5] In "previews" of a gathering of the "Group of Eight" (G8) in Genoa that summer, the Italian media routinely referred to the expected protesters as "Il Popolo di Seattle" (Seattle People).[6] As a protester at the 2002 World Economic Forum (WEF) in New York said, "Seattle was definitely a wake-up call."[7] Indeed, by that time, the *New York Times* had its protest coverage down to a neat formula: The Meeting, The Streets, The Protestors, The Police.[8]

In this final chapter, we offer snapshots of events staged by global capitalists and world leaders from late 1999 to early 2002, and the people's protests consistently mounted against them. Rather than heading straight for the streets, we pause to consider some of the political and economic issues that were at stake. We then take a closer look at mainstream media coverage of the demonstrations. Of course, the world's "captains of finance" and "ambassadors of free trade" meet regularly in private to trade properties, set policies, rub shoulders, and scratch backs. Unlike most meetings of the super rich and powerful, however, these events were highly visible. The media could not ignore the protests against them, but they did strive to symbolically contain them.

## THE MEETINGS: EXCLUSIVE AFFAIRS

In the period under consideration, the mainstream media referred to global trade meetings variously (and sometimes euphemistically) as gatherings, conferences, summits, conventions, forums, and retreats. (The retreat tag was most appropriate to the 2001 G8 Summit, where delegates were scuttled off to boats moored in the Port of Genoa to avoid protesters.) News coverage of most of the meetings tended to focus on eruptions of violence in the demonstrations outside, rather than on the policies debated within. When the media did discuss the meetings, they often treated them as celebrity events or personality parades, focusing on who was invited and who was not, who accepted and who declined. For example, "34 heads of state from the Americas (all except Fidel Castro) declared their commitment to democracy" at the Summit of the Americas in Quebec.[9] They also tended to reduce profound political and economic differences to the level of individual quarrels or conflicting personalities: "The 'BB' (Berlusconi/Bush) factor suggests Genoa is likely to be anything but peaceful."[10] An abbreviated listing of some of the most notable meetings, all of which drew significant protests, attests to our characterization of antiglobalization and indeed anticapitalism as a movement.

Several took place in the United States within months of the aborted WTO meeting in Seattle. In April 2000, representatives of the International Monetary Fund (IMF) and the World Bank met in Washington, D.C. Tens of thousands of peaceful protesters gathered to greet them. Four hundred people were arrested, mostly on charges of creating a nuisance, disturbing the peace, or parading without a permit. In July 2000, President Bill Clinton and Federal Reserve Chairman Alan Greenspan addressed a meeting of the National Governors Association (NGA) in State College, Pennsylvania. Hundreds of students at Penn State University, citizens of the surrounding county, and supporters from across the state protested. Fifteen people were arrested, including a handful of students who hung an anti–global capital banner from a classroom building balcony across the street from a Penn State venue where the governors gathered. Many participants said they planned to continue on to Philadelphia the following August for demonstrations at the Republican National Convention (GOP). There, tens of thousands of protesters were met by heavily armed police, some of whom had infiltrated protest coalitions by posing as activists in the weeks before. More than 300 people were arrested.

In April 2001, President George W. Bush attended the Summit of the Americas to negotiate the proposed Free Trade Area of the Americas

(FTAA). Delegates convened high on the hill of old walled Quebec, which was further buttressed by a 2.5-mile chain-link fence and 6,000 police officers. According to *In These Times,* the FTAA was designed to follow the North American Free Trade Agreement (NAFTA) in giving corporations the power to overturn laws and collect damages from governments whenever they believe a government policy threatens future profits: "It is also likely to give corporations new power to attack public services, forcing deregulation, privatization and marketization of the public sphere." Tens of thousands of people protested, successfully bringing down the chain-link "wall of shame" but "failing" to disrupt the meetings.[11]

Bush embarked on a European tour the following summer, where thousands gathered to protest his policies on missile defense, global warming, and capital punishment. Many top European Union (EU) officials supported them.[12] In June 2001, the EU held a summit in Göteborg, Sweden, in an effort to keep their plans for expansion on track despite Irish opposition. (Earlier that month, Ireland was the only EU member to reject the Treaty of Nice, a complex document designed to open the door for a dozen new members. Ireland was also the only member nation that allowed its citizens to vote on the issue.[13]) The summit drew an estimated 25,000 protesters, including environmentalists and antiglobalization activists. Clashes with police left forty-three people hospitalized, including three with gunshot wounds when police opened fire. The Associated Press reported, "The mayhem forced the EU leaders to change their dinner plans from a posh restaurant to the conference center where the summit was held behind police barricades."[14] Later that month, thirty-two protesters were injured at an anti–World Bank rally in Barcelona, Spain.

In July 2001, in Salzburg, Austria, hundreds of protesters marched on the European Economic Summit, sponsored by the World Economic Forum (WEF) and chaired by billionaire financier George Soros (number twenty-three on the 2001 *Forbes 400* list of "The Richest People in America" with $6.9 billion[15]). The protesters gathered at the local Communist Party headquarters, carried communist hammer-and-sickle flags, and chanted, "Our world is not for sale, put the bankers into jail!" They were turned away by 5,000 police "on duty to make sure mayhem doesn't erupt in Salzburg, the hometown of Wolfgang Amadeus Mozart."[16] Later that month, the G8 convened in Genoa, Italy. Leaders of the world's eight richest nations (the United States, Canada, Germany, Japan, Russia, France, Italy, and Britain) gathered behind a steel cordon "beset by political and economic worries and ringed by protesters determined to drown out their annual summit."[17] Estimates of the number of police officers ranged from 15,000 to 60,000. Navy frogmen;

army sharpshooters; twelve air force helicopters; and specialists in nuclear, germ, and chemical warfare were reportedly deployed. The 2,000 delegates and 6,000 journalists huddled in boats on the harbor, where, as an Irish reporter noted, "We can all sleep easy, safe in the knowledge that U.S. aircraft carrier Enterprise, not to mention various Italian navy boats," will be on patrol nearby.[18] There were 200,000 protesters.

Finally, the World Economic Forum, which had for thirty years convened annually at a ski resort in Davos, Switzerland, was moved to New York City in February 2002. Founder Klaus Schwab made a highly publicized pretense of supporting the city in the wake of attacks on the World Trade Center, but in fact the Swiss government had balked at the cost of providing security for the event, which had begun to draw increasing numbers of protesters. United Nations Secretary General Kofi Annan, Bishop Desmond Tutu, and U2's Bono joined elite leaders of Big Business at the meetings. Serge Schmemann, who covered the meeting for the *New York Times,* charged that the annual event had been "portrayed by outsiders as a gathering of the world's richest and most powerful men shaping a global agenda from which the weak and poor were excluded." As an insider, Schmemann got the impression "of an elite struggling to comprehend the increasingly threatening forces of antiglobalization, militant Islam, terrorism and poverty, forces that gained an immediacy in the inferno of Sept. 11."[19] Police estimated that 7,000 people protested, while demonstration organizers said the number was closer to 25,000. Two hundred people were arrested. Perhaps the most organized protest against the World Economic Forum in New York City was a larger parallel gathering in Porto Alegre, Brazil.

Annan, who addressed both gatherings, reminded those in New York that the title of the Brazilian conference, "World Social Forum," was intended as a criticism of theirs. They are "implying that you are interested only in economics, or in profit, and that you do not care about the social effects of your economic activities," he said. Annan cited a number of channels through which corporations could contribute, including the Global Health Initiative and the United Nations Development Program. In attendance at the forum, Microsoft Chairman Bill Gates (number one on the 2001 *Forbes 400* with $54 billion) agreed that the question of "whether the rich world is giving back what it should in the developing world" was a "legitimate" one. David H. Komansky, chairman of Merrill Lynch (number twenty-five on the 2001 *Fortune 500* list of "America's Largest Corporations" with revenues of $44.8 billion), remarked, "We're trained as businessmen, but we're being asked to pass judgment on the moral and ethical value of these [development] projects."[20]

As the protests of the people in the streets grew louder, global capitalists were continually forced to defend themselves, and, with the help of the media, to set into motion processes of pacification. Nonetheless, as David Moberg predicted, it became "difficult for any politician to talk about global economics without addressing links to labor rights, human rights, food supplies, and the protection of both consumers and the environment."[21]

## THE ISSUES: WHAT ARE WE FIGHTING FOR?

When thousands of protesters marched on Washington to protest the 2000 meeting of the IMF, the mainstream media—always happy to denounce communism—had trouble even coughing up the word "capitalism," preferring the related but far more vague and euphemistic term "globalization." When journalists did feel the need to offer some explanation for the protests, they did so in decidedly dismissive tones: "Parading under an anti-globalization banner, the protesters believe that the operating rules of the WTO, IMF and World Bank are rigged in favor of wealthy multinational corporations at the expense of poor people, labor unions and the environment."[22] All evidence supports these claims. Predictably, however, the news media either blurred or simply buried the issues at stake—the "beliefs" that compelled hundreds of thousands of people to "parade" for causes in which most of them had no personal stake.

The Associated Press crowed when animal rights activists protested the Washington IMF meeting in a peaceful but pungent act of civil disobedience, and the *State College (Pa.) Centre Daily Times* reprinted the story. The headline read, "PETA Dumps Four Tons of Manure near World Bank," and the article beneath it described how the "Department of Public Works carried away the pile in a city vehicle escorted by a police van with siren blaring and lights flashing."[23] The full name of the activist group and a vague reference to their criticisms of the IMF were banished to the last paragraph of the column and topped off with their punishment: "The driver and passenger in the manure truck were from People for the Ethical Treatment of Animals, which is protesting World Bank Agricultural Policies. One was charged with crossing a police line, the other with illegal dumping."[24] The article did not bother to explain that PETA objects to the raising of animals for food—to be processed and packaged for the likes of McDonald's and Taco Bell—not only on the grounds that it is unethical to eat meat, but also because it is destructive to the environment.

The IMF and the World Bank aren't regularly the subjects of top news stories, and these and other protesters helped make them front-page news.

Lacking, however, was any history to help readers put things in perspective. The IMF and the World Bank were formed in the late 1940s and presented as a means of achieving modest financial safeguards in a world reeling from war. They came into the spotlight of international economic policy planning in the 1980s, when they stepped in to stave off global financial collapse by lending money to Third World countries that had borrowed heavily during the 1970s. By utilizing their influence over international lending practices, these organizations imposed a blueprint for economic and social policies to be followed by debtor countries around the world. The basic goal of international finance capital has been to make neoliberalism the economic policy of necessity at the level of the nation-state, which includes market liberalization, export-oriented production, and massive privatization of state-owned industries. At the same time, the austerity plans promoted by the World Bank and the IMF have ravaged the social welfare state with the effect of pulling the floor out from under the poorest segments of a nation's people. Consequently, the gaps between the rich and poor have widened significantly as the gains of popular social movements of the 1960s and 1970s have been reversed.[25]

Furthermore, the internationalist sectors of domestic capital have become increasingly integrated into the global capitalist economy, leading them to identify more and more with the interests of international capitalists and less and less with those of their own national populations. Free trade agreements such as NAFTA and FTAA; global organizations such as the WTO, IMF, and World Bank; congregations of global business and government elites such as the G8 and WEF; and an increasingly interventionist United Nations and increasingly militaristic United States acting as a global police force all serve as pillars of the "New World Order" in which capital reigns supreme.[26]

"The long-standing issues posed by capital's easy mobility—such as job loss, environmental damage, economic insecurity and inequality, sweatshops, 'structural adjustment' squeezes, and threats to farmers and food consumers from agribusiness—have not disappeared, but they are increasingly being consolidated within a broader framework of debate," Moberg explains. The issues are as much political as economic: the human rights of individuals against unfettered freedom of capital, democracy against corporate power and privilege, values of solidarity and justice against a totally marketized society.[27]

## MEDIA COVERAGE OF THE PROTESTS: STORMY WINTERS AND LONG HOT SUMMERS

Media coverage of protests at most of the global trade meetings followed an all-too-familiar pattern, with the initial focus on disruption followed by an emphasis on the restoration of order. Conflict, of course, is an essential news value and the media could not ignore the street battles and larger challenges to the existing economic and political order that the various protest participants represented. The specter of violence haunted journalists even before the street fighting broke out at the WTO meeting in Seattle, because journalists tend to assume that whenever people get together for a political cause or set up a picket line, mob behavior will ensue. This assumption is not without cause, considering the history of massacres of strikers by company guards, the shooting of students by the National Guard at Kent State and Jackson State Universities, or the clubbing of protestors by police at the 1968 Democratic Convention in Chicago.[28] Violence also helps to sell newspapers and boost broadcast ratings, and, often, as in the case of media coverage of Seattle, it becomes a dominant theme.

Media owners and workers themselves, from publishers down to reporters, are deeply integrated into the existing order and therefore have a profound stake in the status quo. Media owners want to amass wealth and exert influence; journalists need to pay off mortgages and car loans. The owners know for sure that they will benefit from the policies of organizations such as the IMF and WTO; most journalists probably assume they will, too. Hence, like the National Guard in Seattle, the media help to restore order after a disturbance of the peace. Journalistic practices that serve this function include symbolically dividing and conquering protesters by casting them as fractious and quarrelsome, and either vilifying demonstrators as violent or dismissing them as failures. Police officers and officials, on the other hand, are generally cast as highly trained professionals doing a difficult and dangerous job or as benign father figures protecting the people. They are also unapologetically celebrated as valiant protectors of private property, which is, of course, the central role of the state under capitalism.

DISTURBING THE PEACE

*A Motley Crew*

One way the media sought to symbolically contain the many protests from Seattle in 1999 to New York in 2002 was by depicting antiglobalization activists as a fractious and disparate lot with too many different causes and internal conflicts to sustain a unified movement. Writing in the *New York Times,* for example, Thomas L. Friedman described the WTO protesters as "a Noah's Ark of flat-earth advocates, protectionist trade unions and yuppies looking for their 1960s fix."[29] The *Philadelphia Inquirer* claimed the protesters had "a stew of grievances so confusing that they drowned any hope of broad public support," while *U.S. News* dismissed them as "all-purpose agitators."[30] When the WTO meeting was shut down, ABC's Peter Jennings remarked that "the thousands of demonstrators will go home, or on to some other venue where they'll try to generate attention for whatever cause that moves them."[31]

Such divisive descriptions and predictions may have begun with Seattle, but they persisted in press coverage of antiglobalization protests even as the movement gained momentum and solidarity in the following years. As organizers prepared for protests at the GOP convention in Philadelphia, for example, the Associated Press reported, "With so many issues apparently vying for attention, there is concern that the demonstrations either will be misconstrued by journalists or will not have enough participants for the message to be heard at all."[32] As the WEF in New York was winding down, the *New York Times* reported, "The collection of causes and protesters was wide: groups as disparate as Save the Redwoods/Boycott the Gap Campaign, the Anti-Capitalist Convergence, Queers for Racial and Economic Justice, the Pagan Cluster and even the Earth and Animal Liberation Coalition attended."[33] The *Irish Times* characterized G8 protesters in Genoa as follows: "Coming from all over Europe, Africa, Australia, India and South America, the ill-defined 'Seattle People' range from hard-line Marxists to Catholic Church groups, passing through anarchist centres along the way."[34] Only occasionally were such descriptions followed by an admission that the protesters "seemed unified by opposition to what they viewed as Bush's American imperialism"[35] or that they "seemed united by a sense that many world problems can be traced to a profit-hungry corporate elite."[36]

### The Specter of Violence

Even before the WTO meeting in Seattle began, the *New York Times* was reporting that police officials in the city feared "some violence." In one reporter's words, "The meeting has become ground zero for anyone with a complaint about the world economy."[37] The day after the meeting convened, the *Centre Daily Times* printed a small Associated Press item on page A4 reporting that the opening activities had been delayed due to a bomb search. The remainder of the article focused on various protest actions and a small number of arrests.[38] The *New York Times* buried news of the meeting on page A14 in a short article headlined "Trade Talks Start in Seattle Despite a Few Disruptions."[39] The next day, 1 December 1999, the *Centre Daily Times* front-page headline read "WTO Protests Turn Violent." The story was accompanied by three color AP photos of police spraying pepper gas on groups of protesters, a longhaired man rubbing his teary eyes, and a woman with blood running down her face.[40]

The *New York Times* front-page headline that day declared "National Guard Is Called to Quell Trade-Talk Protests." The story appeared above a photo of police in Darth Vader–like riot gear drowning protesters in a haze of tear gas.[41] Network television news programs that evening showed video footage of a protester being clubbed and then shot with a rubber bullet at close range. The images belied the text, which spoke little of police misconduct until it officially became "news" when Seattle's chief of police resigned the following week. The larger point here is that the WTO talks themselves—at which a handful of rich and powerful individuals gathered to set government and business trade policies affecting the lives of billions of people throughout the world—weren't front-page news until the protests against them turned violent.

Early media coverage of the protests against the meetings of the IMF in Washington, D.C., were also haunted by the specter of violence. Indeed, the media's pre-rally coverage seemed to serve as a justification for police brutality. "Washington Braces for IMF Protesters," a typical Associated Press story carried by the *Centre Daily Times* announced. Charles Ramsey, chief of Washington's Metropolitan Police Department, was widely quoted: "They ain't burning our city like they did Seattle. They didn't know what to expect in Seattle."[42] Ten days before the IMF meetings, an Associated Press story warned: "The protest groups on the streets as the World Trade Organization meetings collapsed in a cloud of tear gas in Seattle are taking aim at an even bigger target: the April 16–17 meetings of the world's largest multinational lending agencies."[43]

When the meetings convened and the marches set forth, a large, bold-face headline read: "Trade Protest Roils Capital."[44] The choice of words here is rich. According to Webster, "roil" is a verb meaning "to stir up, make turbid, irritate or vex." Capital can be used as a noun to denote either "the Congressional building in Washington, D.C." or "the owners of wealth," or as an adjective meaning "forfeiture of life." The firearm metaphor (protesters "taking aim") was apparently seen by the media as an appropriate way to describe the goals of opponents of global capital—a far cry from news coverage of the Million Mom March for gun control the following May, which was described as a "personal statement" for which protesters "sold muffins for bus fare."[45] Unlike the moms, protesters against the IMF and the World Bank were described as "swarms" who "raged" and "clogged" the streets of the capital.[46] As an *In These Times* commentator put it, "The news media, frustrated at the lack of images of violence and destruction, took vengeance in the only way they know how: They declared the event a victory for police."[47]

Related to the media's focus on violence as a strategy for containing protests is their emphasis on failure when violence doesn't occur. As the mainstream media reported, when protesters in Seattle shut down the WTO meetings, they failed to remain peaceful, and when protesters in Washington, D.C. remained peaceful, they failed to shut down the IMF meetings. The headline of a Knight Ridder story on the IMF meeting carried by the *Centre Daily Times,* for example, announced: "Protesters March, Fail to Block World Finance Meeting."[48] An Associated Press report the next day appeared under the banner: "IMF Protesters Try—and Fail—to Shut Down Meetings."[49]

The Knight Ridder–owned *Centre Daily Times* adopted the failure theme in its coverage of the IMF meeting, publishing a color Associated Press photo of Washington cops in riot gear captioned, "Thousands of marchers failed to stop world finance leaders from meeting." The failure theme was then repeated in the *Centre Daily Times* local coverage of protests against the U.S. National Governors Association meeting in State College the following July. For example, a front-page article about an organizational meeting held by a local activist group, Redirection2000, was headlined, "Protest Preparation Fails to Draw Crowd."[50] As Yale anthropology professor David Graeber wrote for *In These Times,* "If the police manage not to run amok, but are calculating in their application of brutality in repressing constitutional rights, they win, and the newspapers will praise them; if the protesters fail to run amok, they lose."[51]

RESTORING ORDER

*Highly Trained Professionals*

One media strategy for restoring order is to focus on the police as highly trained and disciplined professionals whose difficult job is to keep the peace and protect the people by outwitting protesters. This strategy figured heavily in coverage of security at the IMF talks in Washington, D.C., in the wake of the police debacle in Seattle,[52] and it continued in coverage of the WEF meeting in New York. The journalists covering the police beat for the *New York Times,* William K. Rashbaum and Al Baker, had high praise for the strategic planning of the force: "Using a combination of intelligence, a large deployment of police officers and careful planning, the department seemed to be everywhere at all times—and, much to the chagrin of the protesters, seemed to be able to anticipate their every move."[53] Rashbaum and Baker commended the cops for claiming the streets first, flooding the area around the Waldorf-Astoria Hotel with thousands of officers, surrounding demonstrators with police motorcycles, and monitoring protesters with television cameras mounted high above the Waldorf and on a police helicopter.[54]

When the media departed from their representation of police as security strategists, it was usually to grace the long arm of the law with a firm but gentle father's hand. The police were often depicted in the press as benign parental figures, protecting citizens from protesters and protesters from themselves. For example, the Associated Press reported that Terry Gainer, executive assistant chief of police in Washington, D.C., told demonstrators to "Give yourselves a hand" as his heavily armed force "orchestrated a good-natured arrest of some 400 demonstrators" who had "failed to shut down the two days of meetings of the World Bank and International Monetary Fund."[55] Gainer reportedly gave protest organizer Mary Bull flowers before placing her under arrest."[56] Washington, D.C., Police Chief Charles Ramsey, quoted before the IMF meeting as warning, "They ain't burning our city like they did Seattle," was quoted afterward as saying that most of the demonstrators were "just kids with a cause."[57] According to the *New York Times,* "As the demonstrations ended, both sides claimed a kind of victory and even a certain grudging mutual respect." Police Chief Ramsey declared it "a win-win for everybody."[58]

Coverage of New York police at the World Economic Forum meeting sometimes took on softer tones as well. (New York police officers, after all, had become heroes after September 11.) Even Rashbaum and Baker, fond of military metaphors, opted for allusions to baseball and dance to describe their performance: "Like a fastball pitcher brushing back a batter, the Police Department staked out a claim to its home plate—the streets of New York City—before the World Economic Forum even began, with a carefully choreographed strategy that officials say helped keep the peace by keeping protesters off balance." Rashbaum admitted that the police "were not without critics" and quoted Leslie Brody, a protest volunteer from the National Lawyers Guild, for journalistic balance. Brody criticized the police as if they were overly stern parents scolding mischievous children too harshly: "These are kids who wanted to act out in a creative way, and I think early on they were tagged for dressing or looking differently."[59]

*Protecting Private Property*

Another media strategy for restoring order is to shift the focus away from political and economic issues, and even from human pain and suffering, to destruction and protection of property. The *New York Times* coverage of the Seattle protests centered on "anarchists" and "vandals" who ran "uninterrupted ... smashing windows, spray-painting walls and tossing newspaper boxes and garbage cans into the streets.[60] In fact, the map of "Seattle's Violent Scene" published in the *New York Times* belies U.S. government and Big Media claims that the attacks on property were committed by vandals or anarchists in wanton acts of looting and destruction.[61] The actions of the "Black Bloc" in Seattle were anything but random, as David Graeber of *In These Times* points out.[62] Their targets were carefully selected and represented an attack on the central icons being protected and promoted by what has been referred to as the "World Trademark Organization."

The targets included the store fronts of such brand-name operations as Old Navy, Gap, Nordstrom, Banana Republic, Niketown, Levi's, McDonald's, Starbucks, Warner Brothers, and (the aptly named) Planet Hollywood. Rather than exploring whether there may have been a method behind this "anarchy," the media restored order by signaling customers that all was clear and encouraging them to come back downtown to finish their Christmas shopping. Retailers offered free coffee and free parking along with the usual generous "discounts." With the "anarchists" contained, the National Guard went home while the media continued to restore order.[63]

A week after the protests, the *Centre Daily Times* ran an Associated Press story on the resignation of Seattle's chief of police, referring to him as the "first casualty" of the Battle of Seattle. Civic leaders argued that the police department had not prepared sufficient force and merchants claimed they had suffered nearly $20 million in property damage and lost sales. So Seattle's police chief, who was planning to retire anyway, was offered up as a sacrifice to the media, this time shifting blame from a rogue group to an incompetent individual but still with no significant discussion of the essential systemic issues prompting the protesters' passion.

## CONCLUSION

In an article entitled "Mostly Pleased, but Knowing Few Heard Their Message," reporter Andrew Jacobs covered the protesters' beat of the 2002 World Economic Forum for the *New York Times*. As the headline suggests, the story perpetuates the failure motif that characterizes so much mainstream media coverage of anti–global capital protests. Unlike most reports, however, this one acknowledges the protesters' criticism of the media's sensational coverage of their demonstrations and its failure to analyze the issues that inspired them: "While the marches and rallies drew plenty of attention from journalists, the organizers said the attention was the wrong kind. Most press accounts focused on security concerns and the potential for violence, they said, leaving little room for explanations of why people were protesting in the first place."[64] Jacobs then quotes Antonia Juhasz, an organizer with the San Francisco–based International Forum on Globalization: "The news is not the protesters or the police. The news should have been what issues brought us to the streets. The coverage was just appalling."[65]

Such criticism could hardly have surprised the *New York Times* reporter, but it does appear to have stung him. After dutifully noting the protesters' dissatisfaction, he adds, "But they acknowledged that for many reporters on deadline, the panoply and complexity of issues was too much for a simple sound bite."[66] The image of an elite journalist attempting to persuade a group of grassroots organizers to agree on principle that reporters cannot possibly explain the issues that motivate protesters to the people who read newspapers is a chilling one indeed. It exemplifies an assumption held by many news media reporters and owners that readers are unwilling or unable to grasp anything beyond "a simple sound bite." It is a far cry from the journalistic ideal of beating the bushes to discover and reveal the truth.

Whether because or in spite of the "appalling" media coverage of their actions, protesters did crash the gates of the global capitalist party at the turn of the twenty-first century. In the wake of Seattle, the *New York Times* conceded that labor, environmental, and human rights groups had a legitimate complaint against the WTO as an exclusive businessman's club, and that they deserved a seat at the table.[67] The message was also clear that only those accepting the inevitability of global capitalism were invited. Those who questioned such a future were not welcome. To question capitalism is to ask whether genuine democracy can exist within such an existing order. The answer, as McChesney has argued, is that "the relationship between capitalism and democracy is a rocky one."[68] A genuine democracy requires a degree of equality that permits all members of the citizenry to be involved in political and economic decision making. Under capitalism wealth is concentrated, giving a tiny minority this power. A genuine democracy is based on communitarian values. Capitalism is based on possessive individualism channeled into rabid consumerism. A genuine democracy requires an informed citizenry with access to a wide range of information and culture. Capitalism turns information and culture into commodities, products to be bought and sold in the marketplace rather than shared knowledge to enlighten or pose challenges to citizens.

The struggle for a seat at the table nonetheless seems necessary because the expansionary processes of global capitalism continue unabated. While reserving the right to sit at the table, activists will also have to be ready to excuse themselves and head for the streets. The Big Media will be there, but as we have tried to show in this book, we cannot rely on them to get the message out to the people. Alternative voices will be more important than ever.

## NOTES

1. Sam Howe Verhovek, "Seattle Police Chief Resigns in Aftermath of Protests," *New York Times,* 8 December 1999, sec. A13.

2. Timothy Egan, "Black Masks Lead to Pointed Fingers in Seattle," *New York Times,* 2 December 1999, sec. A1.

3. Starhawk, "How We Shut Down the WTO," *Z Magazine,* February 2000, 18–19.

4. Andrew Jacobs, "The Protesters: Mostly Pleased, but Knowing Few Heard Their Message," *New York Times,* 5 February 2002, sec. A15.

5. Paddy Agnew, "Genoa Braces for Disruption of G8 Summit," *Irish Times,* 14 July 2001, 11.

6. Agnew, "Genoa Braces," 11.

7. Jacobs, "The Protesters," sec. A15.

8. Serge Schmemann, "The Meeting: Annan Cautions Business As Forum Ends," *New York Times,* 5 February 2002, sec. A14; Dan Barry, "The Streets: So Long New York, and Thanks for a Mostly Well-Ordered Bash," *New York Times,* 5 February 2002, sec. A14; Jacobs, "The Protesters," sec. A15; and William K. Rashbaum and Al Baker, "The Police: Shrewd Anticipation Helped Avert Trouble," *New York Times,* 5 February 2002, sec. A15.

9. David Moberg, "Tear Down the Walls: The Movement Is Becoming More Global," *In These Times,* 28 May 2001, 11–14. Note that Moberg is a critical journalist whose tone here is ironic.

10. Agnew, "Genoa Braces," 11.

11. Moberg, "Tear Down the Walls," 11–14.

12. Dana Milbank, "Bush Greeted by Demonstrators, Critics" (Washington Post), *State College (Pa.) Centre Daily Times,* 13 June 2001, sec. A3.

13. Paul Ames, "Demonstrators Riot Outside EU Conference" (Associated Press), *State College (Pa.) Centre Daily Times,* 16 June 2001, sec. A3.

14. Ames, "Demonstrators Riot," sec. A3.

15. "The 400 Richest People in America," *Forbes,* 8 October 2001, 179.

16. Marsha Hill, "World Economic Summit Opens Amid Anti-Globalization Protests" (Associated Press), *State College (Pa.) Centre Daily Times,* 2 July 2001, sec. B8.

17. Agnew, "Genoa Braces," 11.

18. Agnew, "Genoa Braces," 11.

19. Schmemann, "The Meeting," sec. A14.

20. Schmemann, "The Meeting," sec. A14.

11. David Moberg, "After Seattle," *In These Times,* 18 February 2002, 41.

22. Martin Grutsinger, "Protesters Aim at IMF Meeting" (Associated Press), *State College (Pa.) Centre Daily Times,* 7 April 2000, sec. B8.

23. Larry Margasak, "PETA Dumps Four Tons of Manure near World Bank" (Associated Press), *State College (Pa.) Centre Daily Times,* 15 April 2000, sec. A3.

24. Margasak, "PETA Dumps Four Tons," sec. A3.

25. Ronald V. Bettig, *Copyrighting Culture: The Political Economy of Intellectual Property* (Boulder, Colo.: Westview Press, 1996), 191.

26. Bettig, *Copyrighting Culture,* 191.

27. Moberg, "Tear Down the Walls," 11–14.

28. "An Alternative History: Timeline," *The Nation,* 10 January 2000, 8–51.

29. Thomas L. Friedman, "Senseless in Seattle," *New York Times,* 1 December 1999, sec. A31.

30. Seth Ackerman, "Prattle in Seattle," *Extra!,* January/February 2000, 13–17.

31. Ackerman, "Prattle in Seattle," 13–17.

32. Jennifer Brown, "Protests Planned for GOP Convention" (Associated Press), *State College (Pa.) Centre Daily Times,* 7 June 2000, sec. D1.

33. Jacobs, "The Protesters," sec. A15.

34. Agnew, "Genoa Braces," 11.

35. Milbank, "Bush Greeted," sec. A3.

36. Jacobs, "The Protesters," sec. A15.

37. Steven Greenhouse, "A Carnival of Derision to Greet the Princes of Global Trade," *New York Times,* 29 November 1999, sec. A12.

38. "Trade Talks Begin" (Associated Press), *State College (Pa.) Centre Daily Times,* 30 November 1999, sec. A4.

39. Sam Howe Verhovek, "Trade Talks Start in Seattle Despite a Few Disruptions," *New York Times,* 30 November 1999, sec. A14.

40. "WTO Protests Turn Violent" (Associated Press), *State College (Pa.) Centre Daily Times,* 1 December 1999, sec. A1.

41. "National Guard Is Called to Quell Trade-Talk Protests," *New York Times,* 1 December 1999, sec. A1.

42. Derrill Holly, "DC Police Ready for IMF Duty" (Associated Press), 7 April 2000, AM Cycle; and Larry Margasak, "Washington Braces for IMF Protesters" (Associated Press), *State College (Pa.) Centre Daily Times,* 9 April 2000, sec. A1.

43. Martin Crutsinger, "Protesters Aim at IMF Meeting" (Associated Press), *State College (Pa.) Centre Daily Times,* 7 April 2000, sec. 8B.

44. "Trade Protest Roils Capital" (Knight Ridder Newspapers), *State College (Pa.) Centre Daily Times,* 17 April 2000, sec. A1.

45. "Million Mom March a Personal Statement for Some" (Staff and Wire Reports), *State College (Pa.) Centre Daily Times,* 14 May 2000, sec. A69.

46. "Trade Protest Roils Capital," A1.

47. David Graeber, "The Riot That Wasn't," *In These Times,* 29 May 2000, 12.

48. "Protesters March, Fail to Block World Finance Meeting" (Knight Ridder),

*State College (Pa.) Centre Daily Times,* 17 April 2000, sec. A7.

49. Larry Margasak, "IMF Protesters Try—and Fail—to Shut Down Meetings" (Associated Press), *State College (Pa.) Centre Daily Times,* 18 April 2000, sec. A1.

50. Erin R. Wengerd, "Protest Preparation Fails to Draw Crowd," *State College (Pa.) Centre Daily Times,* 25 May 2000, sec. A1.

51. Graeber, "The Riot That Wasn't," 13.

52. "Trade Protest Roils Capital," sec. A1.

53. Rashbaum and Baker, "Shrewd Anticipation," sec. A15.

54. Rashbaum and Baker, "Shrewd Anticipation," sec. A15.

55. Larry Margasak, "Protesters Disrupt Washington" (Associated Press), *Penn State University Daily Collegian,* 18 April 2000, 1.

56. Margasak, "Protesters Disrupt Washington," 1.

57. Margasak, "Protesters Disrupt Washington," 1.

58. John Kifner, "In This Washington, No 'Seattle' is Found by Police and Protesters," *New York Times,* 19 April 2000, sec. A12.

59. Rashbaum and Baker, "Shrewd Anticipation," sec. A15.

60. "Messages for the W.T.O.," *New York Times,* 2 December 1999, sec. A30.

61. Sam Howe Verhovek, "Seattle Is Stung, Angry and Chagrined as Opportunity Turns to Chaos," *New York Times,* 2 December 1999, sec. A14.

62. David Graeber, "Anarchy in the USA," *In These Times,* 10 January 2000, 18.

63. Timothy Egan, "Black Masks Lead to Pointed Fingers in Seattle," *New York Times,* 2 December 1999, sec. A1, A14.

64. Jacobs, "The Protesters," sec. A15.

65. Jacobs, "The Protesters," sec. A15.

66. Jacobs, "The Protesters," sec. A15.

67 "Messages for the W.T.O.," sec. A30.

68. Robert W. McChesney, "The Communication Revolution: The Market and the Prospect for Democracy" in *Democratizing Communication?,* ed. M. Bailie and D. Winseck (Creskill, N.J.: Hampton Press, 1997), 57–78.

# BIBLIOGRAPHY

Ackerman, Seth. "Prattle in Seattle." *Extra!,* January/February 2000, 13–17.

Agnew, Paddy. "Genoa Braces for Disruption of G8 Summit." *Irish Times,* 14 July 2001, 11.

Ahrens, Frank. "The Great Deregulator: Five Months into His Tenure As FCC Chairman, Michael Powell Is Coming through Loud and Clear." *Washington Post,* 18 June 2001, sec. C1.

"America Online Vice Chairman Kenneth J. Novack Elected to Company's Board of Directors." *AOL Corporate.* 25 January 2000. <http://media.aoltimewarner.com/media/> (accessed 5 January 2002).

Ames, Paul. "Demonstrators Riot Outside EU Conference" (Associated Press). *State College (Pa.) Centre Daily Times,* 16 June 2001, sec. A3.

"An Alternative History: Timeline." *The Nation.* 10 January 2000, 8–51.

Andrews, Edmund L. "Bertelsman's Chairman to Leave Board of AOL." *New York Times,* 12 January 2000, sec. C7.

"AOL's Big Byte." *The Nation.* 31 January 2000, 3.

Aronowitz, Stanley. "The New Corporate University: Higher Education Becomes Higher Training." *Dollars & Sense,* no. 216 (March 1998): 32–35.

Aufderheide, Pat. "Open Access or Else." *In These Times,* 26 June 2000, 2.

Bagdikian, Ben H. *The Media Monopoly.* 6th ed. Boston: Beacon Press, 2000.

Baldwin, William. "Capitalism and Its Enemies." *Forbes,* 8 October 2001, 20.

Barringer, Felicity. "CBS News May Face More Cuts." *New York Times,* 9 September 1999, sec. C8.

———. "Does Deal Signal Lessening of Media Independence?" *New York Times,* 11 January 2000, sec. C12.

———. "Other Media Companies' Assets Tied to Those of Deal's Partners." *New York Times,* 13 January 2000, sec. C6.

Barry, Dan. "The Streets: So Long New York, and Thanks for a Mostly Well-Ordered Bash." *New York Times,* 5 February 2002, sec. A14.

Barsamian, David. "Monopolies, NPR, and PBS: An Interview with Robert Mc-Chesney." *Z Magazine,* February 2000, 40–46.

Bekken, Jon. "The Working Class Press at the Turn of the Century." In *Ruthless Criticism: New Perspectives in U.S. Communication History,* edited by Bob McChesney and Bill Solomon, 151–75. Minneapolis: University of Minnesota Press, 1993.

Berenson, Alex. "Investors Seem to Want to Keep AOL–Time Warner Asunder." *New York Times,* 13 January 2000, sec. C1, C6.

Bettig, Ronald V. *Copyrighting Culture: The Political Economy of Intellectual Property.* Boulder, Colo.: Westview Press, 1996.

———. "Who Owns Prime Time? Industrial and Institutional Conflict over Television Programming and Broadcast Rights." In *Framing Friction: Media and Social Conflict,* edited by Mary S. Mander, 125–60. Urbana: University of Illinois Press, 1999.

"The Biggest Media Merger Yet." *New York Times,* 11 January 2000, sec. A30.

"The Big Ten." *The Nation.* 7 January 2002, 27–30.

Bleifuss, Joel. "Communication Breakdown: AOL Time Warner Threatens Public Interest." *In These Times,* 21 February 2000, 2–3.

Boehlert, Eric. "MP3.mess: Petty Single Pulled from Net." *Rolling Stone,* 29 April 1999, 40.

Boettcher, Ken. "AOL–Time Warner Merger Makes Media Critics Nervous." *The People,* April 2000, 3.

Braunsdorf, Douglas. "Knight Commission Report Sparks Debate." *State College (Pa.) Centre Daily Times,* 29 June 2001, sec. B1, B4.

Breznican, Anthony. "Happily Ever After? Not Everyone Enjoys Disney Sequels" (Associated Press). *State College (Pa.) Centre Daily Times,* 17 February 2002, sec. C6.

Brown, Jennifer. "Protests Planned for GOP Convention" (Associated Press). *State College (Pa.) Centre Daily Times,* 7 June 2000, sec. D1.

Brueggebors, Barbara. "'A Taste of Pennsylvania' Gives Governors a Flavor of High-Tech." *State College (Pa.) Centre Daily Times,* 11 July 2000, sec. A7.

"But a Survey." In *Special Report: News and Editorial Independence. A Survey of Group and Independent Editors.* Easton, Pa: Ethics Committee, American Society of Newspaper Editors, 1980.

Carey, Christopher. "Lisa MacFarlane's Story." *St. Louis Post-Dispatch,* 11 July 1999, sec. B1.

Carlson, Matt. "Boardroom Brothers: Interlocking Directorates Indicate Media's Corporate Ties." *Extra!,* September 2001, 18–19.

Carter, Bill. "Media Talk: An Executive with Synergistic Vision." *New York Times,* 11 September 2000, sec. C17.

Carter, Bill, and Geraldine Fabrikant. "Board Dashes Cold Water on Feud at Viacom between Top Executives." *New York Times,* 31 January 2002, sec. C1, C7.

Caruso, Denise. "Digital Commerce: If the AOL–Time Warner Deal Is About Proprietary Content, Where Does that Leave a Noncommercial Directory It Will Own?" *New York Times,* 17 January 2000, sec. C5.

Chatterjee, Sumana. "Chocolate Companies React to Slavery Revelations" (Knight Ridder Newspapers). *State College (Pa.) Centre Daily Times,* 26 June 2001, sec. A7.

———. "Consumers: Why Not Boycott Chocolate?" (Knight Ridder Newspapers). *State College (Pa.) Centre Daily Times,* 26 June 2001, sec. A7.

———. "Chocolate Companies Fight 'Slave Free' Labels" (Knight Ridder Newspapers). *State College (Pa.) Centre Daily Times,* 1 August 2001, sec. A4.

———. "Chocolate Makers to Accept Responsibility for Cocoa Farm Practices" (Knight Ridder Newspapers). *State College (Pa.) Centre Daily Times,* 1 October 2001, sec. A3.

Christians, Clifford G., and James W. Carey. "The Logic and Aims of Qualitative Research." In *Research Methods in Mass Communication,* edited by Guido H. Stempel and Bruce H. Westley, 342–62. Englewood Cliffs, N.J.: Prentice-Hall, 1981.

Christman, Ed. "UMVD Marks 3rd Straight Year As Top U.S. Music Distributor." *Billboard,* 26 January 2002, 51.

———. "U.S. Music Sales Hit a Wall." *Billboard,* 26 January 2002, 1, 76.

Cohen, Mark Francis. "Must-See TV." *Washington Post,* 9 April 2000, 20(W).

Compaine, Benjamin M., and Douglas Gomery, eds. *Who Owns the Media? Competition and Concentration in the Mass Media Industry.* Mahwah, N.J.: Lawrence Erlbaum Associates, 2000.

Cooper, Dick. "Saying 'No' to a Gift of Water." *State College (Pa.) Centre Daily Times,* 5 July 2001, sec. A6.

Cooper, Marc. "The *Progressive* Interview: George Carlin." *The Progressive,* July 2001, 32–37.

"Corporate Spotlight." *Adbusters,* no. 35 (May/June 2001): 93.

"Credit Card Usage Analysis." December 2000. <www.nelliemae.com/shared/ccstat.htm> (accessed 17 October 2001).

Crossette, Barbara. "Experts Scaling Back Their Estimates of World Population Growth." *New York Times,* 20 August 2002, sec. D8.

Crutsinger, Martin. "Washington Pledges To Avoid Repeat of Seattle's Protest Problems." Associated Press, 6 April 2000, AM Cycle.

———. "Protesters Aim at IMF Meeting" (Associated Press). *State College (Pa.) Centre Daily Times,* 7 April 2000, sec. B8.

Cummings, Sue. "The Flux in Pop Music Has a Distinctly Download Beat to It." *New York Times,* 22 September 1999, sec. G60.

DiOrio, Carl. "U Dumps Its Loews Shares." *Daily Variety,* 29 June 2001, 6.

———. "*Potter* Plants WB on Top of Market." *Variety,* 24 December 2001, 12.

Doherty, Ryan. "State College Schools Weigh Soft-Drink Deal." *State College (Pa.) Centre Daily Times,* 5 May 2001, sec. A5.

Domhoff, G. William. "State and Ruling Class in Corporate America." *Insurgent Sociologist* 4, no. 3 (1974): 3–16.

———. *The Power Elite and the State: How Policy Is Made in America.* New York: Aldine de Gruyter, 1990.

Egan, Timothy. "Black Masks Lead to Pointed Fingers in Seattle." *New York Times,* 2 December 1999, sec. A1, A14.

Eisenstein, Elizabeth L. *The Printing Revolution in Early Modern Europe.* Cambridge: Cambridge University Press, 1983.

Eller, Claudia, and James Bates. "Hollywood Box Office Is Boffo." *Los Angeles Times,* 11 November 2001, 1–4. <www.latimes.com> (accessed 3 February 2002).

Eller, Claudia, and Sallie Hofmeister. "Company Town; The Biz; Sony Still Bets on Gizmos, Not Mergers." *Los Angeles Times,* 3 November 2000, sec. C1.

Elliot, Stuart. "A Combined Viacom-CBS Would Cast an Awfully Large Shadow across a Wide Range of Ad Media." *New York Times,* 8 September 1999, sec. C8.

———. "Advertising: The AOL–Time Warner Deal Changes Everything for Those Who Move, and Buy, in Media Circles." *New York Times,* 11 January 2000, sec. C8.

Farah, George, and Justin Elga. "What's *Not* Talked About on Sunday Morning?" *Extra!,* October 2001, 14–17.

Federal Communications Commission. *Subject to Conditions, Commission Approves Merger between America Online, Inc. and Time Warner, Inc.* 11 January 2001. <www.fcc.gov/Bureaus/Cable/> (accessed 18 January 2002).

Forbes, Steve. "Why the List." *Forbes,* 8 October 2001, 30.

———. "The 400 Richest People in America." *Forbes,* 8 October 2001, 127–298.

Frank, Robert H. "A Merger's Message: Dominate or Die." *New York Times,* 11 January 2000, sec. A31.

"Freedom of the Press, Advertising Division." *In These Times,* 24 July 1991, 21.

Friedman, Thomas L. "Senseless in Seattle." *New York Times,* 1 December 1999, sec. A31.

Furman, Phyllis. "MGM Buys Back Movie Rights to Launch TV Cable Channel" (Knight Ridder Tribune). *State College (Pa.) Centre Daily Times,* 16 September 1999, sec. 8C.

Fusfeld, Daniel. *Economics: Principles of Political Economy.* 3rd ed. Glenview, Ill.: Scott, Foresman, 1988.

Gaul, Gilbert M., and Frank Fitzpatrick. "What Was Sacred Is Now Up for Sale." *Philadelphia Inquirer,* 14 September 2001, sec. A1, A14.

"GE Fund Awards Two Grants to Penn State." *State College (Pa.) Centre Daily Times,* 18 December 2000, sec. A5.

Giroux, Henry. "Merger Mania Dazzles Eyes, But Imprisons You and Me." *State College (Pa.) Centre Daily Times,* 13 February 2000, sec. 13A.

Goldberg, Michael. "MTV's Sharper Picture." *Rolling Stone,* 8 February 1990, 61–64, 118.

Goodell, Jeff. "World War MP3." *Rolling Stone,* 8 July 1999, 43.

Goodman, Ellen. "Technology Sets You Free . . . To Work All The Time." *State College (Pa.) Centre Daily Times,* 25 July 2000, sec. A6.

Goodman, Walter. "When Corporate Synergy Becomes Manifest Destiny." *New York Times,* 19 January 2000, sec. E10.

Graeber, David. "Anarchy in the USA." *In These Times,* 10 January 2000, 18.

———. "The Riot That Wasn't." *In These Times,* 29 May 2000, 12.

Graves, Tom. "Movies and Home Entertainment: Current Environment." *Standard and Poor's Industry Surveys.* 10 May 2001. <www.netadvantage.standardandpoors/netahtml/IndSur/mhe/mhe_05001htm> (accessed 19 November 2001).

———. "Movies and Home Entertainment: Industry Trends." *Standard and Poor's.* 10 May 2001. <www.netadvantage.standardandpoors.com/netahtml/IndSur/mhe20501.htm> (accessed 19 November 2001).

Greenhouse, Steven. "A Carnival of Derision to Greet the Princes of Global Trade." *New York Times,* 29 November 1999, sec. A12.

Groves, Don, and Adam Dawtrey. "Hogwarts and Hobbits in Global Grab." *Variety,* 11 February 2002, 1.

Grutsinger, Martin. "Protesters Aim at IMF Meeting" (Associated Press). *State College (Pa.) Centre Daily Times,* 7 April 2000, sec. B8.

Grytting, Wayne. "The New Math." *Z Magazine,* March 1999, 5.

———. "Teach the Kids." *Z Magazine,* May 1999, 6.

Guback, Thomas. "Ownership and Control in the Motion Picture Industry." *Journal of Film and Video* 38, no. 1 (1986): 7–20.

Haddad, Charles. "CBS-Viacom Merger Further Narrows Media." *Atlanta Journal-Constitution,* 9 September 1999, sec. F1, F3.

———. "CBS, Viacom Follow Trail Blazed by Disney, Time Warner" (Knight Ridder Tribune). *State College (Pa.) Centre Daily Times,* 12 September 1999, sec. 15B.

Hafner, Katie. "Schools and Computers: Debate Heats Up." *New York Times,* 5 October 2001, sec. E8.

Hansell, Saul. "America Online Aggress to Buy Time Warner for $165 Billion; Media Deal is Richest Merger." *New York Times,* 11 January 2000, sec. A1, C11.

———. "Not-So-Subtle Engine Drives AOL Profit Forecasts." *New York Times,* 31 January 2000, sec. C1, C12.

Harmon, Amy. "Exceptions Made for Dress Code, But Never for His Internet Vision." *New York Times,* 11 January 2000, sec. A1, C12.

Harmon, Amy, and Alex Kuczynski. "A Bridge Builder for Corporate Culture." *New York Times,* 12 January 2000, sec. C1, C7.

Hayes, Constance L. "District Rethinks a Soda-Pop Strategy." *New York Times,* 19 April 2000, sec. A19.

Hellweg, Eric. "Down with MP3." *Spin,* October 1999, 57.

Herman, Edward. "Market System Constraints on Freedom of Expression." *Journal of Communication Inquiry* 15 (1991): 45–53.

———. "Media Mega-Mergers." *Dollars & Sense,* May 1996, 8–13.

Herman, Edward S., and Noam Chomsky. *Manufacturing Consent: The Political Economy of Mass Media.* New York: Pantheon Books, 1988.

Hill, Marsha. "World Economic Summit Opens amid Anti-Globalization Protests" (Associated Press). *State College (Pa.) Centre Daily Times,* 2 July 2001, sec. B8.

Hofmeister, Sallie. "Lights, Camera, Download? Studios Focus on the Web." *Los Angeles Times,* 30 November 2000, sec. A1.

Holly, Derrill. "DC Police Ready for IMF Duty." Associated Press, 7 April 2000, AM Cycle.

Holson, Laura M. "The Online Generation Courts the Old Guard." *New York Times,* 11 January 2000, sec. C1, C13.

Hopkins, Margaret. "Greenspan Visit Caps NGA Event: Fed Chief Challenges States to Provide Training for Workers." *State College (Pa.) Centre Daily Times,* 12 July 2000, sec. A1.

———. "Six Companies Pledge $1.85 Million for e-Business Center." *State College (Pa.) Center Daily Times,* 14 December 2000, sec. B10.

Horkheimer, Max, and Theodor W. Adorno. *Dialectic of Enlightenment.* Translated by John Cumming. New York: Seabury, 1972.

Horn, Patricia, and Akweli Parker. "AOL Merger Gets Key Approval." *Philadelphia Enquirer,* 15 December 2000, sec. A1, A16.

Jacobs, Andrew. "The Protesters: Mostly Pleased, but Knowing Few Heard Their Message." *New York Times,* 5 February 2002, sec. A15.

Kageyama, Yuri. "Mechanical Mutt: Sony Puppy Robot Good for Laughs, Still Far Call from Lovable Pet." *State College (Pa.) Centre Daily Times,* 24 December 2000, sec. E3.

Katz, Frances. "AOL, Time Warner Deal Sets the Tone" (Knight Ridder Tribune). *State College (Pa.) Centre Daily Times,* 11 January 2000, sec. 1A, 7A.

Katz, Jon. "Invasion of the Billionaire." *The Netizen.* 30 May 1997. <http://hotwired.lycos.com/netizen/97/21/index4a.html> (accessed 21 September 2000).

Kifner, John. "In This Washington, No 'Seattle' Is Found by Police and Protesters." *New York Times,* 19 April 2000, sec. A12.

King, Tom. "Hollywood Journal: Mickey Mouse vs. *Pearl Harbor*—Hoping to Avoid a Costly Bomb." *Wall Street Journal,* 6 April 2001, sec. W1.

Klein, Naomi. *No Logo: Taking Aim at the Brand Bullies.* New York: Picador USA, 1999.

Klinkenborg, Verlyn. "The Vision behind the CBS-Viacom Merger." *New York Times,* 9 September 1999, sec. A28.

Kloer, Phil. "Poof! Harry Potter Is Visible; Movie, Hype Make Wizard Hard to Miss." *Atlanta Journal-Constitution,* 26 October 2001, sec. 1A.

Kolata, Gina. "While Children Grow Fatter, Experts Search for Solutions." *New York Times,* 19 October 2000, sec. A1.

Kuczynski, Alex. "CBS Chief Wanted His MTV." *New York Times,* 8 September 1999, sec. C1, C14.

Labaton, Stephen. "Wide Belief U.S. Will Let a Vast Deal Go Through." *New York Times,* 8 September 1999, sec. C14.

———. "Federal Regulators Give Approval to Viacom's Buyout of CBS." *New York Times,* 4 May 2000, sec. C1.

———. "FCC Approves AOL–Time Warner Deal, With Conditions." *New York Times,* 12 January 2001, sec. C1, C11.

———. "Court Weighs Easing Limits on Big Media." *New York Times,* 8 September 2001, sec. A1.

———. "Appellate Court Eases Limitations for Media Giants: Rejects Longtime Rules." *New York Times,* 20 February 2002, sec. A1, C6.

Lande, Robert H. "Antitrust and the Media—II." *The Nation,* 22 May 2000, 5–6.

Ledbetter, James. "Merge Overkill: When Big Media Gets Too Big, What Happens to Open Debate?" *Village Voice,* 16 January 1996, 30–35.

Lee, W. A. "Student Loan GSE Slams Card Company Marketing." *American Banker* 166, no. 42 (2 March 2001): 8.

Leibovich, Lori. "Choosing Quick Hits over the Card Catalog." *New York Times,* 10 August 2000, sec. G1.

Leroux, Darryl. "Who's Zooming Who?" *Adbusters,* no. 34, March/April 2001, 47.

Levine, Arthur. "The Soul of a New University." *New York Times,* 13 March 2000, sec. A25.

Lin-Fisher, Betty. "Credit Cards for Students Mean Big Business" (Knight Ridder Tribune). *State College (Pa.) Centre Daily Times,* 26 August 2001, sec. C8.

Little, Mark. "Letter to the Editor." *Adbusters,* no. 34, March/April 2001, 6.

"Local Hotel Group to Build on Delaware Campus." *State College (Pa.) Centre Daily Times,* 24 May 2001, sec. A5.

Lohr, Steve. "Medium for Main Street." *New York Times,* 11 January 2000, sec. A1, C10.

Lyman, Rick. "Coming to a Computer Near You: Movie Rentals Direct from Five Studios" (New York Times News Service). *San Diego Union-Tribune,* 17 August 2001, sec. A1, A26.

———. "Coming Soon: *Harry Potter* and Hollywood's Cash Cow." *New York Times,* 4 November 2001, sec. A1, A31.

———. "*Harry Potter* and the Box Office of Gold." *New York Times,* 19 November 2001, sec. E1.

Macleod, Catherine. "Leaders Defiant As Genoa Licks Its Wounds." *Glasgow Herald,* 23 July 2001, 2.

Manning, Steve. "Students for Sale." *The Nation,* 27 September 1999, 11–15.

———. "Zapped." *The Nation,* 27 September 1999, 13.

Margasak, Larry. "Washington Braces for IMF Protesters" (Associated Press). *State College (Pa.) Centre Daily Times,* 9 April 2000, sec. A1.

———. "PETA Dumps Four Tons of Manure near World Bank" (Associated Press) *State College (Pa.) Centre Daily Times,* 15 April 2000, sec. A3.

———. "IMF Protesters Try—and Fail—to Shut Down Meetings" (Associated Press). *State College (Pa.) Centre Daily Times,* 18 April 2000, sec. A1.

———. "Protesters Disrupt Washington" (Associated Press). *Penn State University Daily Collegian,* 18 April 2000, 1.

"Marketing of Junk Food to School Children." *Commercial Alert.* <www .essential.org/alert/junkfood/> (accessed 17 November 2000).

Markoff, John. "Bridging Two Worlds to Make On-Line Digital Music Profitable." *New York Times,* 13 September 1999, sec. C1.

McChesney, Robert W. "The Communication Revolution: The Market and the Prospect for Democracy." In *Democratizing Communication?*, edited by M. Bailie and D. Winseck, 57–78. Creskill, N.J.: Hampton Press, 1997.

McFarling, Usha Lee. "Food Police: Teens Consume Too Much Soda" (Knight Ridder). *State College (Pa.) Centre Daily Times,* 22 October 1998, sec. A6.

"MediaForce Announces Top Ten Pirated Movies for July; Pirates Using Internet to Grow Personal Bootlegged Movies Collections." *PR Newswire,* 16 August 2001.

"The Media Nation: Music." *The Nation,* 25 August 1997, centerfold.

"Messages for the W.T.O." *New York Times,* 2 December 1999, sec. A30.

"MGM Regains Rights to Films" (Reuters). *New York Times,* 16 September 1999, sec. C23.

Mifflin, Lawrie. "Viacom to Buy CBS, Forming 2nd Largest Media Company." *New York Times,* 8 September 1999, sec. A1, C15.

———. "CBS-Viacom Deal Raises Competition Questions." *New York Times,* 9 September 1999, sec. C1, C8.

Milbank, Dana. "Bush Greeted by Demonstrators, Critics" (Washington Post). *State College (Pa.) Centre Daily Times,* 13 June 2001, sec. A3.

"Million Mom March a Personal Statement For Some" (Staff and Wire Reports). *State College (Pa.) Centre Daily Times,* 14 May 2000, sec. A69.

Moberg, David. "Tear Down the Walls: The Movement Is Becoming More Global." *In These Times,* 28 May 2001, 11–14.

———. "After Seattle." *In These Times,* 18 February 2002, 41.

Molnar, Alex, and Jennifer Morales. "Commercialism@Schools." *Educational Leadership,* October 2000, 43.

"Movies and Home Entertainment." *Standard & Poor's Industry Surveys.* 2 October 1997.

Munoz, Lorenza. "Company Town; Movie Industry Ready to Stage a Comeback, Valenti Says." *Los Angeles Times,* 7 March 2001, C6.

Murdock, Graham. "Programming: Needs and Answers." Paper presented at New Dimensions in Television meeting, Venice, Italy, 15 March 1981.

Myers, Jack. *Adbashing: Surviving the Attacks on Advertising.* Parsippany, N.J.: American Media Council, 1993.

Natale, Richard. "Company Town Film Profit Report." *Los Angeles Times,* 30 January 2001, sec. C10.

National Collegiate Athletic Association (NCAA). "A Call to Action: Reconnecting College Sports to Higher Education." June 2001. <www.ncaa.org/databases/knight_commission/2001_report/2001_knight_report.html> (accessed 19 October 2001).

"National Guard Is Called to Quell Trade-Talk Protests." *New York Times,* 1 December 1999, sec. A1.

*NBC Nightly News with Tom Brokaw.* National Broadcasting Company, 7 September 1999.

Nerone, John. *Violence against the Press: Policing the Public Sphere in U.S. History.* New York: Oxford University Press, 1994.

Netherby, Jennifer, and Scott Hettrick. "Warner Wild About Harry; Studio Reaches for Stratosphere." *Video Business,* 11 February 2002, 1.

"Newsflashes." *Adbusters,* no. 30, June/July 2000, 17.

*News Hour with Jim Lehrer.* Public Broadcasting System, 10 January 2000.

Norris, Floyd. "The New, Improved Redstone Still Knows How to Get His Way." *New York Times,* 8 September 1999, sec. C1, C13.

Novack, Megan. "Program Provides Disney Experience." *Penn State University Daily Collegian,* 26 September 2000, 2.

O'Brien, Chris. "AOL Merger May Fuel Silicon Valley Growth" (Knight Ridder Newspapers). *State College (Pa.) Centre Daily Times,* 13 January 2000, sec. 6B.

"Onex Aiming to Acquire Loews Theatre Chain" (Reuters News Agency). *Toronto Star,* 14 November 2001, sec. E11.

"Penn Staters Tinker with Computers." *State College (Pa.) Centre Daily Times,* 25 July 2000, sec. A5.

"People in the News." Associated Press, 7 May 1999, AM cycle.

Perkins, Dan, a.k.a. Tom Tomorrow. Op-Art. *New York Times,* 11 January 2000, sec. A31.

Peters, Cynthia. "Marketing to Teens." *Z Magazine,* April 1999, 23.

Pew Research Center for the People and the Press. "Journalists Avoiding the News, Self Censorship: How Often and Why." 30 April 2000. <www.people-press.org/jour00rpt.htm> (accessed 5 January 2002).

Picchi, Aimee. "AOL Time Warner Too Optimistic?" (Bloomberg News). *Philadelphia Enquirer,* 15 December 2000, sec. C1, C7.

Pollack, Andrew. "Microsoft Makes Another Interactive TV Investment." *New York Times,* 24 January 2000, sec. C4.

Pollack, Andrew, and Andrew Ross Sorkin. "Time Warner to Acquire Control of EMI Music." *New York Times,* 24 January 2000, sec. C1, C12.

Postman, Neil. "Virtual Students, Digital Classrooms." *The Nation,* 9 October 1995, 377–82.

"Potter Proves Power of Cross-Marketing." *Investor's Business Daily,* 23 November 2001, sec. A6.

Press, Eyal, and Jennifer Washburn. "The Kept University." *Atlantic Monthly* 285, no. 3 (March 2000): 39–54.

"Protesters March, Fail to Block World Finance Meeting" (Knight Ridder). *State College (Pa.) Centre Daily Times,* 17 April 2000, sec. A7.

Pulley, Brett. "The Cable Capitalist." *Forbes,* 8 October 2001, 42–54.

Raghavan, Sudarsan. "The Slavery Trap" (Knight Ridder Newspapers). *State College (Pa.) Centre Daily Times,* 26 June 2001, sec. A1, A7.

Raghavan, Sudarsan, and Sumana Chatterjee. "Child Slavery Persists on African Cocoa Farms" (Knight Ridder Newspapers). *State College (Pa.) Centre Daily Times,* 25 June 2001, sec. A1, A7.

"Rapid Media Consolidation Dramatically Narrows Number of Companies Controlling Time Spent Online." Jupiter Media Metrix, 4 June 2001. <www.iup.com/company/> (accessed 7 January 2002).

Rashbaum, William K., and Al Baker. "The Police: Shrewd Anticipation Helped Avert Trouble." *New York Times,* 5 February 2002, sec. A15.

"Raytheon Grant Helps Endow State High Award." *State College (Pa.) Centre Daily Times,* 24 September 2001, sec. A5.

Richtel, Matt. "A New Force in Distributing Music across the Internet." *New York Times,* 8 September 1999, sec. 14C.

"*Rings* Goes to WB for $160 Million." *St. Petersburg Times,* 5 February 2002, sec. 5D.

Robinson, Sara. "Recording Industry Escalates Crackdown on Digital Piracy." *New York Times,* 4 October 1999, sec. C5.

Rowland, Willard D., Jr. "The Illusion of Fulfillment: The Broadcast Reform Movement." *Journalism Monograph* 79 (1982).

Salant, Jonathan D. "Business Lobby Gears Up For Fight Over China Trade" (Associated Press). *State College (Pa.) Centre Daily Times,* 20 December 1999, sec. A8.

Samiljan, Tom. "I Want My MP3." *Rolling Stone,* 18 March 1999, 69.

Schatz, Thomas. "Show Me the Money: In Search of Hits, The Industry May Go Broke." *The Nation,* 5 April 1999, 26–31.

Schiesel, Seth. "A Rush to Provide High-Speed Internet Access." *New York Times,* 12 January 2000, sec. C1, C6.

———. "Vivendi is Said to Have Deal for Expansion in U.S. Media." *New York Times,* 17 December 2001, sec. A16.

Schmemann, Serge. "The Meeting: Annan Cautions Business as Forum Ends." *New York Times,* 5 February 2002, sec. A14.

"School District Ponders Deal for Coke Product." *State College (Pa.) Centre Daily Times,* 2 July 1999, sec. A11.

"School Questions Pepsi Contract." *State College (Pa.) Centre Daily Times,* 6 June 2001, sec. A2.

Schroeder, Ken. "One-derful Channel One." *The Education Digest* 66, no. 1 (September 2000): 72–73.

Schruers, Fred. "Tom Petty: The *Rolling Stone* Interview." *Rolling Stone,* 8–22 July 1999, 88–94.

Sherer, Paul M. "Loews Cineplex to Be Acquired by Onex Group." *Wall Street Journal,* 16 February 2001, sec. A4.

Sherman, Stratford P. "Ted Turner: Back from the Brink." *Fortune,* 7 July 1986, 25–31.

Siers, Kevin. "Contents: Copyright AOL Time Warner" (Charlotte Observer). *State College (Pa.) Centre Daily Times,* 16 January 2000, sec. 9A.

Smith, David. "Nittany Lion Print Foots Too Many Toes." *Penn State University Daily Collegian,* 29 January 1999, 8.

"Star News and Gossip." *TV Guide Live,* 11 December 2001. <www.tvguidelive.com/newsgossip-archives/01-dec/12-11-01.html> (accessed 28 January 2002).

Starhawk. "How We Shut Down the WTO." *Z Magazine,* February 2000, 18–19.

Stark, Andrew. "Taste: Let's Make a Deal—Commerce." *Wall Street Journal,* 31 March 2000, sec. W17.

"State High Teacher Awarded Palm Grant." *State College (Pa.) Centre Daily Times,* 10 September 2001, sec. A5.

Stewart, Barbara. "$9.50 for a Movie Ticket? Who's Up for a Protest?" *New York Times,* 2 March 1999, sec. A20.

Strauss, Neil. "MTV Winner: Neither Rejected nor Censored." *New York Times,* 7 September 1995, sec. C15.

———. "Wal-Mart's CD Standards are Changing Pop Music." *New York Times,* 12 November 1996, sec. A1, C12.

"Students Binge on Credit." *USA Today,* 14 September 2000, sec. A26.

Sutel, Seth. "Giants of Media Join at the Hip" (Associated Press). *State College (Pa.) Centre Daily Times,* 8 September 1999, sec. 1A, 7A.

Tabor, Mary B. W. "Schools Profit from Offering Students for Market Research." *New York Times,* 5 April 1999, sec. A1.

Terenzini, Caroline. "Productive Tinkering." *State College (Pa.) Centre Daily Times,* 18 May 1999, sec. C1.

"THON to Showcase Hilfiger Wear." *State College (Pa.) Centre Daily Times,* 12 February 2000, sec. A5.

Toles, Tom. "Coming to a Screen Near You" (Buffalo News, Universal Press Syndicate). *State College (Pa.) Centre Daily Times,* 13 February 2000, sec. 13A.

"Trade Protest Roils Capital" (Knight Ridder Newspapers). *State College (Pa.) Centre Daily Times,* 17 April 2000, sec. A1.

"Trade Talks Begin" (Associated Press). *State College (Pa.) Centre Daily Times,* 30 November 1999, sec. A4.

"TriStar Strikes Deal with iN-DEMAND." *AP Online,* 28 August 2001.

"TV News in Schools Costs $1.8 Billion in Class Time." *New York Times,* 1 April 1998, sec. B11.

"$25 Million Ad Blitz Planned for *Potter* Video." *Milwaukee Journal Sentinel,* 7 February 2002, sec. 6B, wire reports.

U.S. Bureau of Labor Statistics. *Consumer Price Index Summary.* December 2001. <www.bls.gov/news.release/cpi.nr0.htm> (accessed 2 February 2002).

U.S. Census Bureau. *Statistical Abstract of the United States: 2000.* 120th ed. Washington, D.C.: 2000.

*Variety Portable Movie Guide.* New York: Berkeley Boulevard Books, 1999.

Verhovek, Sam Howe. "Trade Talks Start in Seattle Despite a Few Disruptions." *New York Times,* 30 November 1999, sec. A14.

———. "Seattle Is Stung, Angry and Chagrined As Opportunity Turns to Chaos." *New York Times,* 2 December 1999, sec. A14.

———. "Seattle Police Chief Resigns in Aftermath of Protests." *New York Times,* 8 December 1999, sec. A13.

Walt Disney Company. *Notice of Annual Meeting of Shareholders.* 4 January 2002.

Wasko, Janet. *Hollywood in the Information Age.* Austin: University of Texas Press, 1994.

Waxman, Sharon. "Hollywood's Great Escapism; 2001 Box Office Receipts Set Record." *Washington Post,* 4 January 2002, sec. A1.

Weinraub, Bernard. "A Strained Relationship Turns Sour." *New York Times,* 18 October 1999, sec. C18.

Wengerd, Erin R. "Protest Preparation Fails to Draw Crowd." *State College (Pa.) Centre Daily Times,* 25 May 2000, sec. A1.

Westbrook, Bruce. "*Snow White* to Make Digital Debut; Disney DVD Set Packed With Extras." *Houston Chronicle,* 7 October 2001, sec. 8.

Winston, Brian. *Misunderstanding Media.* Cambridge, Mass.: Harvard University Press, 1986.

Woletz, Robert G. "A New Formula: Into the 'Bin,' Out Comes a Hit." *New York Times,* 2 August 1992, sec. D1.

"WTO Protests Turn Violent" (Associated Press). *State College (Pa.) Centre Daily Times,* 1 December 1999, sec. A1.

Zeller, Tom. "Amid Clamor for Computer in Every Classroom, Some Dissenting Voices." *New York Times,* 17 March 2001, sec. A3.

Zuckerman, Laurence. "As Media Influence Grows for Handful, Can that be a Good Thing." *New York Times,* 13 January 2000, sec. C6.

# INDEX

# ABOUT THE AUTHORS

**Ronald V. Bettig** is an associate professor in the College of Communications at the Pennsylvania State University, where he teaches courses in the political economy of communications. He is the author of *Copyrighting Culture: Intellectual Property in the Filmed Entertainment Industry* (Westview, 1996).

**Jeanne Lynn Hall** is an associate professor in the College of Communications at the Pennsylvania State University, where she teaches courses in film history, theory, and criticism. She is the author of numerous articles on Hollywood and independent documentary film.